Augustus Austen-Leigh

King's College

Augustus Austen-Leigh

King's College

ISBN/EAN: 9783742810939

Manufactured in Europe, USA, Canada, Australia, Japa

Cover: Foto ©Thomas Meinert / pixelio.de

Manufactured and distributed by brebook publishing software
(www.brebook.com)

Augustus Austen-Leigh

King's College

University of Cambridge

COLLEGE HISTORIES

KING'S COLLEGE

BY

REV. A. AUSTEN LEIGH, M.A.

PROVOST OF THE COLLEGE

LONDON

F. E. ROBINSON AND CO.

20 GREAT RUSSELL STREET, BLOOMSBURY

1899

Printed by BALLANTYNE, HANSON & Co.
At the Ballantyne Press

PREFACE

THE materials for a history of King's College consist, in the first place, of the MS. records preserved in the College. Of these, the Account Books go back to the earliest times, and are nearly complete. The Protocollum Books cover the period since 1500 and contain a record of the admission of all Scholars and Fellows, cases of discipline, diversions of the Fellows to exceptional courses of study, and decisions of the Visitor. The Congregation Books, which contain the votes passed by the Governing Body and the annual elections of officers, date from 1722. There is also, in the College Muniment Room, a collection of letters, of the seventeenth and eighteenth centuries, written by Visitors, Provosts, and Fellows, which throw light on some episodes of College history. We possess also isolated accounts of various important occurrences in the College ; but these are unofficial, and the actual date of their composition is sometimes uncertain. Moreover, there are two catalogues of Provosts, Fellows, and Scholars. The one preserved in the College was drawn up by Antony Allen, admitted a Scholar of King's in 1704. He made use of two earlier lists—one the work of Thomas Hatcher, Fellow, who died in 1584, and had carried his catalogue down to 1555 ; the other, a continuation to 1620, by John Scott, Coroner of the College. Allen was a Master in Chancery and enjoyed the friendship and patronage of

Arthur Onslow, Speaker of the House of Commons. His catalogue is completed to the year 1751. Allen's portrait hangs in the Provost's Lodge and is that of a portly gentleman, who looks well satisfied with himself and his fortunes. The other catalogue, preserved in the British Museum, is by William Cole. This is much fuller than Allen's; but though Cole lived till 1782, his record of the members of the College closes in 1731. Cole was a friend of Horace Walpole, with whom he travelled in France, and had begun his antiquarian researches as a boy at Eton. He was at first an Undergraduate of Clare Hall, and then became a Fellow Commoner at King's; he held several Livings in succession, but only resided at one of them, viz., Bletchley, and finally retired to Milton. He is buried under the steeple of St. Clement's Church, in Cambridge, for the erection of which he provided the funds, and where his name is preserved in the motto " Deum Cole."

Of printed books the most important to the historian of King's College is the great work of Willis and Clark on the Architectural History of the University of Cambridge. Indeed, so far as the history of the College buildings is concerned, there is nothing left to be done but to make the best use of this mine of information, and to express admiration of the three volumes. Next to this, perhaps, should be placed Mr. Mullinger's history of the University, at present completed to the accession of Charles I. For the period which it covers it is invaluable. A third source of information is the new " National Dictionary of Biography ; " of this I have made great use, although it has not yet dealt with such prominent Kingsmen as Walsingham, Waller, Whichcote, and the Walpoles. It is hardly necessary to mention the books which the historian of every College must use—e.g., Cooper's " Annals of Cambridge," Fuller's " History of the University," and

Gunning's "Reminiscences." There are also some valuable articles in the publications of the Cambridge Antiquarian Society, especially those by Mr. G. Williams, Mr. Bradshaw, Mr. J. W. Clark, and Dr. M. R. James. The close connection between King's and Eton makes it natural not unfrequently to consult Mr. Maxwell Lyte's history of Eton College, a book to which it is always a pleasure to return. The works written by former Kingsmen, and their biographies, are, of course, numerous; but I must mention Dr. Moule's "Life of Charles Simeon," and Mr. Lane Poole's "Life of Lord Stratford de Redcliffe," as being equally valuable records of two very different men, who must have known one another in College as Don and Undergraduate, and whose portraits now hang opposite to each other in the College Hall.

But my acknowledgments are due to men as well as to books. Like every one else who writes about Cambridge, I have to thank our University Registrary, Mr. J. W. Clark, for much kind help. In particular he drew my attention to the younger G. G. Scott's "Essay on Church Architecture," and also enabled me to use an unpublished memoir of the Thackeray family. Beside this, he has read through the earlier chapters of this book, and has made many valuable suggestions and corrections. If there is any one whose knowledge of the College can rival that of Mr. Clark it is Dr. M. R. James, our Senior Dean. He and my brother, Mr. W. Austen Leigh, Senior Fellow, have taken the trouble to read through the whole book, and have spared no pains to make it less incomplete and less inaccurate than it must otherwise have been. Some parts, too, have been revised by Mr. C. E. Grant, Senior Bursar, whose criticisms have been especially useful on questions connected with the College property. The oldest living Kingsman, Mr. Tucker, formerly Rector of

Dunton-Waylett, has written a lively and graphic account
of Old Court, 1822–1825, from which I have borrowed
largely; and both to him and to Bishop Abraham and
Mr. W. Green I am very grateful for allowing me to make
use of their personal experiences and reminiscences.
Other Kingsmen to whom I owe much are Mr. F. C.
Hodgson, Professor Raleigh, and Mr. Mahaffy. The Vice-
Provost of Eton, Mr. F. Warre Cornish, has furnished me
with some valuable information from the documents contained in the Fellows' Library at Eton. Mr. Lionel Cust,
Director of the National Portrait Gallery, has also sent me
the facsimile of an interesting letter, which will be found
in Appendix E., as it arrived too late for insertion in the
text. To these names I must not omit to add one more—
that of our sub-Librarian, Mr. F. L. Clark, who has
repeatedly called my attention to important records which
I should otherwise have overlooked. Indeed, whatever
the particular topic may be, he seldom fails to unearth
some pamphlet or bundle of old letters which bears
directly upon it.

It was my hope to be able to describe the habits and
manners of resident Kingsmen in bygone days : but the
evidence for this is very scanty. If my readers think that
I have told in too great detail the story of more than one
College quarrel, my excuse must be that it is just from the
accounts left us of such exceptional occurrences that we
catch a glimpse of the life led by our predecessors.
Without this a history of the College is in danger of
becoming a mere chronicle of the buildings together with
a string of biographies. Yet even the biographies are
necessary if we are to form any true idea of what the
College has contributed towards national progress, both in
Church and State. There is a special interest attaching
to the history of King's College, because it is the record of

an almost unique experiment in education. Nowhere else,
at least at Cambridge, were the scholars drawn wholly from
a single school, and exempted from the ordeal necessary
for obtaining a Degree. These anomalies are now universally condemned. But, at a time when it was the custom
for Scholarships and Fellowships to be restricted to particular Schools or Counties, a Society which possessed the
right of recruiting its members from so magnificent a
foundation as that of Eton College had, after all, a toler-
ably wide basis on which to build. It must be remembered,
too, that there was a small but important class of Fellow
Commoners within the College. The College ceased to
receive them just at the time when George Thackeray
became Provost, and perhaps owing to some order of his ;
but there is no record of it. Probably it was felt that
their presence encouraged idleness or extravagance among
the Scholars ; yet the roll of distinguished Kingsmen
would be much shorter if Fellow Commoners had not been
welcomed for three hundred years. No Kingsman, as it
seems to me, has any reason to be ashamed of the position
which his College held in the University till the Restoration, or even till a later date. The Society, which was
cooped up within Old Court, was a prominent one, at any
rate in Elizabethan and Stuart times. Indeed, one is
tempted to say that, as the buildings were enlarged, the
influence of the College declined. Yet in every century
we can show a fair list of great men ; not perhaps of the
very greatest, whose genius seems to be independent of
their surroundings ; but rather of that class who owe much
to the training of School and College.

     If there were shortcomings in the College of former
days, they were probably less due to the closeness of the
tie with Eton than with the want of a closer connection
with the University.   I have tried to collect in an Appendix

the evidence on the origin of the custom by which Fellows
of King's were exempted from the University examination
for a B.A. degree. It is disappointing to arrive at no
definite conclusion. I can only hope that some future
historian of the College may be more successful in finding
fresh evidence, or more skilful in dealing with that which
we now have.

CONTENTS

ILLUSTRATIONS

CHAPTER I

THE MAKING OF THE COLLEGE

HENRY VI. was less than nineteen years of age when, in 1440,* he began his foundation of a college at Cambridge. History is almost silent as to the influence which led him to take such a step. There was nothing in his mother's character to account for it, and the estrangement which followed on her marriage with Owen Tudor must have put an end to any power which she possessed over her son. His great-uncle, Cardinal Beaufort, was rather a statesman than an ecclesiastic; and though we may believe that his preceptor, the Earl of Warwick, carried out the orders of the Council by teaching the King to "love, worship, and dread God," had "drawn him to virtue by ways convenable," and taught him "literature, language, and other means of cunning," yet Warwick had left the King to become Regent of France three years before.

* The site of the Old Court was conveyed by Commissioners to the King on January 22, 1441, and granted to the College by Henry on February 12. According to the old way of reckoning the year began on March 25, and these dates would belong to the year 1440. Moreover, some parts of the site had been acquired by the Commissioners in the preceding autumn. The year 1440 may therefore be considered as the date of the original foundation. Throughout this book the years will be reckoned as beginning on January 1.

A

It was, indeed, traditional in Henry's family to be orthodox and devout. His father had waged war with Lollards as well as with French, and was meditating a fresh crusade at the time of his death; but we naturally look for some one, who may have prompted the young prince in his educational designs, as Bishop Fisher afterwards encouraged the Lady Margaret to found colleges and professorships. And it appears from a list of Benefactors contained in the earliest College Register that the members of the Society recognised such a person in John Langton, Master of Pembroke and Chancellor of the University. He it was who was entitled to their gratitude for the services which he had rendered both in the foundation and in the endowment of the College: "fundari procuravit et possessionibus . . . quam plurimis . . . dotari laboravit." It is not unlikely that William of Alnwick, Bishop of Lincoln, also encouraged the young King's project, for he had acted as Henry's tutor, and he could not but take a special interest in the school founded in his own diocese. Nor would that interest be confined to Eton, when the connexion between the College at Cambridge and the school on the Thames was established in 1443. Whoever may have prompted him, Henry's original aim, as he himself tells us, was to extirpate heresies, to increase the number of the clergy, and to provide ministers of religion whose life and doctrine would give light to his subjects.

The young King had no difficulty in finding the necessary ways and means. The Alien Priories, the rents of which were transmitted to the Abbey of Be in Normandy or to other Foundations in France, had narrowly escaped suppression in the reign of Henry IV.; and in 1414 the estates of one hundred and twenty-two such priories were confiscated, those only escaping which had renounced foreign allegiance and elected their own Head. The rents of the confiscated priories were henceforth paid into the royal exchequer. Before the year 1440 it had become clear that our rule in France was at an end, and it was undesirable that English money should continue to support foreign Foundations. To a man of Henry's devout character it might well seem a duty that the funds, which had been intercepted on patriotic grounds, should be used for some religious purpose at home.

Henry had already granted to the University of Cambridge the manors of Ruislip in Middlesex and Okebourne in Wiltshire, in order that the University Chaplains might pray daily for his good estate during life and for his soul after death. These manors were now made over to his new College, and within a few years many others were added, about half of which still remain in the possession of the College and form the bulk of its landed estates. These are scattered over no less than eleven counties, chiefly in Southern England; and at one time the College owned land as far off as St. Michael's Mount in Cornwall. Its western border does not now extend beyond Sampford Courtenay in Devonshire, a property acquired in Queen Elizabeth's reign by exchange for Withyham in Sussex, which then passed into the hands of Lord Buckhurst.

The College, which the King founded in 1440–41, was to consist of a Rector and twelve Scholars, and to bear the name of St. Nicholas, on whose day (December 6)

Henry had been born. The choice of a site was entrusted to three Commissioners, of whom one was John Langton, while the Bishop of Lincoln took part in framing the Statutes of the new Foundation. The old buildings of Clare Hall at that time abutted on the west side of Milne Street. The south end of this street is now known as Queen's Lane, but in the fifteenth century it was continued northwards till it reached Michael House, the buildings of which then occupied the south-west corner of what is now the great court of Trinity College. Opposite to Clare Hall, and to the east of Milne Street, but at a distance of about ninety feet, stood the new University Schools of Theology and Canon Law. Between these buildings and the street there was a garden belonging to Trinity Hall, and the acquisition of this ground furnished ample space for such a College as the King then contemplated.

On Passion Sunday—*i.e.*, the fifth Sunday in Lent—April 2, 1441, Henry laid the first stone of his new College, and granted the use of materials from the old Castle at Cambridge. The eastern side of the Quadrangle being already occupied by the University Schools, the College consisted of three wings, of which the northern was considerably the longest and overlapped the University Schools. A Chapel of modest dimensions rose outside the Quadrangle on the south, and stood there for nearly a hundred years. Dr. Caius calls it a " mean and inconvenient building "; but it seems to have been of stone ; it consisted of a chancel, nave, and ante-chapel ; it had a western door, and east and west windows, stalls in the choir, a rood-loft, altars of St. Mary and St. Nicholas, and both large and small

organs. It was richly fitted up, and ample provision
was made for the due performances of the church services. The Scholars of some earlier Foundations had
attended one or other of the parish churches ; but such
an arrangement would not satisfy Henry, although he
had not yet conceived the plan of the stately edifice
which within a few years was destined to rise still
farther to the south.

A beginning was made by the appointment of William
Millington as Rector and two Scholars, John Kyrkeby
and William Hatclyffe. But within three years the
King had enlarged his design. Apparently his attention had been drawn to William of Wykeham's two
colleges at Winchester and Oxford. At any rate, now,
in 1443, he takes them for his model, and connects his
Cambridge College with the one already founded at
Eton. The Scholars of the latter, when sufficiently
imbued with the rudiments of grammar, are to be
transferred to the twin College at Cambridge, now
styled the College of St. Mary and St. Nicholas, there
to be more perfectly instructed in the liberal arts and
sciences. In its new form the College is to consist of
a Provost, seventy Fellows or Scholars, together with a
body of Chaplains, Lay Clerks, and Choristers ; and
William Millington exchanges his title of Rector for
that of Provost. At the same time the King nomi-
nates six other " original Fellows of the College." It
was not till two years later that the Society was re-
cruited with students whose connexion with Eton had
been more than nominal ; in 1446 no less than eleven
Scholars were admitted, and so many in the years
following that by 1452, or about the time when the

Quadrangle was completed, the number of seventy may have been completed also.

The site, which was ample for the original body, might well fail to satisfy the new wants, and the King lost no time in acquiring more land to the south. Yet the buildings already begun were so arranged as to accommodate the seventy members. The south and west wings were occupied by chambers; on the north stood the Hall, Butteries, and a Parlour in which the three Bursars dined apart from the other Fellows. Above this Parlour was the Audit-room, and to the west of it the Kitchen with a belfry. The Treasury was over the gateway in the west wing; while at the south-east corner, a passage called "Cow Lane" led from the Quadrangle to the Chapel. In later years the first-floor room over this passage became a Combination-room. Access to the various chambers was given by octagonal staircases projecting into the court. There were three floors; the whole of the south wing, to-gether with the west wing as far as the gateway, was finished; but, before the rest was completed, the King had planned a much larger court on the south side of the Chapel, and hence this remaining part was finished off in a temporary manner. Even so it was probably superior to any previous work in the University, and the gateway in particular was worthy of the Foundation.

The ground-floor was chiefly occupied by Scholars, the Fellows living above; each room held either two Fellows or four Scholars; but the rooms were so con-structed that small studies were partitioned off from the dormitories; and the Statutes especially insist that each

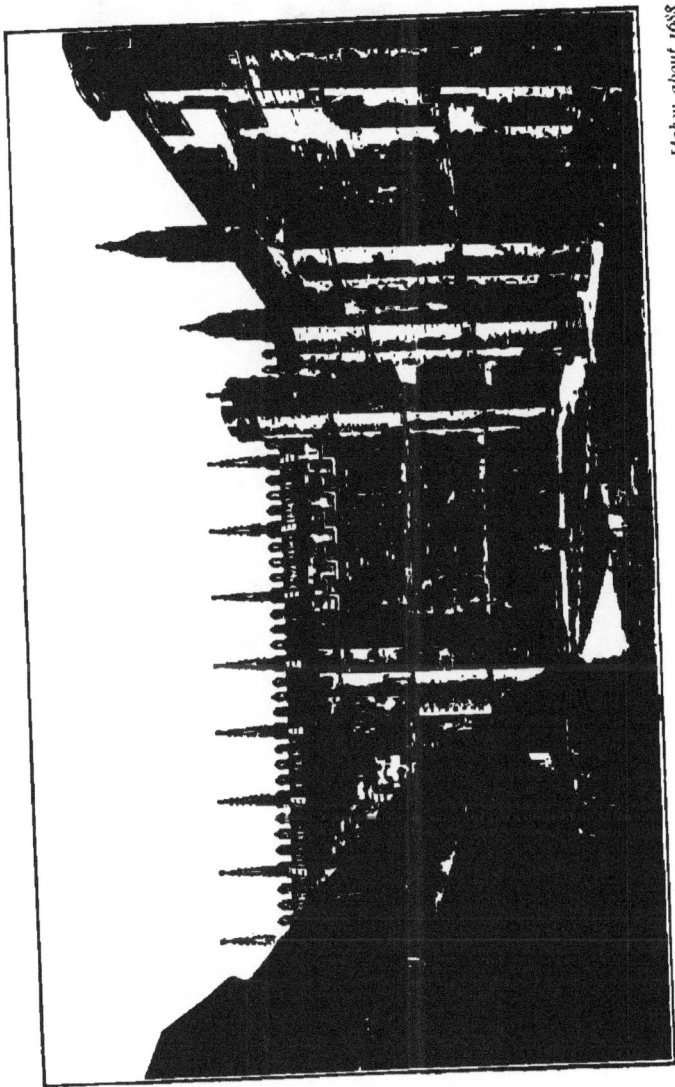

From Loggan's print

OLD COURT

[*taken about 1688*]

Scholar should have a separate bed. The earliest Bursars' Books show that there was a library and a stable; and before 1454, by which time everything seems to have been finished, the College also possessed a pigeon-house and a garden. The Founder had also secured to the College the right of bringing water in underground pipes from a spring in Madingley Parish, and had bound himself and his successors to furnish the Society with a yearly supply of Gascony wine. The latter would, no doubt, have been a boon at the numerous Feast-days which were kept in obedience to the Statutes, while the former would have proved a daily blessing and promoted health as well as sobriety.

While the buildings were in progress, the Society must have suffered great discomfort; what its general condition was, when it was able to occupy a settled home, may be gathered from the Statutes. But these Statutes themselves were not the code originally contemplated. The eminent men, to whom that work had been entrusted, had withdrawn on the plea of stress of business; possibly they disliked the change, by which King's was now linked to Eton. At any rate, Henry took the matter into his own hands, and with the help, as is conjectured, of William Wainflete, an old Wykehamist and Provost of Eton, drew up the elaborate laws which governed the College for more than 400 years. It is to be noticed that Henry's conception of education has by this time grown somewhat wider. It is not merely a College of secular priests which he now contemplates, but a Society in which provision is also made, though on a very modest scale, for the study of law and medicine. Great power was, of course, entrusted to the Provost himself, but it was shared with the Vice-Provost, the three Deans, three Bursars, and six other senior Fellows. The officers were chosen annually by this aristocracy of thirteen ; if the majority of them differed from the Provost, recourse was had to the whole body of Fellows. In dealing with all legislative business of importance this process was reversed ; first the Fellows were summoned ; but, if they were not unanimous, then the decision rested with a majority of the Provost and thirteen Seniors. It seems to have been taken for granted that the Deans and Bursars would always be chosen from among the Seniors ; but the Statute omitted to state whether, in the absence or illness of a Senior, his place should be filled up ; and this omission was a cause of controversy in later times. The Provost alone had the right of proposing business for discussion.

The election to Fellowships was made by the whole body of Fellows, with the Provost's consent ; but the Junior Fellows took no part in the election of Scholars. The Seniors chose two Fellows to accompany the Provost in his annual visit to Eton, a journey for which not more than nine or ten horses were allowed ; and the election, in which they were helped by the Provost, Vice-Provost, and Headmaster of Eton, was to be completed within five days. The electors began by swearing to be impartial in their judgment, and to resist all external pressure which might be applied either by princes or prelates ; a promise which in those days it was easier to make than to keep. Any boy might be a candidate who, having been born in England and being between the ages of fifteen and twenty, had been educated for two years in Eton College, provided that he did not possess an income of five marks and was not a cripple. Some preference was given to boys born in parishes belonging to Eton or King's ; and, failing such, to boys of Buckinghamshire or Cambridgeshire. Those elected to Scholarships pledged themselves to reside as members of King's for at least five years.

On reaching Cambridge they were placed under the care of the Vice-Provost and Deans ; the latter officers presided at the College disputations, the number and character of which were carefully defined ; and other teachers were provided at the cost of the College, whose terminal fee did not exceed 16d. for each Scholar. The examination at Eton had tested their knowledge of grammar, and they were now introduced to the mysteries of logic and rhetoric, which made up the Trivium or undergraduate course. A College order of 1483 gives us some further details. There was a " collector to report to the officers all Scholars and B.A. Fellows who were absent from disputations. Lecturers came into Hall at 6 A.M. and taught till 8 A.M. Every day the last lecture was repeated before a new one was begun. At the end of each week the elder students shewed up to the Vice-Provost, or to one of the Deans, a summary of the week's lectures. Each day the students were bound to get up in private a chapter of logic or physic, and at the end of the week to pass an examination in these chapters. The teaching must have been chiefly oral, for printed books did not yet exist. Books of any sort were scarce and precious, and one College servant was specially occupied in carrying them to and from the University Schools.

Meals were taken in the College Hall, the Scholars

sitting at one table in the middle of the room and the Lay Clerks at another. For the most part they ate in silence and listened to the reading of Scripture; when they did converse, it was in Latin. Dinner ended with a grace, prayer, and an anthem in honour of the Virgin sung by the members of all the various tables. Only occasionally, either on great Feast-days or when there was a fire in the winter time, were the Scholars allowed to stay on in Hall after dinner or supper, and to occupy themselves with singing, and with reading poetry, chronicles, and other improving literature. The College not only boarded and lodged its members, it also clothed them, cut their hair, and shaved them. Once a year the Bursars furnished a sufficient supply of cloth, which was perhaps converted into garments by some of the College servants. Scholars and Fellows were forbidden to sell or pawn their clothes till they had worn them for two years; but after the first year they might give them away to members of the Society whose own suits had come to a premature decay. Even if the Scholars of those days had possessed money, they would have had little temptation to run up a tailor's bill, for they were strictly forbidden to adopt modern fashions in dress, to wear belts ornamented with gold or silver, or red or green boots. A gown reaching down to the heels was indispensable. It was one of the duties of the Porter to trim the hair and cut the beards of all the Society; and neither Fellows nor Scholars were allowed to indulge in a profusion of hair, which was then thought to be inconsistent alike with the academical and the clerical profession.

No encouragement was given to sporting tastes;

dogs, ferrets, and hawks were forbidden. Even such innocent exercises as jumping and ball-throwing were discouraged; though in this case the objection seems to have arisen from a fear that damage might be done to the buildings or glass. If the Scholars went outside the College, they were not to go alone nor to discard their academical dress; and before they could take a walk into the country, leave of the Provost and Deans was necessary. Poverty probably kept them at Cambridge; but they might enjoy a vacation of two months in the course of the year, so long as not more than twenty out of the whole number of seventy were absent at the same time. Even when out of residence they were bound to dress like " clerks," and forbidden to frequent either taverns or public spectacles.

The life, which is described in these Statutes, seems to us hard, monotonous, and sombre; and the election to a Fellowship after three years of probation made but little immediate difference. The Fellow was still a student under strict discipline, though his studies were more advanced. Even when he became a M.A. the College did not loose its hold upon him. For three years he was a Regent, and as such was bound himself to teach others; after that time the College authorities decided whether he should be one of the few who devoted themselves to the study of law, medicine, or astronomy. But theology was the business of the large majority; and it was the duty of the Provost and Deans to see that all M.A.s, with rare exceptions, should within two or three years take holy orders and become Priests. Any failure to obey the Provost's injunctions in this respect was punished with forfeiture of Fellowship.

For the Provost himself a separate house was provided, of which some account will be given in a later chapter. One attendant of good birth and five men servants were assigned to him, and as many as ten horses. Provisions both for horses and men, clothing for servants and master, were found by the College. His income, which the Statutes fixed at £100, though only two-thirds of this sum were actually paid, was large for those days; on great Feasts he was bound to dine in Hall; on other days he might do so if he pleased, and might also entertain guests there. In addition to these emoluments and privileges, he was not debarred from holding other Church preferment, provided that it did not interfere with his residence at Cambridge, where, besides his duties of maintaining discipline and of general supervision, he was bound on great Festivals to celebrate Mass in the Chapel. One absence at least in the year was enjoined on him; at some time before the 1st of October he rode round the estates in company with a Fellow chosen by the College, inspecting the live stock and warning the bailiffs and tenants to send in all moneys due from them, so as to be ready for the Audit. The circuit was not to extend beyond forty days, and the number of horses to be used by the Provost and his companion was specified.

Great anxiety is shown by the Founder that the numbers of the Society should not be allowed to decrease; and frequent diminutions in the amounts for commons are enjoined by the Statutes rather than that one of the seventy should be missing. It is the business of the Provost to see that the ten Chaplains and six Lay Clerks should be maintained; and a fine is imposed on him of 8*s.* 6*d.* a week for each vacancy among the former and of 4*s.* 3*d.* for each missing Lay Clerk. The constitution of the Society was to be protected by a certain veil of mystery, for heavy penalties are imposed on those who show to strangers the copy of the Statutes kept in the College Library, or who allow any part of them to be transcribed. In such a case the Provost is to forfeit half his income, while a Fellow loses his Fellowship. As a general rule the surplus in each year was paid into the common chest, and could only be applied towards enlarging the College property or in legal expenses; but a sum of £200 was reserved, from which loans might be made to members of the Society. Degree fees were paid on behalf of the poorest students, and each Fellow received a certain annual sum which varied from four marks assigned to a Doctor to thirty shillings received by a B.A. The officers also had regular though modest stipends.

Henry had exerted himself to obtain exceptional privileges for both of his Foundations; and on November 29, 1445, Pope Eugenius IV. issued a Bull in favour of King's College. A cemetery was allowed, in which members of the College, and others who wished to have their graves there, might be buried. All the Sacraments of the Church might be performed in the Chapel, even when the town was under an Interdict. The Provost and Scholars were made independent of all parish rights, whether pecuniary payments or the obligation to attend Services. The Founder seems to have thought it inconsistent with the dignity of his College that it should be subject to the ordinary jurisdiction of the Chancellor;

and the College was exempted, under the Papal Bulls, from this jurisdiction, as also from the authority of the Bishop of the diocese, being committed instead to the charge of the Bishop of Lincoln. That Bishop had naturally become Visitor of Eton College, for the county of Buckingham was then within the diocese of Lincoln, and the two Foundations were too closely united to admit of their having different Visitors. Provision was made for frequent visitations either by the Bishop himself or by his commissaries; and even this last office might not be entrusted to the Bishop of Ely. It is remarkable that, whereas at Eton the Archbishop of Canterbury shared with the Bishop of Lincoln the powers of a Visitor, the Bull of Pope Eugenius exempted King's College from the authority of the Archbishop as well as from that of the Bishop and Archdeacon of Ely.

The Statutes, described above, received the royal sanction in 1446, and in the same year William Millington ceased to be Provost. His retirement was not voluntary. We know from a letter which he wrote some years later to Thomas Bekynton, Bishop of Bath and Wells, that his conscience did not allow him to accept the new code. There were many things in it which he disliked, and to two he had an insurmountable objection. As he had already sworn to obey the Chancellor's jurisdiction, he felt that he would be guilty of perjury if he accepted the exemption from such jurisdiction, which was conferred by the Statutes, and still more definitely by the Bulls. Nor could he reconcile himself to the Statute which restricted the Scholarships to Etonians, and gave a preference even among these to boys born in certain parishes. But he protests against the injustice of those who had ousted him, and declares that neither the Bishop of Lincoln nor the King had approved of his deprivation; and the fact that he was one of those appointed to draw up Statutes for Queens' College in 1448 is certainly evidence that he recovered the royal favour if he ever forfeited it. It would seem that Millington did not altogether disapprove of the connexion with Eton. At any rate, he signed the "Amicabilis Concordia," by which the Wardens of Winchester and New College and the Provosts of Eton and King's bound their Colleges for all time to support each other in all causes, trials, and difficulties.

The University did not surrender its authority over the new College without a struggle. In 1453 Scholars of King's were forbidden to take their degrees till they had renounced their exemption from University jurisdiction; and in 1454 there were riots, in which the College was a special object of attack. But Henry was too strong for his opponents; and the University finally gave way in 1457; except that the College jurisdiction was limited to cases which had their origin *within the precincts* of the College.

To us at the present day it does not seem a matter of much moment whether a turbulent undergraduate or dishonest servant was brought before the Chancellor's Court or the Head of his own College; but the exemption from University examinations, which seems to have followed from that of jurisdiction, entailed far more serious consequences. How and when this last privilege was secured is uncertain. The College

Statutes seem to assume that the Scholars will take part in the disputations, which were then the avenue to a B.A. degree; and in the documents by which the University recognised the freedom of the College in the matter of jurisdiction, the Chancellor retains the power of summoning Kingsmen to scholastic acts and congregations. No records are extant to show whether Kingsmen did in fact ever "dispute" for the B.A. degree; and we must be content to remain uncertain whether the custom by which members of the College received their first degree without examination up to the middle of the nineteenth century was established in the fifteenth.* At that period the loss was perhaps not great, for the academical exercises, though they might sharpen the intellect, were no guarantee for any cultivation of the mind. In another half-century the revival of the study of Greek gave an opportunity for a revolution in University studies. Freed from the trammels of a barren logic, the Kingsmen might have devoted themselves to a nobler literature; and it will be found that some of them did so. Yet it cannot be doubted that the exemption was, on the whole, a cause of idleness, and that it was easier to fall below the standard of University culture than to maintain in the isolation of a College a still higher ideal.

* See Appendix A.

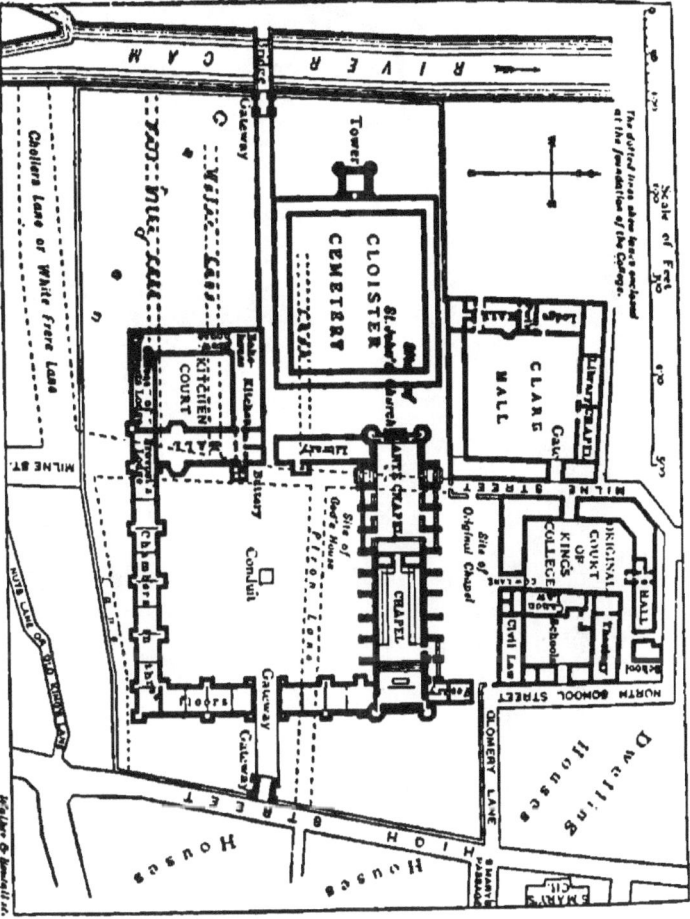

HENRY VI.'S DESIGN, FOR SOUTHERN QUADRANGLE AND WESTERN CLOISTER

CHAPTER II

THE CHAPEL

*" They dreamt not of a perishable home
Who thus could build. "*

As soon as Henry had determined to enlarge his
College at Cambridge and connect it with the one
which he had already founded at Eton, he must have
felt the necessity for a Chapel of more suitable propor-
tions. He had already planned a large church for his
School, and he could not allow his College to be at any
disadvantage in this respect. The document which
goes by the name of his " Will," and is dated March 12,
1448, gives us complete details of his final plan both
for the church and for the southern quadrangle and
western cloister, which he intended to build if his life
and reign had been prolonged. We cannot read the
King's words without feeling how thoroughly he had
put his heart into this work. Every possible precaution is taken for providing an annual supply of
money till such time as both Colleges, at Eton and
Cambridge, should be completed. No appeal could be
more solemn or more pathetic than the concluding
words, in which he charges his executors to fulfil their
task faithfully. Yet, of his great design, the Chapel

B

alone was built; and this, with some exceptions, the most important of which is that the side chapels were not originally meant to extend east of the Ante-Chapel, corresponds to the directions of the Will. The Civil War and the changes in the dynasty delayed the completion of the fabric for more than half a century, but the modifications which this delay caused in the original design are such as are apt to be overlooked except by the eye of an architect.

Henry had gradually acquired a large area reaching from High Street (now Trumpington Street) to the river. The ground was then covered by shops, private houses, hostels for students, and gardens, and there were several thoroughfares leading west from High Street, and across Milne Street, towards the river. By purchase from private owners or by grants from the Mayor and Corporation of the town, he became possessor of nearly all which the College at this day holds on the east of the Cam, except the space now covered by Bodley's building and some ground at the south-east corner. There was one important building, however, which it was necessary to demolish. This was the Church of St. John the Baptist, commonly called St. John Zachary, which stood on the west side of Milne Street, and probably so close to it that the high altar of the church was on ground afterwards enclosed within the western bays of the College Ante-Chapel. The parish of St. John Zachary was of some importance, including as it did the Colleges of Clare and Trinity Hall. Henry made arrangements for its being united with the adjoining parish of St. Edward's; the church was pulled down, and a new one built opposite

Gonville Hall. The necessary area being thus cleared, the King laid the first stone of the new Chapel on St. James's Day, July 25, 1446. The King's presence on this occasion has been doubted, because there exists a letter written by Henry to Abbot Curteys of Bury, telling the Abbot to be at Cambridge on Michaelmas Day, when the Marquis of Suffolk would lay the first stone, the pestilence then prevailing at Cambridge preventing the King himself from coming. But the year of this letter has been wrongly assumed to be 1446, in the course of which year Abbot Curteys died. It was probably written in 1445. Something must have happened to postpone the ceremony, for the College Register distinctly says that the King himself laid the first stone on July 25, 1446. A few months before he had granted to the College a quarry in Thefdale, near Tadcaster, which had already supplied material for a large part of York Minster. Two or three years later part of another quarry of Yorkshire limestone, viz., Huddleston, was allotted to the College ; this was the stone chiefly used in the lifetime of the King, and was no doubt conveyed to Cambridge, as it was to Eton, by water.

Nicholas Close has commonly been considered the architect of the Chapel. He was a man of Flemish family, and one of the six original Fellows. He had for a few years held the cure of the parish of St. John Zachary, and in 1450 became Bishop of Carlisle. He certainly received from the King the grant of a coat-of-arms for his services ; but an equally strong claim might perhaps be made out on behalf of John Langton, Master of Pembroke and Chancellor of the

University, who acted as overseer of the works till
1447, when he became Bishop of St. David's. And
if we accept the view of Mr. G. G. Scott, in his Essay
on English Church Architecture, the man who should
really have the credit of conceiving this great work was
the master-mason, Reginald Ely, appointed by a patent
of Henry VI. " to press masons, carpenters, and other
workers." According to Mr. Scott's view, Close and his
successors did the work which in modern days would
be done, though less efficiently, by a building committee; but they were ecclesiastics, not architects. It
is the master mason, not the more dignified " sur-
veyors," to whom the honour of planning the building
should be attributed.

The third overseer or surveyor was Robert Wodelarke, another of the six original Fellows, who was
made Provost in 1452. He seems to have acted as
overseer till the deposition of the King brought the
work to a standstill ; and finding that there was some
suspicion of his having embezzled part of the funds
allotted to the work, he drew up a statement in which
he tells us the following particulars: When Henry
was taken prisoner at St. Albans, 1455, the Earls of
Salisbury and Warwick promised to supply funds for
the College buildings, and told Wodelarke to collect
stonemasons and workmen. For some time they kept
their word ; and some part at least of the £1000 a
year, promised by Henry from the Duchy of Lancaster,
continued to be paid. But the exigencies of the State
soon absorbed all the revenues of the Duchy; and
Wodelarke found that he had to pay the workmen out
of his own pocket. So far from having made any

profit by his surveyorship, he found, on going into the accounts with Thomas Betts, the College auditor, that the payments exceeded the receipts by £228 10s. 4d.

When the great battle of Towton in 1461 gave the Crown to the young Duke of York, the two Colleges of his rival could not hope for any favour. And, in fact, Edward IV. did not spare either Eton or King's. But the former College seems to have suffered the more severely, much of its property being confiscated for the benefit of the Dean and Chapter of Windsor. Some of the King's College estates suffered the same fate, and the College is said to have lost land to the annual value of £1000, "no fewer than forty of the Fellows and Scholars, besides Conducts, Clerks, and Choristers," so runs the story, being "in one day forced to depart the house for want of maintenance." On the other hand, Edward is said to have restored to the College 500 marks of annual revenue on condition that they should acknowledge him for their Founder. Moreover, the College accounts show that during the twelve years which follow Edward's accession some attempts were made to carry on building operations, and apparently the "Provost's" Chapel in the new church was in use as early as 1470.

The restoration of Henry VI. in that year was only momentary, and could be of no benefit to his Colleges; but towards the close of Edward's reign there are signs of greater activity. This may have been due to the influence of Thomas Rotherham, Archbishop of York and Lord Chancellor of England. It was natural that he should take an interest in the College of which he had been made a Fellow in 1443, and of which he had once been Visitor as Bishop of Lincoln. Moreover, he was a true friend to education. Not only had he founded a College at Rotherham, his own native place, and enriched it with a large collection of books, but he had also re-founded Lincoln College at Oxford ; and at Cambridge he had built ṭthe east front of the new Schools with a Library above, which he had furnished with many valuable books. The College had another friend at Court in Walter Field, who was Chaplain to the King, and who succeeded Wodelarke as Provost in 1479. He was appointed the next overseer of the works, and before Edward's death in 1483 had found the means of spending nearly £1300 on the Chapel. It was at this time that the oolite from Weldon in Northamptonshire was first used ; the stonework of seven of the side windows at the east end was completed, and several of the Chantry Chapels were roofed in, two of them being vaulted with stone. It seems also that about this time the original design was seriously modified. Reginald Ely would probably have taken as his model the Lady Chapel at Ely ; the vault would have been arched, and the great space which is now left between the top of the windows and the spring of the vaulting would have been avoided. But in 1476 John Woolrich had succeeded to the place of master mason, and the vaulting shafts which he placed in the Choir, springing from corbels at the transom level, shew that he had determined to adopt the new fashion of fan vaulting, though the vault itself was built by other hands some thirty years later. He could not raise the windows, some of which were already finished, but he could carry up the wall above them to support his comparatively flat vault. It is, at any rate, certain that, whereas in the two easternmost chapels on the north side, as well as in other chapels, the work of which was already far advanced, we find the earlier and simpler "lierne" vaulting, this is discarded in the body of the church for the more magnificent style which had already been introduced on a smaller scale at Gloucester and in Oxford. The evidence, therefore, points to Woolrich as the man who designed, in the language of Wordsworth's sonnet,

> "that branching roof
> Self-poised, and scooped into ten thousand cells,
> Where light and shade repose, where music dwells
> Lingering—and wandering on as loth to die ;
> Like thoughts whose very sweetness yieldeth proof
> That they were born for immortality."

Although Rotherham himself was disgraced and sent to the Tower on the accession of Richard III. in 1483, yet the new King not only shewed his goodwill to the College by the gift of the estate of Biggin in Hertfordshire, but also ordered that the building should go on with all possible despatch. John Sturgeon is to press workmen, to provide materials, and to commit to prison all who should delay him. Between May and December 1484 about £750 had been spent, nearly all of which was provided by the King. The east window had been glazed with white glass, and the father of a scholar had furnished money for making another window in the Choir. From an extant letter of the Provost thanking the unknown donor, Mr. J. W. Clark has been able to identify the latter. The son's

christian-name was James, and the only James admitted
to the College before 1526 (for the name seems as yet
hardly to have crossed the Tweed) was James Denton,
afterwards Canon of Windsor. Liberality was heredi-
tary in the Denton family, for the son, besides other
improvements which he made at St. George's at his own
expense, "built the long and stately back-stairs from
the bottom of the hill unto the top, commonly known
by the name of the College Stairs," but more familiar
to our own generation as the "Hundred Steps."

Mr. Scott has no doubt that the windows of that
portion of the Chapel, which was finished by 1485, were
glazed with white glass, and a partition erected across
the Choir, so that it might be used for the church services,
as was commonly done in such cases. It must be remembered, however, that the Kingsmen already had a
smaller chapel, which they continued to use on ordinary
occasions, if not on all. At any rate, it is fairly certain
that the five eastern bays of the new building were by
this time finished and covered with a timber roof; and
thus, after nearly forty years, the great church planned
by the Founder was still a fragment, not half completed.

Now followed a period of more than twenty years of
absolute stagnation. It might have been expected
that a grandson of Queen Katherine would readily
adopt the scheme which was so dear to the heart of
Katherine's son; but till almost the eve of his death
Henry VII. took no notice of the College, to which
even Richard had shewn himself a generous patron. It
so happened, however, that in 1506 the King, in company with his mother, paid a visit to Cambridge and

attended service in the unfinished Chapel. This seems to have been the turning-point; at any rate, in the summer of 1508, more than a hundred masons or carpenters were again at work; and in the following spring, only three weeks before his death, Henry conveyed a sum of £5000 to the College, and enjoined his executors to provide as much more as might be necessary for completing the church. After this there was no further interruption in the work, which was of a kind likely to interest the new King, for Henry VIII. was, at that time, if we may trust the judgment of Erasmus, an enlightened and religious prince, and so true a friend to learning that there seemed to the Dutch scholar to be the promise of a golden age in England. It proved indeed to be little better than a "quinquennium Neronis"; but the quinquennium was prolonged sufficiently to secure the completion of King's College Chapel. The vaulting of the Choir and Ante-chapel was now executed with Weldon stone in 1512 and the following years; a "pattern tower" was built at the north-west corner; and, as it was approved, a contract was made for three other towers like it. Another contract provided for vaulting two porches with stone from Hampole in Yorkshire, as well as sixteen Chantry Chapels with Weldon stone. Apparently by July 1515 the fabric of the church was finished, and had cost, in the present value of money, about £160,000.

The design was new in English architecture, but not absolutely original; for in the Cathedral of Albi, in Southern France, as Mr. J. W. Clark has pointed out, as well as in two churches at Toulouse, vast buttresses supporting a great vault are in the same way supported

themselves by Chantry Chapels. At Albi, though the
stone work is plainer than our own, the vault has the
advantage of an extremely rich painted decoration ; such
as was intended, but never executed, at King's. But
the vaulting itself is of a kind peculiarly English ; and
it reappears in Bath Abbey, in St. George's Chapel at
Windsor, in Henry VII.'s Chapel at Westminster, and
in the ambulatory of the choir of Peterborough Cathedral. It is interesting to notice that one of these
buildings, Bath Abbey, was begun by a Kingsman,
Oliver King, who was Bishop of Bath and Wells from
1495 to 1503, and who had pulled down the old Abbey
Church. It was not only in the vaulting of the College
Chapel that the change of style appeared. The double
niches in the windows, and the profusion of heraldic
badges with which both the exterior and interior of the
Ante-chapel are enriched, if not overloaded, are examples
of the exuberance of detail which marks the last stage
of Perpendicular architecture. This was certainly a
departure from the Will of Henry VI., which directs
that the building should be constructed "in large
fourme, clene and substancial, settyng aparte super-
fluyte of too grete curyous werkes of entaylle and besy
moldyng." But probably the executors of Henry VII.
introduced these Tudor badges as evidence to future
generations that they had faithfully discharged the
trust committed to them.

With the exception of one bay at the east and two
at the west end, the main building is flanked by low
chapels. The Founder's will directs that an altar should
be placed in each of these "closets," and that there
should be a vestry on the north side "departed into

two howses beneath and two howses above." No such Vestry was built ; but some of the Chapels answered the same purpose, though most of them served as Chantries, where Masses were sung for the souls of individual Bene-factors. In two of these on the south side, opening into the Ante-chapel, and in one farther east on the north side, there is some painted glass of the fifteenth century. A vague tradition tells us that part of this came from Ramsey Abbey. It is at least as likely that it was taken from the church of St. John Zachary, which had been demolished to make room for the Chapel.

When the fabric was finished, no time was lost in glazing the windows. Bishop Fox, afterwards Provost, was originally entrusted with the supervision. He was executor to Henry VII., who may possibly have seen and approved the design; and as almoner to Henry VIII. Fox is believed to have used his influence in favour of a petition which the Provost and Scholars had presented for pecuniary aid. If only funds could be procured, the time was favourable for an artistic use of them. During the last half-century many illustrated books had appeared, chiefly in Holland and at Nuremberg, which provided the glass stainers with models for their subjects. The art of glass-staining too had itself ad-vanced; and, owing to the artist's increased mastery over his material, or from some other cause, the single figures characteristic of the fourteenth century had given way to large pictorial subjects. Barnard Flower, the King's glazier, received £100 in November 1515, and the same sum in February 1517; it seems that he completed four windows, one of which was that over the north porch. His death and other causes delayed matters, and it was not till 1526 that another contract provided for the completion of the remaining twenty-two windows within five years. Among the names of the glaziers we find some who seem to have been Flemings ; and it has been suggested that the designs were by foreigners and the execution by English hands. Such a man as Bernard van Orley may very possibly have had a share in the work. The scenes representing the Death of Ananias, and Paul and Barnabas at Lystra, remind us of Raphael's cartoons, and may even be derived from them.

The contract of 1526 specified the windows of the King's new Chapel at Westminster as the model to be followed ; the price was to be 1s. 6d. per foot, and the windows were to be secured with double bonds of lead " for defence of great wyndes and outragious wetheringes." The windows were to represent the "story of the old lawe and of the new lawe." Above and below the transom in each are two separate pictures, each pair being divided by a " Messenger," who bears a scroll with a legend giving the subject represented. In the lower tier the windows, from north-west to south-west, represent the Life of the Virgin, the Life of Christ, and the History of the Church as recorded in the Acts of the Apostles. The upper tier has scenes from the Old Testament or from Apocryphal sources, which prefigure the events recorded below. But the whole of the east window is devoted to the Passion and Crucifixion ; the first window of the series is filled with scenes connected with the Birth of the Virgin ; three of the later windows on the south side are entirely taken

up with the History of St. Paul or St. Peter; while the
two last of the series, at the south-west corner, represent the Death and Assumption of the Virgin, together
with the appropriate types; so that the general plan
is not strictly preserved throughout. The series of
scenes from the Acts is perhaps due to the influence of
the approaching Reformation; at any rate, St. Paul
had been but little prominent hitherto in medieval
art.

The Last Judgment would in all probability have
formed the subject of the west window, as it does at
Fairford Church in Gloucestershire. The windows of
that church date from about 1490; and, like our own,
are a combination of English and foreign workmanship, if
we may judge by their characteristic details; like our
own, too, they represent the story of the Law and the
Gospel; but the plan is different, perhaps owing to the
smaller size of the windows. On the north side stand a
series of Prophets, each bearing a text, and opposite to
them are the Apostles holding sentences from the Creed.
Within the Chancel Screen the windows depict the
story of the Virgin, the Passion, and the Resurrection;
and to make the history more complete, in the cleres-
tory are represented on the north the persecutors, and
on the south the martyrs of the Church. The Fairford
windows are said to have been taken down and concealed in 1643, when Essex was marching upon Ciren-
cester. The story, in this case, is not improbable; at
any rate they survive, and besides their own intrinsic
beauty they furnish a most interesting and instructive
parallel to our own glass.

Before the windows were quite finished an estimate,

was made for filling the fifty-four niches with statues
and for painting and gilding the great vault. As the
plan of our windows follows that of Henry VII.'s
Chapel, it is probable that the plan of the statuary,
which still remains in that Chapel, would also have
been followed. We can but guess what would have
been the combined effect of glass, painted vault, and
statues, for the two latter works were never executed.
Money perhaps fell short. What there was, was
applied to the erection of the rood-loft and lower
portion of the stalls. As the rood-loft has the arms,
badge, and initials of Anne Boleyn, its date must be
between 1533 and 1536. It is generally considered to
be of Italian workmanship; but Mr. Scott thinks it
French rather than Italian in character, and compares
it to the stallwork of the church of St. Bertrand de
Comminges in the Pyrenees, which bears the date of
1537. The " Will " of Henry VI. ordered thirty-six
stalls on each side, exclusive of those placed against the
rood-loft, for seventy Fellows and ten Conducts. No
sub-stalls were mentioned, but if distinguished strangers
were present, they were to occupy some of the stalls,
while the Fellows stood below. The number of stalls
was eventually reduced to sixty, and these were as yet
without their canopies, except those adjoining the
rood-loft. But the walls throughout were probably
covered with hangings.

A high altar was erected in 1545, but was removed
four years later, on the publication of King Edward's
first Prayer-book. The brass lectern, given by Robert
Hacumblen, who was Provost 1509–28, was already in
the Choir, which was paved with grey English marble,

the gift of the King. About this time also a clock-house was placed at the north-east corner of the Chapel; it was a wooden building with a tiled roof surmounted by a tapering spire, and there it stood till 1817.

Even if no organ as yet stood in the rood-loft, some simple instrument was doubtless used from the first to accompany the Choir. Provision was certainly made for another kind of church music; for five bells were sent by the Founder in 1443, and were hung in a wooden belfry a little to the west of the Chapel. They are said to have been the largest in England; one story makes Pope Calixtus III. their donor, and another tells us that they were taken from a French Church after the battle of Agincourt. Whatever their origin, Mr. J. W. Clark's researches into the College accounts shew that they were replaced by at least one fresh set before 1470. The campanile projected by the Founder was never built, and the wooden belfry proved an insufficient protection. Early in the eighteenth century it fell into decay, and was removed in 1739. For a time the bells stood in the Ante-chapel, but in 1754 they were sold for the sum of £533 10s. 3d., two of them being cracked and the others considered useless.

The new church was probably ready for constant use by 1536 or 1537; and it was in one of those years, by a singular coincidence, that the old Chapel, which had provided the means of worship to so many genera-tions of Kingsmen, fell one evening, happily after the conclusion of Vespers, so that no one was hurt. The great Chapel and its services will generally be recog-nised as the most striking features of King's College; the deepest and widest influences exercised by the

College during three centuries and a half are due to them, and the question is naturally asked, why the building is so impressive. Certainly, it has not escaped criticism ; but the fault which is found with its exterior lies not in its construction but in its isolated position. It is, in fact, a fragment of the Founder's great design. Had the church been connected with a quadrangle on the south and a cloister on the west, the four turrets of the main building leading up to the great campanile of the cloisters, the general effect would have been very different.

Even as it stands, however, it is a marvellous work. In one sense it is unique, for it is a Cathedral in size and a College Chapel in plan. It is striking also from its apparent unity of design. We have seen that important modifications were, in fact, introduced during the seventy years which elapsed between the laying of the first stone and the completion of the fabric ; but to the uninitiated eye it might have been the creation of a single night; and in this respect it offers a contrast to most English Cathedrals, which charm us by the varieties of their architecture almost as much as by their intrinsic beauty. It is interesting also as the meeting-point of the last Gothic with the earliest Renaissance work. And the effect produced by the combination of the great stone vault with the long line of rich glass is one which can hardly be felt elsewhere, except, indeed, at York Minster, where, alone among English Cathedrals, there is the same happy union of old stone work with old glass ; and there, though both architecture and glass are earlier and in themselves perhaps more interesting than at King's, yet they are

CHAPEL: INTERIOR (LOOKING EAST)

not brought into such close contact with each other. Like other really great works, King's Chapel produces an impression which is instantaneous and at the same time permanent. It does not disarm criticism, but it compels admiration. And if any one is inclined to criticise, let him look at the exterior on a moonlight night from the south side of the Quadrangle, or from the top of Trinity Street; or let him take his stand within the Ante-chapel at the north-west corner on a bright summer's day, and cast his eye along the coloured glass and stone vaulting till he catches a part of the east window rising above the stately rood-loft; and if he does not feel that there is an inspiration in the building which is above criticism, he must be a

" Man that hath no music in himself."

c

CHAPTER III

THE NEW LEARNING

WHILE the Chapel was growing in beauty, the Society was gradually making itself felt in the University. But the close of the fifteenth century was not remarkable for activity of mind, at least in the English Universities. Bishop Fisher, looking back from the year 1506, says that

"a weariness of learning and study had stolen on the University, whether owing to quarrels with townsmen, or the prevailing fevers, or that there was a lack of helpers and patrons of letters."

One is tempted to connect with this complaint the fact that a large proportion of those admitted to King's College threw up their Scholarships and left Cambridge without proceeding to a degree; but as this habit continued till late in Elizabeth's reign, it must have been owing to other causes than those which Fisher enumerates. It does not seem to have been due to a lack of intellectual or practical ability in the Provosts Robert Wodelarke (Third Provost) was prominent in the University, as well as energetic in carrying on the building of his own College Chapel in dark days; while by founding St. Catharine's Hall he at least shewed his

willingness to promote education. His successor, Walter
Field, had been Chaplain to Edward IV., and during
the first part of his Provostship, which lasted twenty
years, was even more successful than Wodelarke in
obtaining supplies for the building; and John Argentine
was enough of a scholar to propose a series of subjects
for his "Act," as incepting Master of Arts, in Latin
Hexameters. Up to this time, however, Latin must
have monopolised the attention of Cambridge students,
and the Latin of the Schoolmen more than that of
classical authors; and it may be that the early Provosts
of King's were administrators rather than teachers. Of
Richard Hatton, who was Provost from 1507 to 1509,
a curious story is told, which rests on fairly good
evidence.

"He was a very high coloured man in the Face, which
happened to him after this Manner, and for which he could
never get any Cure. When he was Bursar, being on the
Road to London upon College Business, and having a considerable charge of Money about him, he was tempted to
take some Repose under the shade of some Trees during
the excessive Heat; but happening to fall asleep, a Welsh
servant that attended him, endeavouring to cut his Throat,
awaked him; upon which he striving to defend himself,
the Villain struck him across the face with a Dagger; but
being overmatched by his Master in the Struggle was by
him carried to the next Town, and from thence to the
County Gaol, where the Law had its course against him.
After he was chosen Provost he rarely wore his Doctor's
Robes; and being asked the Reason of it, he replied that
a Scarlet Gown did not become so bloody a Colour, at the
same time pointing to his face."

The new learning was now beginning to dawn upon Cambridge. Erasmus began his residence as Lady Margaret's Professor in 1511. Among his earliest friends were two young Kingsmen, John Bryan, who was afterwards a champion of the genuine text of Aristotle, and Robert Aldrich, who went with Erasmus to Walsingham in Norfolk, where they made fun of the relics. The character of Aldrich was perhaps hardly on a par with his intelligence and learning; but he was a successful man, was employed on missions to the Pope and the King of France, and became Provost of Eton and Bishop of Carlisle. He is said to have complied with all the changes of religion, and in the reign of Mary acted as a Commissioner for the suppression of heresies. His office of Bishop took him away from Eton during the session of Parliament, but it does not seem to have kept him much in his diocese, for in 1541 the Privy Council found that he was "lingering at his comfortable residence at Eton," and commanded him to return to Carlisle, "there to remain for the feeding of the people both with his preaching and good hospitality."

Erasmus left Cambridge in the late autumn of 1513, disheartened by his apparent want of success. But the seed was sown; and seven years later, he declares that sound theology is flourishing at Paris and Cambridge more than at any other University, "because they are receiving the new learning not as an enemy but courteously as a guest." A welcome, too, was given at many Cambridge Colleges to Erasmus's great work, the *Novum Instrumentum*, printed at Basle in 1516, in which not only a more genuine text of the Greek

Testament is furnished to students, but the comments
of Erasmus set forth the real teaching of Christ and his
Apostles in glaring contrast to the doctrine and practices
of clergy and monks.

It was about this time, in 1518, that Bryan of King's
in his lectures as a Regent M.A., turned aside from the
old disputes on nominalism and realism, and taught
from a genuine Greek text of Aristotle himself.   But
now a greater champion of Greek appeared from the ·
same College in the person of Richard Croke.   This
remarkable man had certainly not been a " home-keep-
ing youth."   Soon after taking his B.A. degree he had
removed to Oxford in order to study Greek under
Grocyn.   After this he had gone abroad and taught
the language at Cologne, Louvain, and Leipsic.   It was
at this last University that his reputation reached its
highest point.   Erasmus, writing in 1515, says, " Crocus
regnat in Academia Lipsiensi " : and at Erfurt a foreign
scholar found himself famous simply because he had
been a pupil of Croke, " qui primus putabatur ita
docuisse Græcam linguam in Germania ut plane perdisci
illam posse . . . nostri homines sese intelligere arbitra-
rentur."   An Englishman teaching Greek to Germans
strikes us as rather a strange phenomenon.   By the
year 1519 Croke had returned to Cambridge, taken a
M.A. degree, and been appointed Greek Reader to the
University.   Compared to his predecessor Erasmus, he
started with a great advantage ; for he was young and
vigorous, an Englishman dealing with English students,
and one who added to this the prestige of a brilliant
career on the Continent ; and there were " Trojans "
enough at Cambridge to make such advantages valuable

to a champion of Greek. His inaugural lecture is, in
part, an apology for the study of the language. It was
delivered in Latin of Quintilian's style. He urges that
Greek is the tongue of a superior race; in itself and in
its literature to be preferred to Latin. He professes
not to undervalue the Schoolmen and the old-fashioned
disputations; but Greek is useful for the studies both
of the Trivium and the Quadrivium, and invaluable for
that knowledge of the New Testament which has a
paramount claim on theologians. And, after all, Greek
is not so very difficult; time can be found for it if men
will deduct a little from what is now given to sleep,
sports, play, and idle talk. A few years later the poet
Skelton complains that the new learning has driven out
the old; and as Croke was elected Public Orator for life
for the two reasons curiously coupled together, that
"primus invexit literas Graecas et regi carus est," we
may be pretty sure that his lectures were really successful. The University of Oxford, where he had first
learned his Greek, offered him a large stipend to reside
and teach it there. Archbishop Warham and Sir
Thomas More pressed him to consent, but Fisher's
influence succeeded for the time in keeping him at
Cambridge. Probably it was Fisher's influence also
which had provided him with a Fellowship at St. John's;
and if so, it was the more ungracious, not to say
ungrateful, in Croke that he protested against a proposal to hold an annual service in commemoration of
the man who had done so much both for St. John's
College and the University. Some years later, in 1531,
Croke became a Canon of Wolsey's new College at
Oxford, which had not yet taken the name of Christ

Church. But in the interval he had made himself conspicuous by his efforts on the question of the divorce of Queen Catherine, consulting MSS. at Venice or Bologna for passages in support of Henry's view, and administering gratuities to win or to reward the goodwill of the learned men with whom he conferred at the Italian Universities. It is to be feared that the sunshine of royal favour had converted the scholar into a courtier, and that there is some truth in Dr. Caius's description of him as " homo certe doctus sed in gloriam suam officiosissimus." One cannot but regret that the last recorded act of his life was that he testified to Cranmer's heresy at Oxford in September 1555. He had begun by urging the duty of studying the New Testament. He had boasted to Cromwell of the number of sermons which he had preached in favour of the King's supremacy. It is possible that his Protestantism stopped here, and that his own religious convictions remained the same as those of his royal master.

If King's College had given Richard Croke to St. John's, the latter College repaid the debt by giving John Cheke to King's. It was he, more than any one else, who carried on the work of Erasmus and Croke, and made Cambridge students familiar with the poets, historians, and philosophers of Greece. But his career as a teacher belongs to the history of his first College. It was not till 1548 that he became Provost of King's. Naturally there was some resistance to his election, as he had none of the qualifications required by the Statutes ; but, ten years earlier, the Fellows had accepted another alien in the person of George Day, and it was not safe to resist the King's will. Cheke had resigned his Greek Professorship a year before, and was now a Member of Parliament, and a statesman, though he still remained Tutor to Prince Edward. He must have felt some scruples in taking the place of his own old Tutor, Day, still Bishop of Chichester, though now in disgrace and prison ; and a few years later we find him writing a touching letter to King Edward on behalf of the late Provost, and at the same time recommending Walter Haddon as successor to his own office at King's. At this time Cheke believed himself to be dying ; and perhaps it would have been better for his own happiness and fame if his life had not been prolonged. But he recovered from his illness ; he was knighted, and became Secretary of State to Lady Jane Grey ; and it was at his Lodge that the Duke of Northumberland was arrested. The part which he took at this crisis was naturally fatal to his own fortunes. After a short stay in the Tower, he was allowed to go abroad ; but he was deprived of his Provostship and of his private estates, and reduced to support himself by teaching at Strasburg. Three years later he was arrested in Flanders, and sent to the Tower once more. This time he was not to be spared except on one condition, viz., that he should recant the Protestantism of which he had been a champion. In a weak moment he gave way ; but remorse for his weakness affected his health, and he died at a friend's house in London in 1557.

Neither Cheke nor Croke seem to have been of the stuff of which martyrs are made ; but all testimony goes to show that Cheke, at least, was a warm-hearted and honourable man. And it may be that for men of the keenest intellect and greatest learning it was

doubly difficult to attain such certainty on points of
controversial theology, as would enable them to stake
everything on the truth of the views which they had
themselves sincerely adopted. At any rate, these two
men had done much to give their College a prominent
position in the University and to secure the teaching of
Greek within its walls. Every College had indeed been
ordered, in 1535, to provide a daily public lecture both
in Latin and Greek; but it appears that, after the
foundation of the Regius Professorship in 1540, King's
was one of the only three Colleges in which the Greek
lecture was still maintained. No doubt the comparative wealth of the College was much in its favour.
When Parliament, in 1534, granted Henry VIII. the
first fruits and tenths of ecclesiastical foundations, a
valuation of College incomes was made. At Cambridge
King's came first with £751; St. John's next with
£507. The stipend of the Provost was so much above
that of other Heads that a Master of St. John's did not
hesitate to accept the Provostship of King's.

By 1545, when a dissolution of Colleges was threatened, and the University begged the Queen (Katherine
Parr) to intercede for them, the revenue of King's
College had risen to £1010; and the list of members
which follows must have made an imposing show
compared to other foundations. It consists of a Provost, Vice-Provost, Dean of Divinity, two Deans of Arts,
three Bursars, a Sacrist, four Fellows who were Priests,
fifteen not Priests, nineteen B.A. Fellows, twenty-four
Scholars. Considering the requirements of the Statutes,
the number of four Priests seems small, but probably all
or most of the eight officers were also in Priests' orders.

The large proportion of young members of the College
is also noticeable; forty-three out of seventy had not
resided more than seven years in the College, and the
average number of vacant Scholarships in each year
must have been eight.   The list of stipendiary members
is made up of ten Priests Conducts, six Clerks, sixteen
Choristers, an Auditor, a Clerk of Accounts, Stewards,
a Clerk of Sacristy, and thirteen servants.

During this period we find evidence that the provisions of the Statutes requiring two of the Fellows to
study medicine had borne some fruit.   Provost Argentine was physician to the two sons of Henry VII. ; John
Blythe, who had married Sir John Cheke's sister, and
must therefore have ceased to be an actual Fellow of
King's, was the first Regius Professor of Physic ; and
before the close of the century two more Kingsmen
held the same Professorship.

CHAPTER IV

BISHOPS AND MARTYRS

EVERY Scholar of King's College, on completing his three years of probation, was bound by the Statutes to swear that he would never throughout life favour the errors or heresies of John Wyclif, Reginald Pecock, or any other heretic. It was now to be seen whether this obligation would bear the strain of a religious revolution. The revival of the study of Greek and the publication of Erasmus's New Testament had given the first impulse to the spirit of inquiry, and in 1520 Luther's three famous treatises appeared. Pecock had questioned the authority of Fathers and Schoolmen, but had stoutly maintained that of the Pope. Luther appealed from the Pope to a General Council, and demanded that the teaching of the Schoolmen should be superseded by that of the Bible. Within a year the three treatises were burned at St. Paul's Cross, and the meetings of reformers at Cambridge were necessarily held in secret. The White Horse Inn, which adjoined the Bull Hotel on the north, was the place chosen, and received the nickname of " Germany." A young Scholar of King's, John Frith, was among those who frequented this place; but the leading spirit was Thomas Bilney, of Trinity Hall, and it was he who, a

few years later, converted Hugh Latimer. The Bishop
of Ely at this time was Nicholas West, who was in
many ways a typical mediæval prelate. The son of a
baker in Putney, he was now second only to Wolsey,
the butcher's son, in his magnificence. He became a
Scholar of King's in 1477, and if we could believe
Fuller's account

" was so desperately turbulent that, discontented with the
loss of the Proctorship, he endeavoured to fire the Provost's
lodgings; and having stolen some silver spoons departed
the College. Afterwards he became a new man, D.D., and
Bishop of Ely, who to expiate his former faults gave many
rich gifts and plate to the College, and built part of the
Provost's lodgings."

It is difficult, however, to accept the first part of this
story in the face of the facts that he held his Fellowship till 1498, that he was appointed to the College
living of Kingston in 1502, and that he became Dean
of Windsor in 1510. In the early years of Henry VIII.'s
reign he was often employed in the highest diplomatic
missions, and accompanied the King to the Field of the
Cloth of Gold. At Ely, where he became Bishop in 1515,
he had 100 servants in rich liveries to attend him, while
200 poor were daily fed at his palace gates. And his
magnificence survived him in the rich Memorial Chapel
which he raised for himself at the south-east corner
of the Choir of the Cathedral. It was likely that such
a man would come into collision with the Cambridge
reformers ; and the fame of Latimer's preaching induced
him to pay a surprise visit to St. Mary's. Latimer was
equal to the occasion, changed his text, and preached

on the contrast between the lives led by the superior clergy and the life of their Master. The Bishop afterwards thanked Latimer for expounding the duties of the Episcopal office, but begged him to preach one more sermon in the same place against Martin Luther and his doctrine. Latimer excused himself on the ground that he did not know Luther's doctrine, and that at Cambridge they were not allowed to read his works ; he was sure, however, that what he had that day preached was Scripture doctrine. For the moment the Bishop was checkmated, but he had his revenge by preaching himself against Latimer at Barnwell Abbey, and he followed this up by inhibiting Latimer from preaching. Strange to say, this inhibition was shortly afterwards removed by Wolsey. Four years later, in 1529, Latimer's two " sermons on the Card " (in which he borrowed terms from the games which marked the festivities of Christmas in order to illustrate the duties of a Christian life), provoked the Bishop to attack him once more; but this time Buckenham, a Dominican Prior, was Latimer's chief antagonist. The contest, however, was stopped by a letter from the King's Almoner, Edward Fox, who was now Provost of West's old College. When Bishop West died in 1533, another Kingsman, Nicholas Hawkins, was nominated as his successor. There would probably have been changes in the Palace at Ely had he lived to be consecrated, for as Archdeacon he had sold, at a time of famine, all his plate and goods to relieve the poor of the Isle of Ely, and was content himself to be served in wooden dishes and earthen pots.

One more Kingsman may be mentioned, who was

certainly not on the side of the reformers. This was Richard Master, of Maidstone, who had served the office of Proctor, and left the College as a B.D., with the character of an excellent scholar and philosopher. His philosophy, however, was not equal to the ordeal which awaited him, when he became Rector of Aldington, in Romney Marsh, a living to which Archbishop Warham had once presented Erasmus, and the tithes of which were still paid to Erasmus as a pension. One of his parishioners, a servant-girl, Elizabeth Barton, was popularly supposed to have been miraculously cured, and to be an inspired prophetess. There were men in the county who could not resist the temptation to make use of her for their own ecclesiastical or political purposes. She was removed to Canterbury, and as the Nun of Kent she denounced the views of the reformers, but especially the King's marriage with Anne Boleyn, and prophesied his speedy death. She may have begun by being hysterical; she certainly ended by being an impostor. During the earlier part of her career she was encouraged by Master; her fame brought pilgrims and gifts to his parish; but it is quite possible that his belief in her was genuine, for Fisher would not disown her, and Warham thought her claims serious enough to be brought before Wolsey and the King himself. The sequel was tragical enough. An act of attainder was passed against the unfortunate maid and her patrons, and Master himself was one of those who were executed as traitors.

About this time, 1525-27, Cardinal Wolsey was founding at Oxford his College, which bore the names of "Cardinal" and "King's" before it gained its final designation of Christ Church. The Master of Pembroke was invited to choose Cambridge men to go as colonists to the new settlement. Whether by accident or design, several of the Kingsmen chosen were men whose minds were ripe for Lutheran doctrine. Of Richard Cox and John Frith mention will be made hereafter, but Fuller adds to these John Fryer and Henry Sumptner. Fryer seems to have been a man of versatile gifts, for when he was committed a prisoner to the Master of the Savoy, he "did much solace himself with playing the lute, wherein he had great skill." He then escaped, went abroad, and became an eminent physician; but he ultimately returned to England and to the Roman Catholic obedience. Henry Sumptner was less fortunate, for he was thrown into a cave under the College, where the salt fish was kept, and died in 1527 from bad food and foul air.

In Nicholas West we had an instance of a prosperous prelate who would make no terms with the reformers. Two Kingsmen must now be mentioned, who in different ways and with marked success adopted the cause of Protestantism. These were Edward Fox and Richard Cox. Six or seven years only separated them at College; but Fox, the senior, died before the crisis of the religious troubles when under fifty years of age; Cox lived on far into the quieter times of Queen Elizabeth. Fox appears chiefly as the champion and advocate of Henry's divorce from his first wife. As secretary to Wolsey he first gains his introduction into political life. In 1528 he is sent to Rome with Bishop Gardiner to induce Clement VII. to grant a Bull for the divorce of Catherine. The next year he introduces

Cranmer to the King as a man who will be a useful ally; and in 1530 he takes a chief part in persuading the University of Cambridge to pass a vote favourable to Henry's prime object. Mr. Mullinger's account of the way in which this result was achieved shews us that Fox and his friends were far from scrupulous about the means which they employed in gaining their end. Fox's exertions in the cause did not, however, stop here; at Oxford and at Paris he helped to obtain similar decisions from the Universities. He had his reward, for he was made Provost of King's in 1528 and Bishop of Hereford in 1535. It was in this last year that he went to Smalcald to win over the Protestant Princes to the "King's Cause"; at Wittenberg he had an interview with Luther, who was too honest to promise more than a fair inquiry into the merits of the case; and at Frankfort he waited till the German divines dismissed him with an answer which seemed to condemn both the King's original marriage with Katherine and his subsequent conduct in divorcing her. In 1538 Fox died. It is impossible to feel sympathy for the cause to which he devoted his life; but he was undoubtedly a subtle and able negotiator, and among his contemporaries his talents and eloquence gave him great influence. He was called "the wonder of the University and the darling of the Court." Some of his sayings sound like anticipations of aphorisms in Bacon's essays.

If Fox's name is identified with the Divorce question, Richard Cox was no less the champion of the Book of Common Prayer. As Tutor and Almoner of Edward VI. he naturally took a part in compiling both editions of the book; and during his exile in Mary's reign he had

an opportunity of showing the strength of his attach-
ment to the English liturgy. At Frankfort a number
of Protestant refugees were collected, who had been
persuaded by John Knox to discard their Prayer Book.
Cox came to the rescue in March 1554, and for a year
the controversy raged. Cox insisted on repeating the
responses and in reading the Litany from the pulpit.
Knox, when he got his turn, inveighed against the
Prayer Book, and twitted Cox with the number of
ecclesiastical offices which he had held. Cox had
undoubtedly been a pluralist, but he gained his point,
and Knox was forbidden to preach and requested by
the authorities to leave the town. Nearly ten years
before this Cox had done good service to the Universities
as well as to the Church. In 1546, Parliament had
placed the properties of the Colleges at the disposal of
the King, and it was partly owing to a spirited protest
made by Cox to Sir William Paget, Secretary of State,
to "stay impropriations," that confiscation was averted.
He was never afraid to speak out; he told Queen
Elizabeth that his conscience would not permit him to
officiate in her chapel if she continued to use lights and
a crucifix; and he risked his influence with her still
further by defending the right of Deans and Canons to
marry, urging that enforced celibacy would result in
their non-residence. In this last matter he certainly
practised what he preached, for at seventy years of age
he married a second wife; an offence so grave in the
Queen's eyes, that he was brought before the Star
Chamber and narrowly escaped imprisonment. But, as
a general rule, his words were braver than his deeds;
and he had no notion of toleration either for Romanists

or for Protestant "Sectaries."   Another blot also rests
on his memory.   He was one of the Commissioners
who destroyed valuable books and MSS. in the Oxford
libraries under the pretext that they tended to Popery.
It would seem that neither as Headmaster of Eton nor
as Dean of Christ Church, both of which offices he held,
had he learned to respect literary documents; and Sir
J. Harington tells us how

" an Oxford doctor said merrily to a Cambridge man that
Oxford had formerly a good Library till such time as a
Cambridge man became our Chancellor, and so cancelled,
catalogued, and scattered our books as from that time to
this we could never recover them."

As Bishop of Ely Cox had much difficulty in defending
the estates of the See from the encroachments of the
Crown and courtiers.   He did, indeed, succeed in preventing Lord North from appropriating the Palace of
Somersham and Manor of Downham ; but, after a hard
fight, he had to surrender his house at Holborn to Sir
Christopher Hatton.   At last, worn out with years and
troubles, he desired to resign his Bishopric, and retire
to the Palace and Manor of Doddington with a pension
of £200.   His enemies accused him of avarice; but
Leland, when asked if he could find a perfect character,
chose Cox, of whom he wrote :

> " Is vir judicio omnium piorum
>   Omni ex parte fidelis integerque."

Leland, however, only knew him in his younger days,
and there may be truth in Sir J. Harington's verdict,
" Cœpisti melius quam desinis."

Such men as Cox probably escaped the stake by
voluntary exile; but there were others who either could
not, or would not, adopt this course. John Frith was
the first member of the College who suffered death for
his religious opinions, when hardly thirty years of age;
the friend and assistant of William Tyndale, and a man
in whom even his enemies could find no flaw. He was
the son of an innkeeper at Sevenoaks, and as a B.A. of
1525 was one of the batch of Cambridge Scholars who
were established at Wolsey's College in Oxford. Here
his opinions got him into trouble; but he was allowed
to go abroad, where he lived for several years at Mar-
burg and in Holland. His abilities were such that
Henry VIII. was ready to promote him if he would
renounce his opinions. Instead of doing this, he wrote
a treatise on Purgatory which was sure to bring him
into collision with Sir Thomas More and Bishop Fisher.
In 1532 he came over to England, having some business
to transact with the Prior at Reading. There he was
seized as a vagrant and put in the stocks; but a benevolent schoolmaster, struck by his learning, exerted
himself to obtain his freedom. However, he was too
well known to escape for long; and being arrested in
London, and sent to the Tower, he there occupied himself in writing his views on the Sacrament of the Lord's
Supper, a work which was the real cause of his death,
for he repudiated Transubstantiation, and maintained
the doctrine subsequently adopted in the English
Prayer Book. Sir Thomas More got possession of
a copy of his treatise and wrote an answer to it;
Frith himself was examined by various Bishops; and
Cranmer, who afterwards adopted Frith's views, tried to

persuade him to renounce them. But Frith stood firm, and was burnt at Smithfield, July 4, 1533.

More than twenty years later three other Kingsmen followed in his steps. One of these was Laurence Saunders, a man of good family, who was apprenticed to a London merchant; but, having a distaste for business and an irrepressible yearning for religious truth, he soon returned to Cambridge, and studied Greek, Hebrew, and the Scriptures. He became first a lecturer in Divinity at Fotheringay, and then Rector of a London church. It is said of him that on Mary's accession he met a certain Dr. Pendleton, and that Saunders confessed that he doubted his own strength to bear much suffering. The doctor reproved him ; but when the ordeal came, it was Pendleton who failed and Saunders who stood firm. He might have escaped when Sir Thomas Wyatt with his army reached Southwark, but he considered the insurrection illegal, and would not take advantage of it. After fifteen months of imprisonment he was taken to Coventry to be burned.

At Coventry, too, suffered Robert Glover, a layman and a man of some property in the Midlands. His arrest was accidental, for his elder brother was named in the warrant, but had escaped ; and Robert, who was in bad health, was seized in his place. It is evident from Glover's letter to his wife that love for her and anxiety for his young children's welfare made it difficult for him to die. But he refused to recant. Out of weakness he was made strong. The fourth Kingsman, John Hullier, left the College when still a Scholar ; but he afterwards became a Conduct or Chaplain of the College, and Vicar of Babraham ; and he is interesting

as being apparently the only resident who suffered at
Cambridge in Queen Mary's reign.   He was burned on
Jesus Green.

Meanwhile, a Commission appointed by Cardinal
Pole, among whom were the Master of Trinity and the
Provost of Eton, were visiting Cambridge in order to
extirpate heresy at its source.   Their headquarters were
at King's College.   According to Fuller, they

"resorted to King's College because the same for the
worthiness thereof was chief and sovereign of all the
residue, or else because that house especially, before all
others, had been counted time out of mind never to be
without a heretic (as they term them) or twain.   And at
that present time, albeit that many now of late had withdrawn themselves from thence, yet they judged there were
some remaining still."

At King's they began their proceedings by hearing a
Mass of the Holy Ghost, two of them occupying the
Provost's stall and two the Vice-Provost's.   There also
they dined ; but, being anxious to appear as judges
rather than guests, they "ordered that not more than
three kinds of meat at most should be prepared."   Yet
"one capon chanced to be served more than was prescribed, and they thrust it away in great displeasure."
The Provost, Dr. Brassie, who had already shewn his
independence of spirit as Vice-Chancellor, by resisting
a movement on the part of the impoverished University to sell to the townsmen the privileges which the
University possessed in Sturbridge Fair, is described
as a " worthy old man both for his wisdom and his hoar
hairs."   He protested against the jurisdiction of the

Commissioners, and declared that the reformation of his house belonged solely to the Bishop of Lincoln. Such a protest was not likely to weigh much with men backed by the authority of a Cardinal, but it does not seem that the Commissioners did much harm. Provost Atkinson, a staunch Romanist, who had succeeded Sir John Cheke in 1553, and had died of the Plague three years later when on a College circuit, had already replaced the high Altar, and had perhaps not left much for the Commissioners to do. They examined books, but it does not appear that they followed Cox's example by destroying any. All that is recorded is that the Provost and many Fellows "received injunctions and penance very grievous to some."

CHAPTER V

THE SPACIOUS TIMES OF GREAT ELIZABETH

THE accession of Elizabeth must have been welcomed by the Universities, as well as by the nation at large, with feelings of relief and hope. Neither learning nor discipline was flourishing at Cambridge, and in the year 1558–59 only twenty-eight students proceeded to the B.A. degree. Dr. Caius, who revisited the University at this time after a long absence, was struck by the change for the worse. He missed the dignified elders of former days proceeding to the disputations in the schools, attended by the chief members of their respective Colleges.

The undergraduates no longer respectfully saluted their seniors from afar and made way for them in the streets; many seemed to have discarded the long gown and cap. They wandered about the town, frequenting taverns and wine-shops; their nether garments were of gaudy colours; they gambled and ran into debt. Though the study of Greek had been introduced half a century ago, yet the number of the parish clergy who understood even Latin was small. Elizabeth and her Ministers were determined to improve this state of things, and in particular to promote the study of theology at the Universities. The character of that theology could not fail to be affected by the Continental Protestantism which the exiled divines now brought back to England; and it was perhaps in order to shew that she did not mean to break entirely with the past that Elizabeth authorised the use of a Latin version of the Prayer Book in College Chapels. A competent translator was found in a Kingsman, Walter Haddon, who was reputed to be the best Latin writer of his time, and who had lately held the Mastership of Trinity Hall and the Regius Professorship of Civil Law.

In most Colleges the existing Heads declined to take the oath of Supremacy, and either resigned or were expelled. At King's College it so happened that Provost Brassie died. The place had been promised by Queen Mary to Richard Grey, Vicar of Withyham; but Elizabeth, while still at Hatfield, nominated Philip Baker, a native of Barnstaple, and at this time Rector of Elsworth in Huntingdonshire.

The choice turned out an unfortunate one, and Baker, as Vice-Chancellor in 1562, made a bad beginning by committing to prison the Vice-Master of Trinity, on grounds which proved to be insufficient when an appeal was made to the Chancellor.

The interest which the Queen took in her two Universities was shewn by a visit to Cambridge in the summer of 1564. At 2 P.M. on August 5, the Queen rode in from Haslingfield, and found the members of the University lining the street from Queens' College to the west door of King's Chapel. Within the Ante-chapel stood Provost Baker and others in copes. The church itself was hung with tapestry, and the floor

covered with rushes and carpeting. As soon as Elizabeth reached the west door, William Master, a Fellow of
King's, and Public Orator, delivered a long Latin speech,
which the Queen, still seated on her horse, occasionally
interrupted by comments partly in Latin and partly in
English. When at last Master stopped, she commended
him, wondered at his memory, and said she would reply
in Latin, but her Latin would be false, and they would
laugh at her. Then the choir sang in English, and the
whole party moved up into the inner chapel, the Queen
taking her place under a canopy at the east end. The
Provost began the *Te Deum* in English, which was
solemnly sung in pricksong, the organs playing; this
was followed by evensong. The Queen then went out
by a passage made through a window of the north-east
side chapel to her lodgings at King's Lodge, receiving
on her way a present of gloves and comfits.

The Lodge was a long, low building, standing
between the east end of the Chapel and the High Street.
The greater part of it had been built at the same time
as the old Court; and an inventory of 1452 specifies
seven rooms besides a pantry, buttery, and a stable in
which five horses were kept. To these rooms an oratory
was soon added; but before the end of Henry VIII.'s
reign more extensive improvements were made at the
south end, including a large room and a gallery, and
money was spent in hangings and wainscoting. Carter,
writing as late as 1753, says of it, that "tho' it make
not so grand an outside appearance as some do, yet
within few exceed it for grandeur and convenient
apartments." We may therefore conclude that the
Queen could not have found more comfortable quarters

elsewhere. The lower hall was used as a guard-chamber; the room above it became the chamber of presence; the gallery and adjoining rooms served for the Queen's lodging. The three days which followed the Queen's arrival were devoted to church services, plays, and University disputations. On August 6, being a Sunday, Elizabeth was naturally present in King's Chapel at a Litany and sermon; in the afternoon she was not expected, and the service had already begun, when she appeared; on her arrival it was stopped and begun over again.

On the evening of Sunday the *Aulularia* of Plautus was acted in the Ante-chapel, the Queen sitting against the south wall, and some ladies occupying the rood-loft. The other plays acted by members of the College were *Dido*, written by a Kingsman, John Rightwise, formerly High Master of St. Paul's School, and *Ezechias*, an English play by Nicholas Udall, a former Headmaster of Eton. In the disputations held in the Schools, or in St. Mary's Church, Kingsmen were again prominent; for while Bishop Cox and Dr. Haddon presided in their respective faculties, Thomas Preston was the man who made the most favourable impression on the Queen. He had the advantage of youth and good looks, and acted so well in *Dido*, and "did so genteelly and gracefully dispute before her that she gave him a pension of £20 a year besides viii. angels and her hand to kiss." The more solid abilities of Cartwright, the other chief disputant, were quite eclipsed by the handsome Preston, and it is said, though probably without any truth, that the disgust which Cartwright felt on this occasion was the cause of his subsequent disaffection to the Church.

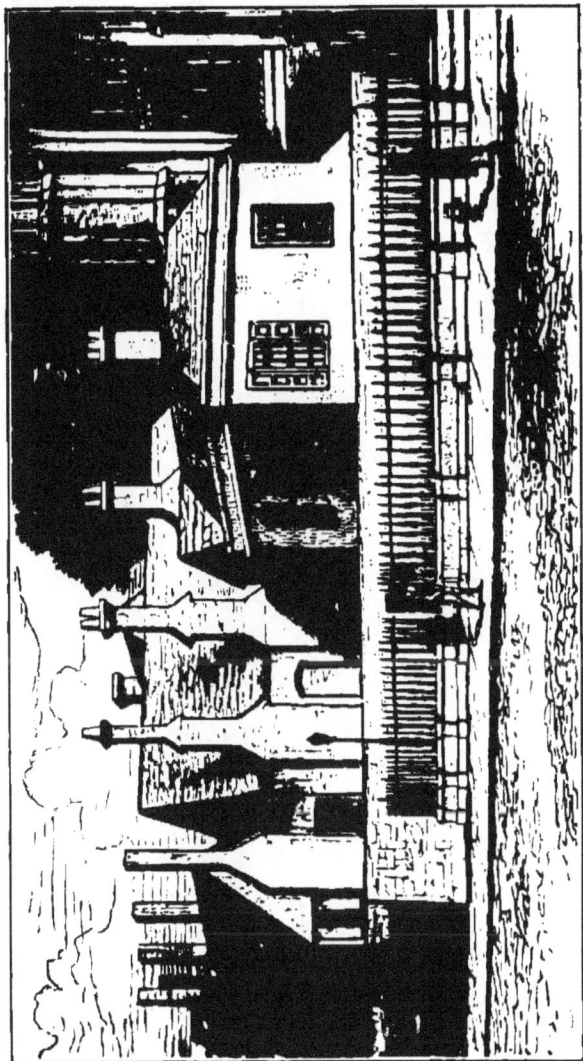

From a Print by Malton]

OLD PROVOST'S LODGE

[taken about 1798

If the prominence of Kingsmen on this occasion was merely accidental, it is the more remarkable that much the same thing happened when the Queen came again into the neighbourhood of Cambridge. This was in July 1578, at Audley End. The Vice-Chancellor and Heads repaired thither in their gowns and hoods, and the Public Orator, Mr. Bridgewater, of King's College, knelt down and made a speech. After the Queen's departure a disputation in philosophy was held before Lord Leicester ; and Mr. Fleming, of King's, maintained two theses, one of which was " Astra non imponunt necessitatem." Whether his argument was directed against Astrology or in favour of Free Will is not recorded ; but probably both were burning questions at that time ; and, if we may accept Sir Walter Scott's description of Leicester in *Kenilworth* as an authentic likeness, the Lord High Steward himself must have been tempted to enter the lists against Mr. Fleming in defence of Astrology. Another Kingsman was Moderator ; but the Chancellor practically took this duty on his own shoulders.

But before this second visit took place, more practical controversies had arisen at Cambridge ; for signs of disaffection to the Ecclesiastical Settlement were already visible in the opposition to wearing a surplice, an opposition which was especially conspicuous in St. John's and Trinity. From this controversy King's College was free ; and one of the Fellows, Bartholomew Clark, LL.D., wrote to the Chancellor, protesting against the " trifling" " of these surplice and hat fanatics," and complaining that the time, which used to be devoted to good arts and sciences, was now taken up with janglings

" de lana caprina." But the Kingsmen had troubles of
their own. For just at this time they were engaged in
sending to their Visitor, Bishop Bullingham, a complaint against their Provost; and in 1565 the Bishop
held a visitation. At the same time, feeling perhaps
that it was a bold measure to impugn the conduct of a
Head who had been chosen by Elizabeth herself, eleven
of the Fellows wrote to the Secretary, Cecil, to make it
clear that it was no objection to the "habits" that
induced them to act so; but

" our care is for the promoting of *Religion,* which for a long
time hath been of little or no account with us; and our own
private domestic *Concerns* are now become in so bad and
difficult a state that the safety of the whole College is in
danger."

The charges brought before the Visitor against Baker
were, that he never preached, though a D.D., that he
had no regard to Divinity in others, nor had caused the
Fellows to study it; that no Sacrament was adminis-
tered, but once, or at most twice, in the whole year.
The Conducts and singing men were manifestly Papists,
his own guests the most suspected Papists, and it was
added that he used one Mr. Woolward, then a Conduct
and afterwards a Fellow of Eton, " verie extremely,"
because he refused to celebrate the service at the Communion with his face towards the East and his back
towards the Congregation. It further appeared that
Baker had already been deprived of the Living of St.
Andrew's, in London, for refusing to renounce the Pope
and his doctrine. The Visitor admonished the Provost,
and enjoined him to destroy a great deal of Popish

stuff, as Mass books, graduals, copes, crosses, pixes, &c., "which the Provost did not perform, but kept them in a secret corner"; for, as he shrewdly remarked on another occasion, "that which hath bin may be againe."

Four years passed, and the complaints were renewed, but this time the Fellows applied to Grindal, Bishop of London, and Visitors were appointed by the Queen. New charges were now added to the old list. The Provost was said to have shown favouritism in preferring a Junior Regent to be Proctor, and tyranny in stopping the B.A. degrees of four young Fellows who had opposed him; it was added that he had taken bribes in letting College leases, and in other ways had fraudulently enriched himself at the cost of the Society. He would let no one go with him to the College Courts, kept all profits to himself, and charged five times as much for his circuit expenses as had heretofore been done. In performing his duties in the University he was, to say the least, slack.

"His rare frequenting of sermons, and continuall absence from all disputations is so intolerable that in every sermon almost he is cried owte of, and sometimes touched by name to the no small infamie of the College. Whereas he should be a disputer at Commencement, two or three days before he flieth the towne, so that herein he is as infamous as in his not preaching."

So notorious was his conduct that at one Commencement he had been described as "pistori quam pastori similior." The fact that Baker was at heart a Romanist will account for most of his shortcomings. A man with

his views could neither preach himself, nor could he
conscientiously insist on the punctual performance of
the Reformed Service in his Chapel. Possibly he might
have been able to answer the charges of peculation.
But it would have been useless. He was evidently out
of harmony with the new order of things. He hardly
waited to be deprived of his office, but fled abroad,
giving, however, a last proof of his integrity by resigning
the College money and plate which was in his custody,
and even sending back the College horses which carried
him to the seaside. " Nothing in his life became him
like the leaving it."

The field being now clear, the College lost no time in
applying both to the Chancellor and to the Queen for
leave to elect Roger Goad, a former Fellow, who was
now Master of the Grammar School at Guildford.
Leave was given ; and in 1569 the new Provost began
his long reign of forty-one years. The influence of a
strong will soon made itself felt. The Statute, which
required Fellows of a certain standing to be " diverted "
to divinity, law, or physic, had been much neglected.
It was now enforced, and the number of clerical Fellows
and qualified Preachers rapidly increased. The Library
had been " utterly spoiled."   Goad caused a " fair new
Library to be made in the Southern side chapels, and
furnished it with books, especially of divinity." The
" old copes and Popish stuff" which the last Provost
had secreted were sold for this purpose, and no charge
entailed on the College. The Deans having failed to
lecture diligently, two of the younger M.A.s were
appointed to read Philosophy Lectures to Bachelors and
senior students.   There was a Greek Lecture daily,

and Hebrew Lectures for divinity students. The Provost himself read a Divinity Lecture three times a week at morning prayers in Chapel; and every Thursday, between 4 and 5 P.M., one of the clerical Fellows catechised, the whole College being obliged to attend.

It would be interesting, if it were possible, to ascertain how the undergraduates employed their time when left to themselves. Perhaps something may be inferred as to their habits from the list of *prohibitions* which we find in a compendium issued by Goad, as Vice-Chancellor, in 1595. The "hurtful and unscholarly exercise" of football was forbidden *except* within each College and between members of the same College. Students were forbidden to keep a dog within College or without, or to resort to bull-baiting, bear-baiting, common bathing-places, &c. ; to carry guns, cross-bows, or to shoot in Cambridge or out of it. No student was to wear long or curled locks, great cuffs, velvet breeches, or any other coloured apparel, but their caps, hoods and habits. Bachelors and undergraduates were forbidden to cover their heads at sermons. The objection to bathing strikes us as particularly strange, and it was one of the Provost's earliest enactments. For there is a College order of 1571 forbidding *all* members of the College, including servants and Choristers, to enter any stream, pool, or water, within the county of Cambridge, for the purpose of swimming or bathing, either by day or night. The penalty for a first offence was a severe flogging in Hall in the presence of the whole Society ; while seniors, who broke this law, sat in the stocks in Hall for a day. A second offence entailed expulsion.

It had so happened that a very promising son of Walter Haddon, admitted to the College in 1567, had been drowned while " washing himself in a Place in the river Cham called Paradise "; and this accident may in some measure account for the severity of the new rule. Mr. Mullinger, however, observes that the river did possess considerable attractions, though of a kind differing from those of the present day. The fishing belonged to the town; but the members of the University seem to have been shameless poachers; and perch and pike were freely caught and eaten. They even went so far as to break the nets of the men to whom the Corporation had leased the right of fishing, and to drive them out of their boats. The prohibition of fierce birds within the College perhaps indicates that the students were given to hawking as well as fishing. Mr. Wordsworth thinks that undergraduates enjoyed about as much liberty as public-school boys now do. They had to attend morning and evening prayer in Chapel, as well as early dinner and supper in Hall. Their dormitories were not altogether private. In King's College the Scholars and young Fellows were quartered in chambers, each of which accommodated four inmates, and bore some distinctive name, such as " The Tolebothe," " Horskeeper's Inn," " Barber's Inn," &c. The Fellows' chambers held two instead of four beds. Something like bullying seems occasionally to have gone on within these chambers; for in 1624 a B.A. was accused of maltreating " et verbis et pugnis " a M.A. Fellow " in propriâ ipsius camerâ et lecto exis-tentem." Of course the appeal to the fist was more common in those days; one Scholar, in 1590, is in trouble " pro percussione enormi Jacobi Scarlett Chorustæ "; and there is more than one instance of an undergraduate dealing in the same way with one of the butlers. But the offences detailed in the College Records are for the most part slight. Absence without leave from Chapel or from College, indecorous dress, quarrelsome conduct, impertinence or disobedience to the authorities were common enough ; and sometimes a Fellow would take advantage of a sermon at St. Mary's, or an exercise in the Chapel, to speak disrespectfully of his College officers. But there are periods during which there is no sign even of the most trivial misdemeanours.

A change had, moreover, taken place in the class of students who resorted to Colleges ; they were no longer universally poor. Rich men's sons, if they had come to the University at all, had formerly frequented hostels ; but the comforts of College life had now induced many of them to become members of Colleges ; and the introduction of such a class would naturally tend to a demand for greater liberty and more amusement. To a certain extent this would be counteracted by the age of the students, which was still that of schoolboys rather than undergraduates. It may be doubted, however, whether this social change had greatly affected King's College ; the class who passed from Eton to King's probably remained much the same as before, and the age at which they came to College continued, as in the earliest days, to vary from 15 to 19.

But, besides the Fellows and Scholars, there was in the College a small but important body of Fellow-Commoners. Their number, which depended on the accommodation in certain chambers assigned to them, was never to exceed twelve. Strict rules were made in 1577 and 1578, by which the Tutor was made responsible for a Fellow-Commoner's dues to the College, and was liable (together with his pupil) to be put out of Commons if he failed to pay the Bursar. Only those were admitted Fellow-Commoners who on examination were found fit for "logique," according to the University Statutes. They began by giving a silver cup of four marks' price, which they used themselves in Hall, but which afterwards became the property of the College. At dinner and supper they took their places after the Masters and Bachelors; in Chapel they sat in the lower stalls next beneath (i.e., immediately to the east of) the Choir. At Christmas 1598 there were six Fellow-Commoners, and two who are called Scholar-Commoners. This last was a position which a boy elected to a Scholarship from Eton would sometimes hold while waiting for an actual vacancy in the Scholarships; but it seems clear that most of the Scholar-Commoners corresponded to the Pensioners of the present day. At Eton, in the same way, the original Commensales were either of the Fellow-Commoner class, and dined in Hall at the second table with the Chaplains, Usher, and Clerks; or else took their meals, at a lower tariff, with the College boys. But, whereas at Eton this last class grew into the hundreds of Oppidans, at King's, on the other hand, the Scholar-Commoners, for whom it must always have been difficult to find room within the College buildings, do not seem to have lasted beyond the close of the seventeenth century.

From the list of 1598 it appears that, besides the regular number of Deans and Bursars, there were four Lecturers; the Greek Lecturer, Miles Raven, being also a Student of Astronomy. There were two students in law and one in medicine. The rest of the Society was occupied with theology or arts; but so young were the members, that out of seventy as many as twenty-three were still B.A.s, and the same number undergraduates. The oldest Fellow, who was also Vice-Provost, had come up from Eton in 1577, eight years after the election to the Provostship of Roger Goad, who must have seemed a patriarch to those over whom he presided.

About the time of Goad's election an important exchange had been made in the College property. The Manor of Withyham, in Sussex, had been made over to Lord Buckhurst, and the College had acquired in its stead the Manor of Sampford Courtenay, in the heart of Devonshire. The new property was the most distant, and almost the largest which the College now owned. The College had not been in possession for many years before pressure was put on them to grant a lease of it to the Queen. The Fellows were inclined to give way, but the Provost stood firm. This was not a solitary instance. A few years before, the College had found it necessary to write to Lord Burghley, the Chancellor, begging him to use his influence with the Queen, to excuse them from leasing the Rectory of Barton to one Skinner. They urged that they had already promised to let part of the tithes to an old Kingsman, who had done special services to the College, and part to a present member who was about to quit the University. Moreover, they felt bound to add something to the stipend of the Vicar, so that the parish might enjoy a resident Minister " qui et moribus suis ad virtutem et doctrina sua ad religionem plebeculam Bartonensem adhortari possit." Ten or twelve years before this they had given the Queen and Chancellor a different reason for not granting a lease to a member of the Carey family. In this case the farm was said to be one out of which exceptional profits could be made, and without such extraordinary receipts it was impossible for the College to pay its way. A Tudor Sovereign like Elizabeth, whose father had confiscated ecclesiastical property without shame, was not likely to feel any scruple in trying to make a little profit out of Colleges, either for herself or her friends ; but it is more remarkable that the College saw no harm in doing a good turn to individual Fellows or ex-Fellows at the cost of the common purse.

We must now turn to the College dissensions which unfortunately mark the history of Goad's Provostship. Their origin is obscure. One naturally suspects, in those days, some difference in religious doctrine or discipline, but there is little or no trace of this in the records which have come down to us. Perhaps the previous anarchy obliged the Provost to exert a strictness which made him unpopular ; and the *youth* of the Fellows, which has been already mentioned, might induce them to be turbulent, while it would make it more difficult for them to appreciate the views of one so much their senior. This is the explanation which Fuller gives :

" no wonder," he writes, " young Scholars swelled against him, who bound them hard to the observation of the

Statutes. He had many contests with the young Fire of this College, chiefly because he loved their good, better than they themselves."

We shall see, too, that the pressure of poverty, or at least a desire for a larger share in the receipts of the College, had something to do with the troubles.

These began in 1576, when four Fellows preferred articles against their Provost, which the Visitor (Bishop Cooper) declined to entertain. He wrote to Lord Burghley to this effect, whereupon the Chancellor himself took up the matter, and pronounced the charges to be false and scandalous. Two of the four complainants were imprisoned in the Gatehouse at Westminster, and the apologies which they made are still extant. The charges had turned chiefly on supposed peculations, and Latin libels had been posted on the door of the Lodge, imputing such faults to Goad. But some of the accusations were evidently of a more frivolous kind, to judge by the Provost's answers. He justifies himself for having a wife at the Lodge, and says she has never twice been within the "Quadrant" of the College. He had not dined in Hall on Easter Day, and it was said that he meant to absent himself from Hall on all festivals ; his answer is, that he had been requested by the Vice-Chancellor to preach at St. Mary's ; and it may be inferred that he stayed at home to write, or think over his sermon. He was also accused of excessive riding ; but he naturally asks, why should he not use the "geldings" which the College kept for him ? Fault was found because a new dove-house had brought no profit to the College ; he replies that, " thei which have eni experience know it must have a time to be stored, being but lately buylt." Even Burghley may have found it difficult to hear such charges with gravity, especially if he was told of a certain Mr. Lakys, who joined the four ringleaders in their mutiny. The Provost had punished him with a week's loss of commons for wearing next under his gown a

"cut taffety doublet of the fashion with the sleeves out, and a great payer of gallygastion hose. And yet this punishment hath ever sence stuk in his mynd, as hath appeared. by his sundry expostulacions with me about that matter; such is his stout nature and impatience to be reproved when he doth amisse."

There was, however, one of the four complainants who, if we may judge by his later career, was not likely to bring absolutely trivial accusations. This was Giles Fletcher, and in his apology of May 22, 1576, made to the Chancellor, he still maintains that he had seen the most promising students neglected and spoiled by bad examples, while the idle and profligate escaped punishment; though he admits that the Provost himself is an excellent man, and, if he would trust to his own judgment, perfectly fair. Fletcher's real complaint seems, therefore, to have been against the officers of the College who had misled the Provost, and whose influence had caused misgovernment. Another of the four, and a much less respectable witness, was Robert Lilesse, who was not content with making mischief within his own College, but having libelled some M.A. was, in 1583, summoned before the Vice-Chancellor and Heads, and banished for ever from the University. This expulsion entailed the loss of his Fellowship, and ten years afterwards he induced the Chancellor to take some steps for his restoration. The question was referred to the Visitor, who writes to Lord Burghley from Buckden, Sept. 27, 1594, that he found Robert Lilesse undeserving of restoration, and begs Lord Burghley to withdraw from his encouragement, with the hope and confidence of which Lilesse " began to be swoln and puffed up."

By this time, *i.e.*, in 1594, the old dissensions had reappeared in the College in an aggravated form ; and the Visitor, Bishop Wickham, writing to Lord Burghley, speaks of his sorrow at finding on a visit to Cambridge "most strange insolencies and immodesties far different from the ancient reverence and humility towards their superiors." In December of this same year he read to the College a memorandum containing orders for the better management of public meetings, for securing a due distinction between Seniors and Juniors (the new Parlour and Laundress Yard being reserved for the use of the former), and for preventing the habit of discussing the private affairs of the College before strangers. Some of the Fellows had not confined themselves to dangerous language. They had even snatched money from the Bursars, and laid hands on bread and beer at the Buttery. Six or seven had taken horses violently out of the stable and ridden them abroad at their pleasure.

This was the last effort of Bishop Wickham as a peacemaker, for he was translated to the See of Winchester the next year and died within a few months. He had once been a Fellow both of King's

and Eton. Sir John Harington tells us that, as Vice-
Provost of Eton, he would teach the School in the
Headmaster's absence, and that he shewed a fatherly
care of the boys. He was

" a very milde and good natured man, and esteemed a very
good Preacher, and free from that which St. Paul calleth
Idolatry, I mean covetousness; so that one may say
probably, that as the first William Wykeham was one of
the richest Prelates that had been in Winchester a long
time and bestowed it well, so this was one of the poorest
and endured it well."

His charity was in advance of his generation ; for when
he preached at the funeral of Mary Queen of Scots,
Martin Marprelate taunted him with having expressed
a hope that his auditors might hereafter meet the departed Queen, "an unrepentant Papist," in heaven.
Such a man was not likely to use his Visitatorial powers
with undue harshness, and perhaps a firmer hand and
the adoption of more stringent measures might have
averted the serious outbreak, which must be described
in the next chapter.

CHAPTER VI

THE LAST DAYS OF ROGER GOAD

IN the spring of 1602 civil war again broke out in the College. The Fellows were dissatisfied both with the management of the College property and with their own share in the profits. They complained that they received only £3 15s. a year apiece; many of them not having a penny besides for apparel, books, &c. From this discontent a custom had arisen of attaching some condition to their votes at the sealing of leases, so as to intercept part of the fines paid by the tenants, which would otherwise have gone into the Common Purse. It was, in fact, a movement, irregular and unconstitutional in character, towards the modern system of dividends.

The Provost, at a meeting in February of this year, gave notice that he would not allow any Fellow henceforward to give "a conditional or ambiguous voice"; but several such votes were immediately given, and on the same day thirty Fellows petitioned their Visitor to reconsider an interpretation of the 46th Statute, which Bishop Wickham had made. This was to the effect that on all important questions the whole body of Fellows must be summoned; and that, if they were not unanimous on any matter, it should be settled by a majority of the thirteen Senior Fellows. The Junior party would have accepted this decision if, in the absence of any of the thirteen, the next in seniority had been summoned to the final decision; but the late Visitor's words had made it clear that this was not to be done, so that the Provost and seven others might conceivably impose their will on . the whole Society, without even hearing arguments on the other side. The petition was rejected, and in May of the following year, 1603, the Provost and Seniors themselves asked the Visitor, Bishop Chaderton, to intervene, and urged that there was a kind of mutiny among the younger Fellows. A visitation immediately followed, with the usual forms of "articles of inquiry" and "presentments."

It was evident that the desire for a dividend lay at the root of the quarrel. To this the Provost and Seniors reply :

" As for the surplusage remaining in the year's end there is some competent quantity left in the charge of the Baker and Bruer. But as for other surplusage to be divided (as divers of the company have dreamed they might have) the truth is, this is so farr of, that the College runneth more and more in great detryments yearly above Statute allowance . . . to the sum, of late years, of neer £300 per annum . . . which intollerable burthen, as it increaseth yearly, so it had great need be provided for in time, or else it will prove a Canker consuming and eating out the Bowells of this College."

Accordingly they request the Visitor's "effectual help," and complain that the more part of the company, instead of practising frugality, have broken out into open dissension for their dividend.

The Provost had also several charges to prefer against individual Fellows. One had made an offensive oration in the public schools, aimed at the present state and government of the College; another had used his sermon at St. Mary's for the same purpose; a third had presumed to come to meals in Hall when he had been put out of commons. A fourth "has a scandalous report for his trade of usury." Three Fellows had used "unlawful gaming," even drawing some of the young Bachelors to play with them, and had frequented a house in the town for the purpose of card playing, not without a suspicion of more serious immorality. One Fellow, a Mr. Hinde, having received a legacy of £20 a year, persisted in retaining his Fellowship.

Within a few days the Visitor called the Society into the Chapel and delivered an address. While some points were reserved for future consideration, he proceeded to inflict penalties on the chief offenders without delay. Presently he called forth three Fellows, Woodyere, Saunders, and Hinde, as idle misspenders of their time and non-proficient in their studies, and discommuned them "usque ad condignam emendacionem." This was more than the mutineers could bear. Woodyere said, "We do appeal to the King," and this cry was taken up clamorously by many others. The Provost reminded them that such an appeal was contrary to their oaths, but they persisted. Some of them

"took exceptions against my Lord of Lincoln as a partiall and suspected Judge, for being a mere friend to Mr.

Provost, for admitting him to sit as assistant in examinations, and for treating of the lesser matters and omitting the weightier."

Woodyere followed this up by challenging the Provost openly for alienating the College lands, and for retaining farmers' money for the space of nineteen years. Another Fellow, Griffin, joined Woodyere in exclaiming against the Provost for oppression and injustice. It was a scene of wild confusion, and the Bishop was hardly equal to the emergency. Eventually, " being therewith very much disquieted," and not being able to restore order even by offering to respite the punishments, he left his seat and departed.

It was probably on the next day that the Provost and Seniors determined to send a petition to the Privy Council, and in particular to warn the Archbishop of Canterbury and Mr. Secretary Cecil, that the younger Fellows were on the point of appealing to the King. The Juniors, however, were determined to be beforehand in getting the ear of the authorities in London. So, rising at 4 A.M. on May 9, they went to the College stables, overpowered or intimidated the stable-boy, and violently took out

" two College geldings, which Mr. Provost should have used to London the same day, taking them against Mr. Provost's prohibition, alledging that they had a warrant from the more part of the Fellows."

Lisle and Griffin were the two who rode off to London to transact their business; and on their return, which seems not to have been till June, they added insult to injury by presenting their bill of charges to the

Provost, and claiming that it should be paid as College business.

It must have been an uncomfortable summer at King's; but, to make matters worse, a new controversy arose in August. A frequent but unwelcome visitor, the Plague, had appeared in Cambridge ; and the Provost and Seniors decided, on the 13th, that the College should break up till November 1 ; each Fellow receiving 2s. 8d. per week, and each Scholar 2s., in lieu of commons. This decision was confirmed by the Visitor, who sent Commissioners to the College on August 19 to announce the fact. Then there ensued in the Chapel a second edition of the tumult of May 7, with cries of " There is no authority nor Statute to drive us from the College, and we will not go but withstand it."

Between twenty and thirty of them, one being Samuel Collins, the future Provost, appealed to the Visitor, urging, among other pleas, that " We are many poor, many orphans, and friendless, many Londoners, and know not whither to go but into places still more dangerous." Of course the Provost also wrote to assure the Visitor that the danger was serious, and he complained of fresh misconduct on the part of Lisle, which occurred under the following circumstances : The Electors at Eton, considering Hinde's Fellowship as vacant, had announced and filled up seven vacancies. On August 25 there was a meeting in the Hall to admit the new Scholars, when Lisle behaved so turbulently that the Provost retired to the Lodge to complete the business. Nor was Lisle's language more conciliatory than his conduct ; for when one of the Seniors asked him what authority he had for disbelieving the Provost, who affirmed that there were seven vacancies, he answered, " What if Mr. Provost say it is night, when I see the sunshine at noonday, am I bound to believe it ? "

Some of the younger Fellows, in spite of College orders, and although most of them had already received their money allowance in lieu of commons, persisted in remaining in residence till the end of August, taking their meals in the Hall, and bread and drink at their pleasure out of the Buttery ; so disturbing the Seniors that the latter " were fain to withdraw themselves and take their dyett in the Provost's lodging."

After this the College seems really to have been broken up for a time, and towards the end of October the Provost and Seniors found it necessary to extend the period till January 13, that being the day fixed by the University, and the King having given strict orders to the County Justices to avoid all occasions of spreading the contagion.

The new notice had probably not reached all whom it concerned. At any rate some returned to College, and the Provost called them to the " Wainscot Hall " in the Lodge on November 3 ; and, after objecting to the presence of Mr. Hinde as being no Fellow, explained to them the necessity of obeying the order, confirmed by the Visitor, to be absent till January ; and he offered to pay the travelling expenses of any who had come back in ignorance. However, Messrs. Sheaf, Griffin, and Woodyere insisted on their right to remain ; and Woodyere said that, as the Provost had lately dined at an inn with the Vice-Chancellor and Proctors, and also kept his family in College, there could be no great danger of infection. The meeting was now becoming disorderly, and the Provost had to retire into the next room, and

" so entring the door, which he would have pulled after him, Mr. Sheaff laid hould thereupon to keep it open, to what end is not known, but to have followed him in with his trayne, had not the auditor Mr. Brooks been sitting apparent and to be seen."

The presence of the Auditor may have been a momentary check to bad manners, but the Audit itself gave the malcontents some further opportunities of distinguishing themselves ; especially to Hinde, who intruded into meetings, and presumed, in preference of his claim to commons money, to set upon Mr. Raven, one of the Bursars,

" mistrusting no such matter, in his own chamber, and violently throwing him down on the floore drew out his knife and cutt of the bottom of a bagge, which he held fast in his hand, with the College money in it, and took thereof the sum of 27 shillings."

Things had now reached such a pitch that King James thought it time to interpose. A Stuart King was not likely to regard with favour any movement against authority, and he wrote to the Bishop of Lincoln to say that he was shocked by the state of things. " We have some reason to impute part of these continued disorders to your sufferance and remissness." The Bishop is charged to visit the College and to take strong measures, reporting offenders to the Council if necessary ; these dissensions having " caused great scandal and evil example to the whole University."

The Bishop accordingly held another visitation in the Chapel on January 25, 1604; but the rebels declined to give way, declaring that the King had been misled, and appealing "from the King misinformed to the King better informed." At the same time John Griffin and William Woodyere did not lose the opportunity offered by the Bishop's visit to drive home their countercharges. If there was a weak joint in the Provost's armour, it was in his management of the property, and here Griffin and his partner directed their main attack. That the Provost had left off going on circuit might be excused on the score of his age; but he had persuaded the Society to buy a farm at Coton, which he promised would bring in £80 a year; and the purchase had turned out a bad bargain. More serious than this misjudgment was the fact that for twelve years he had kept in his own hands a farm at Grantchester, paying the College the old rent for it, though it was now worth much more. A former Visitor had told him that he ought either to take a fresh lease for it or let it to others. But this direction had been ignored. It was not the first time that the Provost had been accused of feathering his own nest. When Queen Elizabeth had applied for the lease of Sampford Courtenay, it was said that the Provost "had the commodities for fines of copyholders to himself," and that this was the real reason why the application was refused. If there was any truth in this story, it must mean that some percentage of the fines was retained by the Provost; and the fact that such a story could be told may perhaps throw some light on his conduct in the case of the Grantchester Farm.

Scrupulous delicacy in money matters does not seem to have been a common virtue in the Elizabethan age.

The Bachelors of the College had also grievances to present to the Visitor. The Provost and Vice-Provost are accused of favouritism in assigning chambers. The complainants averred that they were discouraged from all familiarity with their elders ; that they were strictly obliged to wear caps within the College, and that in all weathers, and before any company, they must " cap " a M.A., even if he is at the farthest end of the court. They can never take their commons out of Hall as others do ; and they are expected to be in their rooms from 8 to 9 P.M., to receive visits from the Deans, and have sometimes thereby missed a Hebrew Lecture. In modern days the visit is generally paid by the person *in statu pupillari,* and the loss of a lecture would probably not be urged as an aggravation of the burden.

But the end of the civil war was at last in sight, for on Feb. 9 the whole body of Fellows joined in a petition to the Visitor " for peace," asking him to compose all differences, and promising to pursue an inviolable peace with the Head and members of the Society. On the following day the Visitor delivered a series of injunctions, many of which were repeated or amplified at a visitation held six years later, in October 1610, under the title of " Articles of good husbandrie " and " Reformation of manners."

The attempt of the Juniors to have a place on the Seniority, or to attach conditions to their votes, was repudiated. All were ordered to dine and sup regularly in Hall, except by special leave of the Vice-Provost ; the habit of taking commons out of Hall having helped

F

to create faction and dissension. Still less might men carry their commons into the town, a practice which had caused the loss of College Plate. A Fellow might, however, still bring a friend to the Buttery hatch " in moderate sorte," to refresh themselves. The fact that Latin is still to be spoken in Hall, and that servants are to take their commons there, reminds us that we are hardly yet out of mediæval times. While such measures were ordered to promote economy or unity, others aimed at the development of the College estates. Two yearly circuits are enjoined. Inquiry is to be made as to the management of woods, and competent legal advice to be taken on the still more serious question of granting copyholds. And here the advice of Mr. John Lowe, of the Inner Temple, confirmed the College in its traditional practice, and emphatically condemned the notion of converting copyhold into leasehold tenures. His view was that, if such a policy were adopted, the tenements and lands would be in such a deplorable state before the copyholds fell in, that the College would find no tenants. And if the College would gain nothing, society in general would certainly be injured ; the depopulation of the country which would result from ousting the copyholders would be a national loss ; and there would be much distress, begging, and vagrancy among the ejected families.

The Visitor's injunctions also provided for greater regularity in lectures and exercises, it being the duty of the "Presidents of Lower Chambers" to superintend the studies of the Scholars who inhabited them, and to take care that there were no "non-proficients." Idle Fellows and Scholars were to be punished and reformed,

and none to be allowed to practise merchandising or
other trading. No one was to frequent taverns. Those
who came in after the keys had been carried to the
Provost were to be mulcted or discommuned. Cards
and all gaming were forbidden. Only the thirteen
Seniors might use the Seniors' Parlour, Orchard, or
Garden; and so far from granting any relief to the
Juniors in respect of their head-dress, the Visitor
ordered all Bachelors and Scholars to take off their caps
to M.A.s in the Chapel yard and walks, not putting them
on till they had leave; and not to wear caps at all in
the presence of any M.A. Fellow within the Inner Court.

Such was the general settlement. But the hand of
justice fell heavily on individual offenders. John
Griffin and William Woodyere were ejected from their
Fellowships by the Visitor at once. Lisle escaped for
the moment, but four years later was declared by the
Provost to have forfeited his Fellowship by being in
possession of a Manor at Great Wilbraham worth more
than £5 a year. As for Edmund Hinde, his case had
already been heard, on July 12, 1603, by the Provost
and officers. It was found that he had inherited a
"faire Inn near Holborne Bridge" called the Queen's
Arms, the annual value of which was more than £5;
and though Hinde fenced with the questions put to
him and tried to evade any admissions fatal to his
cause, the evidence was too strong; he was ejected, and
the decision was ratified by the Visitor on Jan. 30,
1604. One Henry Howgrave also got into trouble for
insulting the Provost. A report had arisen that Goad
was to be made Dean of Windsor, on which Howgrave
remarked that Mr. Provost had been a thief all his life,

and would now be a Dean of thieves. Howgrave's own account of the conversation gave it rather a different colour; but he was discommuned, and had to make an apology. He was probably an extreme Puritan, for a few years later he was again punished for libellous language against the Bishops, and for calling Archbishop Bancroft "Antichrist."

The last event recorded in Roger Goad's long reign indicates that the disorders of King's College had infected other Colleges also. A comedy was being acted before a distinguished company in the Hall on February 28, 1606. Stones were thrown at the Hall windows, a crowd of Scholars and others hooted and shouted for two hours; windows were broken, and a post of timber was pulled up and used as a battering-ram to break a strong gate. The Vice-Chancellor and Heads made order that any one convicted of having taken part in the riot should have his degrees suspended, or be corrected with the rod in the Schools, or (if a townsman) be put in the stocks in the bull-ring.

One cannot but regret that the closing years of Provost Goad's rule, which in the opinion of so great an authority as Mr. Mullinger "was attended with the utmost advantage and credit to his College and the University," should have been darkened by the long and acrimonious dissensions which have been described. In spite of this, however, no Fellowships were more prized than those at King's, whether for their value or their social advantages. Music, rather than theology, is said to have been the favourite study of the Fellows. The practice of music, however, did not, in this case, produce either harmony or unison.

The worth of a College must be judged in no small degree by the character of the men whom it sends into the world outside, and there was no lack of prominent Kingsmen during Elizabeth's reign. In Church and State alike they did good service. Mitres were, no doubt, plentiful at the opening of this era; but still it is remarkable that within one year Archbishop Parker consecrated three Kingsmen. Of these, Cox has been already described. Edmund Guest, who became Bishop of Rochester, had a large share in the Revision of the Prayer Book in 1559, and in framing the Thirty-nine Articles; unlike Cox, he seems to have leant towards Luther's view of the Eucharist, and he was unlike him also in dying poor and unmarried. William Alley, who during Mary's reign had supported himself by practising medicine in Northern England, now became Bishop of Exeter, and took part in the translation of the Bible in 1561. A generation, however, passed before another such appointment was made, for it was not till 1595 that William Day became Bishop of Winchester. His elder brother, also a Kingsman, had been Bishop of Chichester and was a staunch Romanizer. William adopted quite opposite views, and rose to be Provost of Eton in 1561, where he lost no time in pulling down a tabernacle of stone in the body of the church and in whitening Dr. Lupton's chapel. In his exercise of patronage he does not seem to have been so much of a Puritan, for when on one occasion he broke his leg, by a fall from a horse that started under him, some waggish Scholars observed that it was a just punishment, because the horse was given him by a gentleman to place his son at Eton. It may be hoped, however, that the present was made as a token of the father's gratitude, and after the boy's admission to College.

But the most eminent Kingsman of this reign was Francis Walsingham, who, after an education at his own home near Chislehurst, entered King's as a Fellow-Commoner in 1548. There he resided during parts of two years, under the care of Thomas Gardiner, one of the Fellows. He did not stay to take a degree, but travelled on the Continent, where, by making himself master of foreign languages and customs, he fitted himself for the important parts which he afterwards played both as a diplomatist and a Minister. He did not forget his old College, although the connexion had been so short, but presented the Library with a copy of the Antwerp Polyglott of 1569–73. To the College lately founded by his brother-in-law, Sir Walter Mildmay, he made the more substantial gift of the Advowson of Thurcaston in Leicestershire. Perhaps he felt more confidence in the Protestant character of Emmanuel theology, or he may have thought that his own College was already sufficiently endowed with livings.

Another notable servant of the State was Thomas Wilson, who was Tutor at King's to the two brothers Henry and Charles Brandon. As relations of the royal family they might have been useful patrons to Wilson in after life; but unhappily the two lads, while undergraduates, were attacked by the sweating sickness. They were hastily removed to the Bishop of Lincoln's Palace at Buckden, but died within twelve hours of each other. Both of the Brandons had attained a remarkable proficiency in learning; and Peter Martyr

considered the elder to be the most promising youth
of his day, with the exception of Edward VI. During
Mary's reign Wilson studied civil law at Padua and
Ferrara, but he was imprisoned at Rome on a charge
of heresy, and only escaped when the prison took fire
and the populace broke open the doors. Tradition
says that for some time Wilson tried in vain to get
employment from Lord Burghley. At last Elizabeth,
wishing to animate her subjects against Philip of
Spain, inquired for some one who could translate the
Philippics of Demosthenes, and Wilson was chosen for
the purpose. The story must be legendary, for before
this time Wilson was Master of St. Catharine's Hospital,
M.P. in 1563, and Ambassador in Portugal in 1567;
but it is true that a translation of the Philippics by him
was printed in 1570. However, Wilson's literary fame
rests on two earlier works, the *Rule of Reason* and *Arte
of Rhetorique*, both of them very able and witty
treatises, which were popular in the sixteenth century.
In the *Rhetorique* he tells, or perhaps invents, a story
of his own early days :

"When I was in Cambridge and student in the King's
College, there came a man out of the town with a pint of
wine in a pottle pot, to welcome the Provost of that
House, lately come from Court."

The speech that was made by the man is quoted by
Wilson as an example of the absurd misuse of long
words. It begins quite in Dogberry's vein :

"Knowing that you are a worshipful Pilate, and keeps a
bominable house, I thought it my duty to come incanti-
vantee, and bring you a pottle of wine."

Wilson afterwards became a Secretary of State, and
was employed by Elizabeth both in the Low Countries
and also to investigate the Queen of Scots' connexion
with the Duke of Norfolk's plot.

Success came still earlier in life to Bartholomew Clark,
made Dean of Arches before he was 36 years of age.
The Earl of Leicester, who for some reason was his
enemy, tried to oust him from his place on the ground
of his youth; and it must have seemed to Clark a just
retribution when he was employed on a mission to the
Low Countries to inquire into the charges made against
the Earl's government there.   He had a friend in Lord
Buckhurst, who encouraged him to write the History of
Queen Elizabeth.   This he did not do, but he wrote
an answer to Sandars, who had attacked both the .
English Church and the right of Elizabeth to the
throne.   Clark was an Italian and a French scholar, so
proficient in the latter tongue, that he was offered a
Readership at Angers.

Sir John Harington is one of the most picturesque
figures of these times.   His father and mother had
been fellow prisoners with Elizabeth in the Tower in
1554, and he himself was the Queen's godson.   Harington entered King's as a Fellow-Commoner in 1576, and
he speaks of "My learned Tutor Dr. Fleming," the
same person, doubtless, who disputed before Lord
Leicester in 1578, and who died in his pulpit at
Cottenham Church in 1620.   In his tastes and abilities
Harington may perhaps remind us of a better known
Kingsman of the eighteenth century, Horace Walpole.
Like him, Harington was fond of society, and a
favourite in it; a great gossip, and a lively letter-

writer. But Walpole's vanity never betrayed him into the indiscreet actions which mark the career of the Somersetshire squire. Harington was an Italian scholar, and translated part of the *Orlando Furioso*, and the translation was circulated at Court. Elizabeth reproved her "saucy poet" for corrupting the minds of her maids of honour, but, with characteristic inconsistency, condemned him to translate the rest of the poem. Her poet's improprieties might have been pardoned if in one of his writings he had not appeared to reflect on the Earl of Leicester; he was thereupon ordered to leave the Court till he "had grown sober." This he can hardly be said ever to have achieved, for besides being implicated in Essex's proceedings in Ireland he had the audacity, in 1606, to propose himself, though a layman, to Sir Robert Cecil as a candidate for an Irish Archbishopric.

Harington must have been a strange medley of ill-assorted tastes and qualities. He could write sensibly on serious subjects, but he was capable of being both indecent and profane. His style is generally clear and bright, but it is disfigured by puns which would disgrace a schoolboy. While in Ireland with Essex he wrote an account of the Irish campaigns which is said to have been shewn to the Queen, contrary to the author's wishes, and to have led to the ruin of the unfortunate Earl. Perhaps the most interesting of his works are the letters in which he gives a lifelike description of Elizabeth in her old age, and of James I. soon after his accession.

Harington was no friend to the Puritans, and, fearing that Prince Henry of Wales might be

disposed to fulfil the prediction of the then current
couplet :

"Henry the VIII^t pulled down monks and their cells,
But Henry the IXth shall pull down Bishops and bells,",

he drew up, for the Prince's instruction, biographies of
many of the Bishops since Parker's time, some of whom
he had known personally. In a letter to the same
Prince he professes to give, out of old family records,
some specimens, both of prose and verse, written by
Henry VI. These would be interesting relics if we
could trust the source whence they come. Of Harington's own epigrams the following is well known ;

"Treason doth never prosper :—what's the reason ?
Why, if it prosper, none dare call it treason."

Of Giles Fletcher something has been already said.
He was a lawyer of sufficient eminence to become
Chancellor of more than one diocese, but he was better
known as a diplomatist. After being employed in
Scotland and Germany, he went, in 1588, on a special
embassy to Russia, then an almost unknown country.
Here he succeeded in obtaining great concessions for
English merchants, but he was himself treated with
such indignity that Elizabeth sent a formal complaint
to the Czar. Another result of his ill-treatment was
that in 1591 he published an account of Russia so
uncomplimentary that it had to be suppressed, for fear
of the consequences to the English merchants trading
in Russia. Poetry ran in the Fletcher family, and in
the case of Giles it took the form of a Latin poem
"de Litteris antiquæ Britanniæ," part of which is

devoted to an account of Cambridge. The early history of his own College is described in the following lines:

> " Fortunata domus nimium, si cetera primis
> Aequa forent! Musis invidit cetera Mavors.
> Aspice quæ moles et quæ fundamina primi
> Interrupta manent operis! vix ista feruntur
> Edvardi flexisse minas quin, victor ab hoste
> Cum redit infestis ducens hostilia signis
> Agmina, nil meritis inferret bella Camœnis,
> Innocuosque furens incenderet igne Penates."

King's College has always been a nursery of schoolmasters, and in this century five out of the first eight Headmasters of St. Paul's School were Kingsmen. One of these, William Malim, had already been Headmaster of Eton. He had travelled in the East, and adopted Oriental methods in dealing with boys; for he was a great flogger, so much so that some boys ran away from Eton, and this incident is said to have induced Roger Ascham to write his treatise on *The Scholemaster*.

Another High Master of St. Paul's, Rightwise, besides composing the tragedy of *Dido*, acted by his Scholars before Wolsey, was the author of those poems of the Latin grammar, *As in præsenti* and *Propria quæ maribus*, which were familiar though probably not dear to many boys of the early Victorian period.

But the greatest of the Schoolmasters seems to have been Richard Mulcaster. It was at the newly founded Merchant Taylors' School that he made his name; and, besides his Eton and Cambridge training, he had acquired at Oxford a knowledge of Oriental languages.

In two respects he anticipated modern ideas. He asserted the right of girls to receive as good an education as boys, and he advocated a system of special training for Schoolmasters. Fuller's account of him deserves to be repeated:

" In a morning he would exactly and plainly construe and parse the lesson to his Scholars; which done, he slept his hour (custom made him critical to proportion it) in his desk in school; but woe be to the Scholar that slept the while. Awaking he heard them accurately; and Atropos might be persuaded to pity as soon as he to pardon, where he found just fault. The prayers of cockering mothers prevailed with him as much as the requests of indulgent fathers, rather increasing than mitigating his severity. His sharpness was better endured, because he was impartial; and many excellent Scholars were bred under him."

One of these was Bishop Andrewes, who ever retained a warm affection for his old master, and had his portrait hung over his study door. Mulcaster had held office for twenty-five years, when he determined to resign. The Company pressed him to continue; but his answer was, "Fidelis servus perpetuus asinus." This did not prevent him from undertaking the Mastership of St. Paul's School when he was already sixty-five years of age.

The study of mathematics was not yet a prominent feature of Cambridge life, although the Commissioners of 1549 had introduced it into the "Trivium" in place of grammar, a knowledge of which was now supposed to precede admission to the University. But one Kingsman of these times is mentioned by an old College chronicler as having "arrived at great skill in the Mathematicks." This was Robert Dunning, who was one of Roger Goad's first accusers, and was committed to the Gatehouse at Westminster. There he repented, and wrote to Lord Burghley:

"that he wondered at the Blindness of his own mind and confessed that because he hated the Provost therefore he had raised most false accusations against a man worthy to be seen and heard by Princes."

His repentance seems either to have been superficial or to have come too late, for our chronicler goes on:

"he behaved so as to be expelled. Remarkable it is; you seldom find men of moderate parts run into such enormous extravagancies. Your slow dull fellows usually live longer, behave better, and are more usefull and exemplary in their generations, than those volatile and elevated geniuses."

CHAPTER VII

SAMUEL COLLINS

ONLY five years separate the Provostships of Roger Goad and of the equally eminent Samuel Collins. This short interval is filled by two Provosts, Fogge Newton and William Smythe, both of whom gave promise of doing good service to the Society. Newton was son-in-law to Goad, and is described as "a most learned, meek, and good man." Meek as he was, he was called upon to withstand James I. in an attempt which the King made to secure a Fellowship for a Scotchman. Newton wrote to explain that the College Statutes forbade the election of any one born outside the realm of England. Strict loyalty to the Statutes would equally have prevented any royal interference in the election of Scholars from Eton; but there is evidence to show that such interference was not uncommon, as indeed we might infer from the language of the following letter written only eighteen years later:

" WESTMINSTER PALACE.
        " *10 December 1628.*

    " *The King to the Provosts of Eton and King's College.*

    " Whereas we are given to understand that one Isaa Oliver, a student of our College at Eton, hath spent man

years in the course of his studies there and is as well in
respect of his time as of his proficiency in learning very fit
to be removed to our University of Cambridge ; We have
therefore thought fit, both in regard of the industrious
expense of his time in the course of his studies as for his
better encouragement to proceed in his commendable
endeavours for the time to come, by these our letters to
desire you whom it may concern, that at the next election
of Scholars of that College you choose elect and admit him
into the first place of a Scholar of King's College in Cambridge according to the usual custom of that House. And
we shall take your readiness to give us satisfaction herein
in very thankful part at your hands."

Isaac Oliver was accordingly admitted a Scholar,
though not till 1630, and proved rather an expensive
acquisition to the College, for the records tell us that
he

" went distracted and so continued above thirty years, and
which was very reasonable was allowed the full profits of
his Fellowship as if he had been resident."

It is added, however, that he was an excellent scholar,
so that perhaps he would have been admitted without
royal intervention.

But Oliver was not the only Scholar admitted in
1630 on the King's recommendation. Two years later,
a strong opposition was made by some members of the
College to the appointment of Nathaniel Vincent as
Poser ; and among other objections it was urged that,
when he had served that office in 1630, he had dis-
pleased the King by refusing to elect boys on the royal
recommendation. Vincent's rival at this time was one

Thomas Roe, and a written statement was made by the former, to the effect that in 1630 Roe had exhorted Vincent not to be pusillanimous, and had then accused him to Lord Holland of resisting the King's will. After all, Vincent's opposition was ineffectual, for in 1632 the Fellows of the College made the following declaration:

"We may trewly say that more Schollers were expedited at that time upon his Majestie's Commandment, wherein hee of all Princes of the earth hath been most sparing and moderate, than commonly are in scores of years, 4 Schollers being contented in their desires at once, for whom his Majestie then vouchsafed to write."

Then follow the names of Isaac Oliver and three more.

Provost Newton was Rector of Kingston in Cambridgeshire, when he was made Provost; there he died and was buried, as his Inscription says, by his own wish:

" Moriens, ' ubi
Pro Christiano feceram excubias grege,
Hic nostra ' dixit ' ossa conquiescite.
Edormietis sæculi noctem brevis.' "

William Smythe then succeeded to the Provostship in 1612, and held it for three years. In this case also the election was determined by the interference of the Crown. James I. wrote to the College, warning them not to act in filling the vacancy caused by Provost Newton's death till he had ascertained "where The Right lyeth"; and then, being satisfied of his own right to nominate, he bids the College to elect Smythe, whom he (King James) had inclined to elect instead of

Newton, but "wee were misinformed of something concerning him, which since we have found to be untrue."
The new Provost had for some time been Master of
Clare, and perhaps, if he had lived, the controversy
which presently arose between the two Colleges might
have been conducted with less acrimony. Of him it is
recorded that " he was a good housekeeper, and the loss
of him was much lamented as well by the Fellow-
Collegiates as by the College Tenants generally."

His successor, Samuel Collins, was the son of a
Kingsman, Baldwin Collins, who ended his life as
Fellow and Vice-Provost of Eton; in which office " he
took the opportunities to prefer many poor but good
Scholars; a man of wonderful learning and as great
humility." For himself he refused preferment, but he
went up and down " preaching gratis at one neighbouring village or another almost every Sunday, as long as
health and strength of nature would permit him." He
just lived to see his son become Provost. Samuel
inherited his father's love of learning, without the
humility. He must have been a precocious boy, if
there is any truth in the story that he was elected

" against six eminent competitors by Dr. Goad who, upon
his translating a piece of Horace, clapping his hands on his
head, said, 'This is my child, who if he lives shall be my
heir and successor.'"

This was in 1591, when Collins was only fifteen years
of age. He gained the reputation of being the best
Latinist of his days, and in 1613 he kept a celebrated
Act for his Doctor's degree, when the Elector Palatine
and Princess Elizabeth, then just married, were present,

G

his opponent being Williams, afterwards Visitor of Collins's own College as Bishop of Lincoln, and finally Archbishop of York and Lord Keeper. " No flood," says Hacket,

" can be compared to the spring-tide of Collins's language and eloquence, but the milky river of Nilus with his seven mouths. . . . What a Vertumnus, when he pleased to argue on the right side or the contrary."

Four years later Collins became Regius Professor of Divinity, and read Lectures twice a week for thirty-four years, " wherein " (says Fuller) " never any two alike." Yet the same authority, contrasting him with Samuel Ward, who was the Margaret Professor, adds:

" Dr. Collins had much the speed of him in quickness of parts, but let me say (nor doth the relation of a pupil misguide me) the other pierced the deeper into underground and profound points of divinity."

It appears that he was sometimes too ready with his tongue; for Hacket, who wrote the Life of the Visitor, Bishop Williams, tells us that in 1628 on some disgust conceived against him the Fellows petitioned the Bishop to visit the College, who accordingly accepted the invitation ; but

" the cause went for the right worthy Provost, in whose government the Bishop could perceive neither carelessness nor covetousness. The most that appeared was that the Doctor had pelted some of the active Fellows with slings of wit; at which the Visitor laughed heartily, and past them by, knowing that the Provost's tongue could never be wormed to spare his jests, who was the readiest alive to gird whom he would with innocent and facetious urbanity."

The Visitor did, however, make, or at least recommend, a change of some importance in the administration of the College, which will be noticed in a later chapter.

A man of Collins's disposition may have had a taste for controversy. If so, he was able to indulge it in one which he maintained with the Jesuits in defence of the book which Andrewes had written against Cardinal Bellarmine. The titles given by these combatants to their respective pamphlets, such as *Ephphatha* and *Obmutesce*, suggest that they did not spare each other. Collins, however, was a scholar as well as a theologian, and to the end of his life continued to study his favourites, Ovid, Pindar, Cicero and Isocrates, as well as such writers as Bembo and Politian. Unfortunately we do not know whether he succeeded in inoculating the members of his College with his own love of literature. We have a pleasant picture of Provost Collins at home in a letter from his brother Provost of Eton, Sir Henry Wotton. Sending a portrait of Paolo Sarpi as a present, Wotton writes:

"You have a luminous Parlour, which I have good cause to remember, not only by delicate Fare and Freedom (the Prince of Dishes), but by many good Authors. In that Room,* I beseech you to allow it a favourable Place for my sake."

* Sarpi's portrait has unfortunately disappeared. But in the dining-room of the present Lodge there is one of Collins himself; and one can easily imagine that it is the likeness of an impulsive, self-reliant, and witty man.

Wotton also sent to Collins a MS. of Horace, which had once belonged to Pietro Bembo, and which is still preserved in the College Library.

Bishop Williams was himself quite capable of appreciating the Provost's wit, and his letters show that he began his Visitorship with a high opinion of the Provost's character.   He writes in 1626:

"I would have all men to know, I loved and respected you extraordinarilye, for your many excellent partes, and amongst the rest your great sweetnes and mildnes in Governement."

And in the following year :

"I observed nothing in any thinge you saide or did, but what became a man of as great a Depthe in Judgment and Prudence as in Learninge."

A longer experience, however, and the frequency of the appeals or petitions presented by Fellows, who thought themselves aggrieved or the welfare of their Society endangered, seem to have altered this favourable opinion.

It was in May 1629 that two Fellows, Thomas Roe and Ralph Winterton, approached the Visitor with a complaint.   Winterton wished to be allowed to "divert" to the study of medicine; the Statutes limited the number of such students to two ; but Roe was anxious to give up medicine for theology, thereby creating the necessary vacancy.   This seemed to the Visitor a reasonable arrangement, and he writes to the Provost:

"The matter is not of that moment but I maye resemble their suyte to that of Pamphilus and Charinus in the

Comædie; the place of a Physitian is the Mistresse that
looks to be courted. And the case is this,

'Hic pavet ne ducat illam, alter autem ut ducat.'

Mr. Roe's request is full of reason, if he hath a resolution
for the Ministrie, and you and I must be no adversaries to
that resolution, if any other be willing and able to supply
the other facultye."

He goes on to show that Winterton is excellently
qualified for the study of medicine, and it seems
impossible that

"you wold not give way of your own accord to this per-
mutation, were not somewhat concealed, under soe many
good partes, which cannot as yeat be visible. This made
me move some questions to Mr. Wynterton, from whom I
receiv'd humble and ingenuous Awnswers. And such as
persuade me, that he is your true and faythfull beadesman,
and doth runne into noe irremissible error. Εἰ δέ τι ἠδίκησέ
σε—τοῦτο ἐμοὶ ἐλλόγει."

The result of this letter was that the two diversions were allowed on August 20, 1629. Unhappily,
further trouble soon arose in the case of both these
men. A sermon having been preached by the Vice-
Provost in Chapel on Oct. 19, 1631, which appeared to
Roe "very unseemly, tending to the breach of charity
and the dishartning of young men in their studies,"
Roe took advantage of a disputation, which he held in
the Chapel a few days afterwards, to "testifie" his
dislike of the sermon. For this "indiscreet exercise"
Roe was reprimanded; and as the Visitor would not
listen to him, he went to the Chancellor, Lord Holland,
and, according to the College account, he

" openly protested in ye Lord of Holland's Chamber that he neither valued King's College nor any in it more than he did the rushes under his foote."

Lord Holland gave him no more encouragement than the Visitor had done. But the next year he had a new grievance. It was the custom of each of the four Senior Fellows to keep a servitor, who waited on him and was fed on the remains of the Hall dinner; and "your petitioner," so Roe tells the Visitor,

"being one of the fower hath brought into the said Colledg one Balls, a civil and studious youth, to be his poor Scholler. . . . But Dr. Goad at this time being Dean of Arts hath . . . warned the said Balls to be gone, and doeth every day molest and threaten the poor boy."

The Visitor writes on this petition, that if Dr. Goad's intention was to turn out all the four poor Scholars as encroachers on the Foundation, he approved of such a design; if not,

" I doe holde it reasonable that Mr. Provost doe keepe him in possession of all privileges as his predecessor hadd. And must suspect the justice of Dr. Goad's proceedings in that kinde."

A more serious controversy arose when the College in 1631 refused Winterton the degree of M.D. The Provost and Fellows signed an explanation of their refusal, which they sent to the Visitor. They were aware that divers Heads of other Colleges had taken up Winterton's cause, but declared that

" as for diverse other passages of his distempered cariage among us, whereof happly they of other Colleges could not so well take notice, conversing not so neer with him, so especially because in our judgment he hath lived turbulently and seditiously in ye College, we hold him unfitt for that honor and unworthy of the same."

Ralph Winterton was evidently a difficult person to live with. The College records describe him as "somewhat disordered in his senses" while an undergraduate. And this was attributed to his intense grief at the death of a brother in the wars abroad. But this cannot have been the cause of his earliest eccentricities, as his brother was one of the English volunteers in the army of Gustavus Adolphus, and did not die before 1631, eleven years after Winterton had become a Fellow. It is said that ill-health and sleeplessness had first made him study medicine; and that he was also an excellent Greek scholar and musician. At any rate, he was now recognised in the University as a person of some importance; and his treatment by the College was a matter of general interest. This appears from a curious letter of John Hacket to Collins, dated June 25, 1632. Hacket was chaplain to Bishop Williams; and, while staying at Buckden Palace for a few days, he writes to the Provost of the general indignation caused by the stopping of the grace for Winterton's degree, a man

" whose learning in that science, in anatomy, and in all parts conducing to it, is most exquisite. For pittie sake, and justice sake, good S^r, let this not bee so. For what is Mr. Winterton's offence? unless that he subscribed to a Petition for ye reformation of grave abuses crept into your most famous College, wherein he did the part of a good Patriot."

Hacket adds that the Visitor himself shares this indignation :

" I have heard his Lordship call this malice, not justice ; and thinkes ye case so worthy of his protection that if it be not redressed, it wil make him come to King's College in a more angry mood than hitherto he hath don. . . . I hard him say that if there were as great a tyrant Bishop of Lincoln as you shew yourself tyrannical in your place, few men in your College according to district justice would be able to hold their places. . . . As you tender your own safctie let Winterton's grace pass within an hour after you have read this letter."

Hacket was evidently much impressed with the acuteness of the crisis, but he could hardly expect that his last piece of advice would be taken; and the Bishop's own letter, three days later, reveals some irritation and impatience. He wishes the Provost would let Mr. Winterton go and seek his fortunes as a physician, " and for you to live quietly and peceablye at home, and free me from these unnecessarye molesta- tions." The business, he says, is " not worth a chippe, unless Dr. Goad thinkes he shall be forced to take physicke from Winterton when he is Doctor." But he insists on knowing the names of those who refused the grace, and that they should set down the " enormityes " of Winterton which justified their refusal. Then he passes on to another recent incident, which he thinks very discreditable to the College :

" Whereas I heare of a base and unworthye question in Divinitye, given in your College by one Mr. Vintner, that ' Ebrietas non est gravius peccatum quam schisma ' . . .

I pray you, Mr. Provost, lett me understand, whither you
have heard thereof, as alsoe, how he hath been punished
and the Deane who admitted and allowed of that Question.
If you have not heard of it, enquire into it, and lett them
both be suspended or otherwise punished (I mean the
partye and Moderator) untill they have in all humilitye
acknowledged their Brutishe offence."

Some time after the Visitor's letter the Provost so
far gave way that he propounded to the College a grace
for the disputed degree, but it was refused by the
Fellows. Thereupon Winterton applied to the Chancellor, Lord Holland, and at his mediation the matter
was at last settled. But this was not done without the
intervention of Archbishop Laud, who, finding the
Court "full of this business," wrote to the Provost on
Dec. 12, 1633, to say that Winterton's worth and
learning were very well known to him, and that there
must be no more delay.

It is evident that Winterton had made himself
unpopular in the College; indeed he was punished
more than once, in 1631 and again in 1633, for
indecorous and rude conduct in the College Hall. But
he must have been a man of mark, for he became
Regius Professor of Physic as soon, apparently, as he
became a M.D. Perhaps his self-assertion and combativeness were among the qualities which made him a
vigorous reformer in his own Faculty. And the times
called for reform. In consequence of an outbreak of
the plague at Cambridge there had been a great
increase in the number of doctors, who, as Fuller tells
us, graduated in a clandestine way, without keeping any
Acts, " to the great disgust of those who had fairly

gotten their degrees with public pains and expense."
Dr. Collins, as Vice-Chancellor, in admitting a man of
real ability to the Doctorate, made a distinction
between what he called the " cathedra pestilentiæ " and
the "cathedra eminentiæ." Winterton, during his
short tenure of the Professorship (for he died in 1636),
did his best to amend this state of things. He tells
us that hitherto any one, such as a

"serving man, an apothecary, any M.A., have had license
to practise in Physic. Some of these had also been
ordained, so that if one profession failed another might
supply them. The Minister hath neglected his own
calling and trespassed upon another's, not without en-
dangering the souls of the people of God and the loss of
the lives of many of the King's subjects."

Henceforth, no one was to have a licence or obtain a
degree *without keeping one Act at least*. But little
good, so Winterton adds, would be done unless pressure
were brought to bear on Dr. Clayton, Regius Professor
at Oxford, to adopt the same rule.

A few years senior to Collins was John Lancaster,
who deserves to be remembered for his simple piety.
He is thus described by a contemporary writer:

" A very humble and self-denying man, who tho' by birth
he was a good gentleman, and had some time been Fellow
of King's College in Cambridge, where he had read sundry
public lectures, and made many speeches, and (as Dr.
Collins that master of languages used to say) delivered
himself in as pure Latin as ever Tully spoke, having no
other notes to help him but what he wrote upon his own
nails ; yet this good man thus accomplished with all

learning contented himself with a living not worth £40 per annum, and in his preaching made no noise of learning at all. When I was young, I knew this Master Lancaster; he was a very little man of stature but eminent, as for other things so especially for his living by Faith. His wife would many times come to him, when she was to send her maid to Banbury Market to buy provisions and tell him she had no money. His usual answer was, ' Yet send your maid and God will provide'; and tho' she had no money, yet she never returned empty, for one or other that knew her to be Mr. Lancaster's maid, either by the way or in Banbury town, meeting her would give her money, which still supplied their present wants."

Another country clergyman, who about this time did honour to his College, was Phineas Fletcher, son of the Russian traveller, Giles Fletcher. He was Rector of Hilgay in Norfolk, and Isaac Walton's words are a sufficient description of the life which he led there :

" There came into my mind certain verses in Praise of a mean Estate and an humble Mind : they were written by Phineas Fletcher, an excellent Divine and an excellent Angler, the Author of excellent Piscatory eclogues, in which you shall see the picture of this good man's mind."

His chief poem, which appeared in 1633, was the *Purple Island*, an allegory on man's physical and mental composition, told by a young shepherd to his mates,

> " Where by the garden wall
> The learned Cam with stealing water crawls
> And lowly down before that royal temple falls."

Nearly half the poem is devoted to a description of the human body. Even Lucretius himself could hardly have made anatomy poetical, but an occasional episode or simile in the earlier cantos shews what Fletcher might have done if his subject had been better chosen. When he comes to personify the mental faculties and to describe the fight between the virtues and vices he has more scope for his imagination. He has a passion for antithesis, the frequent repetition of which becomes wearisome, though some of the lines, such as his description of the tongue:

"Mother of fairest truth and foulest lies,"

are forcible. Milton may have owed something to the author of the *Purple Island*, who, at any rate, anticipates the great poet when he writes of the Fallen Angels:

"In Heaven they scorned to serve, so now in Hell
    they reign."

Fletcher professes to take Virgil and Spenser as his models. In politics he was an admirer of the Earl of Essex, and attributes Elizabeth's death to her regrets on his account; in theology he inclined to the Arminian view, for he personifies the Will as "fair Voletta,"

"Whom neither man, nor fiend, nor God constrains;
Oft good, oft ill, oft both, yet free remains."

CHAPTER VIII

THE EVE OF THE CIVIL WAR

IT was in Provost Collins's time that further progress was made with the furniture of the Chapel. The stalls did not, indeed, receive their canopies till after the Restoration; but in 1625 Thomas Weaver, a former Fellow, gave the coats of arms carved in elmwood which form the back of the stalls. He had already done work of the same kind for the Chapel at Eton, of which College he was a Fellow.

Even more important was the work undertaken at the east end of the Chapel at King's. What had stood there since the removal of the High Altar in 1560 we do not know, but now a wooden screen or reredos was raised, on which were carved the arms of the College and other devices. This screen had a canopy adorned with fine carved work, and stood at a little distance from the east wall; there were doors in it leading to the void space behind, which was used for the interment of Senior Fellows. The back of the Altar seems to have been hung with damask, and the Altar itself covered with a purple velvet Communion-cloth with silk and gold fringes, partly paid for by the Provost. The cost of these alterations was more than £200.

But a more permanent change had been made in the

appearance of the Chapel a generation earlier, when the organ was placed on the rood-loft. Some sort of organ, but of a humble kind, had no doubt been used from the first, for the Statutes required that one of the chaplains, or else a lay clerk, should be competent "jubilare in organis"; and the College Accounts show that a modest sum of money had been spent on the repair of the organ and as a stipend to the performer. The instrument which was in the Chapel at Elizabeth's accession had been sold by order of her Commissioners. During the two years, 1596–97, which Orlando Gibbons spent as a Chorister under the charge of his elder brother, it is doubtful whether there was any organ in the Chapel, and the music which he composed for certain festivals, and for which he received from the College payments of 2s. or 2s. 6d. in 1601–1603, may well have been sung without accompaniment.

In 1606, however, a new departure was made. John Tomkins was appointed Organist, and was probably the first who held that title. His salary was about £14 a year, and he seems, in addition, to have had rooms and commons in College. It was part of his duty to instruct the Choristers in music. On his appointment, and probably under his superintendence, if not at his instigation, a new organ was built by a Dallam or Dalham; more than half a century later there were three of this name employed in building organs for York Minster, for New College, Oxford, for St. George's, Windsor, and other places. It was probably the father of these three who was employed at King's. Dallam and his men were lodged in the town of Cambridge for more than a year, and boarded in the College Hall;

from one item, for suppers on Fridays, it would seem that they required extra dishes when the College fare was meagre. The cost of the organ was about £214, and that of the case £156. Nothing of Dallam's organ remains, but the case has undergone only slight alterations, and is a beautiful specimen of Jacobean woodwork.*

It was now the springtime of English Church Music; which, after a temporary check under the chilling influence of Puritan ascendency, was soon to reach its maturity in the compositions of such men as Blow, Purcell, and Croft. With a new organ and a really great organist it is probable that the College Services became more widely attractive. Within the last hundred years the Chapel had been the scene of Latin Stage-plays, of Provost Goad's catechetical lectures, and of the Visitor's judgments, sometimes delivered to a disrespectful and tumultuous audience. Now it began to be in some degree the Cathedral of Cambridge. A regulation of James I. in 1619, the object of which was to secure the due maintenance of services in the various College Chapels, forbids the ladies of Cambridge to repair to any such services except the ordinary Prayers in King's Chapel. There was still room for improvement; at least in the opinion of one of the Heads, who in 1636 sent to Archbishop Laud a complaint of various ecclesiastical irregularities at Cambridge, and observes that at King's College

* Dr. M. R. James, whose judgment is entitled to the greatest weight, is confident that some parts of the organ-case date from the reign of Henry VIII. If so, it is probable that the first organ used in the Chapel stood in the rood-loft. It may have been placed on one side, so as to leave the centre free for the rood itself, as is the arrangement in the Church of St. Bertrand de Comminges.

"some of the Choir, both men and boys, are mute and come without surplices when they list ; that the singing is hasty and slovenly."

Even in modern times it is not an uncommon thing for some members of a choir to be too old, and some too young, to be effective singers, and we need not attach great weight to the remarks of a solitary critic, who perhaps had not much experience on which to base his criticism.   John Milton left the University in 1632, and is believed to have written *Il Penseroso* within the next five years.   One cannot but believe that a reminiscence of King's College Services helped to inspire the lines,

> "There let the pealing organ blow
> To the full voic'd Quire below,
> In service high, and Anthems clear,
> As may with sweetness, through mine ear,
> Dissolve me into ecstacies,
> And bring all Heav'n before mine eyes."

About this time the monotony of College life at King's was enlivened by a quarrel with their nearest neighbours.   In 1637 the authorities of Clare Hall, being about to rebuild their College, wished to retire from Milne Street and move their Quadrangle westward.   By so doing they would at once gain for themselves and confer on King's the benefit of more light and air.   But Clare had at that time no property to the west of the Cam.   The ground on the far side of the river was the property of King's, and Clare, naturally desiring an outlet to the open fields beyond, wished to secure a free passage through Butt Close (the name by which the area now known as the "Quarters" or "Scholars' Piece" of King's, together with the old Clare Garden, was then called). The proposal made by Clare was that leave should be given them to make a causeway running west from the bridge which they meant to build, or else that an exchange of property should be arranged, whereby King's would acquire a piece of ground at the north-west corner of the Chapel and should surrender part of Butt Close to Clare. Apparently without waiting for an answer, they applied to the King not merely for a passage but for a piece of ground, and the King directed that their application should be granted. The Kingsmen not unnaturally resented this method of cutting the knot, and a controversy ensued. It was argued, on the part of King's, that their Statutes forbade them to alienate land, that the close neighbourhood of the Clare buildings was a protection against west winds and violent storms; and that Butt Close was the exercise-ground of a hundred persons, besides giving pasturage to ten horses which they were bound by Statute to keep. The matter was referred to Lord Holland, the Chancellor, who seems to have persuaded the College to withdraw their opposition. At any rate, a letter from the King, March 17, 1638, ordered the exchange to take place. But there was to be no actual sale. Each College was to lease ground to the other for terms of twenty years, to be renewed without any fine; King's College paying 12*d.* a year for their new acquisition, and receiving in return £5 yearly rent for the part of the close which they surrendered to Clare.

It is rather remarkable that in 1633 and 1634 three out of the four Regius Professorships were held by

H

Kingsmen; for, besides Collins and Winterton, one of
the Goad family was Professor of Civil Law. Not long
before him the same office had been held by another
Kingsman, who may be said to have thrown down the
gauntlet in the cause of Absolutism. This was John
Cowell, who became Professor in 1594 and Master of
Trinity Hall in 1598. As a Scholar of King's he had
distinguished himself by his regularity; and it is
recorded as a College custom of the following century
that on every 7th of January the senior Scholar after
supper visited the College authorities with a request for
a "Dor," *i.e.*, for leave to the Scholars to lie in bed till
late next morning "in memoriam Doctoris Cowell who
then and never else overslept himself and missed early
prayers." The book by which he gained notoriety was
not published till 1612; it was called the *Interpreter*,
and its professed object was to explain the meaning of
legal terms. But, as Dr. Johnson afterwards made his
Dictionary a vehicle for expressing his political sentiments, so to a much greater degree did Cowell in
giving his explanations of such words as "King,"
"Parliament," "Prerogative," to the effect that the
King was superior to the Law, that in asking the
Houses of Parliament to pass laws he was waiving his
own absolute power, and that subsidies were granted to
him in consideration of this condescension on his part.
The House of Commons was immediately on the alert,
instigated, it was said, by Coke, who was believed to be
jealous of Cowell, and who was certainly jealous of the
Civil Law; but, before Parliament had time to act,
James had summoned the rash Professor before the
Council, and had called upon him to justify some other

passages in his book, which "do as well pinch the
authority of the King, as the other points were
derogatoric to the liberty of the subject"; and had
decided that Cowell impugned the Common Law of
England, and that in opposing Prerogative to Law he
had attacked both King and People together.   Cowell
was committed to the custody of an Alderman, his
book suppressed, and burnt by the common hangman.
Two months later he resigned his Professorship, and
before the end of the year he died.

If Cowell was a champion of political theories which
led to civil war, Richard Mountagu was equally
prominent in maintaining those Church views with
which the Stuart cause was intimately associated.   He
became a Fellow of King's in 1597.   In the year 1610
he was at Eton, engaged in editing the works of
Chrysostom and other Greek Fathers for Sir Henry
Savile, the Provost, who had set up a printing-press
there.   Three years later, at the age of thirty-six, he
became a Fellow of Eton, and other preferment followed.   Before long he was engaged in a controversy
with the Roman Catholics, whose emissaries he had
found endeavouring to pervert one of his parishioners
at Stanford Rivers in Essex.   But even before this he
had undertaken, at King James's request, to write a
reply to Cardinal Baronius.   His book was so displeasing to Archbishop Abbot that for a time it was
suppressed.   When it appeared in 1622, it was found
to be a learned Latin inquiry into the origin and early
history of the Faith, with the view of showing that
Anglican doctrine was derived from primitive sources.
This was not a line of argument likely to please the

Puritans, especially as Mountagu, in the controversy in which he had embarked on behalf of his parishioners, while maintaining that the Church of Rome was not a sound branch of the Catholic Church, hesitated to call the Pope Antichrist. Not that he had any scruple about using hard words; for he named his anti-Roman pamphlet, *A new Gag for an old Goose;* and in describing to his friend Cosin what he had done, he says, "Answere it I have . . . . bitterly and tartly, I confesse, which I did purposely because the asse deserv'd so to be rub'd." But he declined to fight Rome with Puritan weapons, his own position being that of an Anglo-Catholic. He went so far as to defend auricular confession, though only as a voluntary practice; and the use of pictures and images to excite devotion, not as objects of adoration.

These doctrines roused the indignation of two Ipswich clergymen, who complained to the House of Commons. The House referred the matter to the Archbishop; Abbot remonstrated with Mountagu, but King James took his part. "If that is to be a Papist," said he, "I am a Papist." At the crisis of the controversy the old King died; and Mountagu, who had been encouraged to write a fuller vindication of his views, now produced and dedicated to Charles I. his well-known *Appello Cæsarem.*

In this work he neither retracts his opinions nor softens his language. It is a masterly treatise, written in vigorous English; especially the fifth chapter, which deals with the burning question of predestination. He protests that his own object is to "make up if it were possible the breaches and ruines of the Church"; but he will have nothing to do with the Puritans' "comfortable Doctrine of Election and Reprobation." He retorts on them the charge of disloyalty :

"you seem to cloze with the Church of England in her Discipline, to use the Crosse, and wear the Clothes; but her Doctrine you wave it, preach against it, teach contrary to that which you have subscribed."

Being himself perfectly at home in classical and patristic literature, he does not conceal his contempt for Puritan ignorance :

" If you with your new learning (for old you have none) can teach me more than yet I know, I will yeeld and thank you for such instruction.
    " If I have any occasion hereafter to speak of *learned* and *moderate* men, I will ever except and exempt you and yours."

He sums up his views by saying that

" Popery is for *Tyranny*, Puritanisme for *Anarchy ;* Popery is originall of *Superstition ;* Puritanisme the highway unto *Prophanenesse ;* both alike enemies unto Piety."

For two or three years the controversy continued. Parliamentary inquiries and theological conferences were held, and at one time Mountagu was in the custody of the Serjeant-at-Arms.   So far as argument went he was at least a match for his numerous opponents, and he had the support of the King.   But he had spoken disrespectfully of the Synod of Dort, and (though he disclaimed the title of Arminian) he was a thoroughgoing antagonist of the predominant Calvinism. Even the excellent Bishop Morton, whom Mountagu speaks of with respect and not unfrequently quotes in his *Appello*, could make no terms with him on this crucial question. At last, in 1628, when he was in imminent danger of impeachment, some sort of peace was restored by the suppression of the obnoxious treatise, and by a royal declaration imposing silence on both parties. At the same time Mountagu was raised to the See of Chichester, and it was clear on which side the King's sympathies really lay.

Mountagu's letters to his friend Cosin, afterwards Bishop of Durham, reveal both the earnestness of purpose and the recklessness of language which were alike characteristic of the man, his self-confidence and his disdain for his opponents. It must be added that the letters also show him to have been a loyal friend and an affectionate father. He saw clearly enough the double danger which then threatened the Church of England:

" I hope God will every day raise up some to stand in the gapp against Puritanisme and Popery, the Scilla and Charybdis of antient piety."

But, though circumstances had driven him into controversy with Rome, he recognised that the more pressing danger came from the side of Geneva:

" If it be but *calamo tenus*, all the Calvinists in the world come on, I care not."

" This riff-raff rascals make us lyable to the lash unto our other adversaries of the Church of Rome, who impute the frantick fitts and froth of every Puritan paroxysme to the received doctrine of our Church, as this beboone doth with whom I have lately had to do, Sr Goose the Gagger."

And the danger was a personal one :

" Let me understand at full the Puritan charity, what it is, as Arminius found amongst the brethren in the Nether- lands.   From their doctrine, discipline, and charity, Good Lord deliver me and all honest men."

The answers to his *Appello* were numerous, and to one of his antagonists, Dr. Prideaux, Rector of Exeter College and Regius Professor of Divinity at Oxford, he was especially uncomplimentary :

" Prideux hath thretned to write against me.   *Utinam,* But I think he distrusteth himself and his pen. . . . For those Oxford braggarts I fear them not ; ther pens nor pratinge."

Allowance must be made for the fact that Mountagu is unbosoming himself to an intimate friend; but those who read his letters will readily understand the criti- cism of Davenant, Bishop of Salisbury :

" I wish he had a more modest concept of himself and a less base opinion of all others who jump not with him in his mongrel opinions."

The closing words of the *Appello*, " Do thou defend me with thy sword, and I will defend thee with my pen," gave Mountagu's enemies some excuse for repre- senting him as relying on royal prerogative, and on try- ing to set King against people.   But Mountagu was no politician.   His whole mind was given up to ecclesias- tical questions.   As Bishop, first of Chichester and then for a short time of Norwich, he was diligent in the duties of his diocese without abandoning his literary work.   Towards the close of his life, 1635–36, he was represented by Panzani, the Papal envoy, as being forward in promoting union with Rome, and as willing to accept all Romish doctrine except Transubstantiation. It is rather surprising that this exception should be made, for his views on Eucharistic Doctrine might easily be interpreted so as to bear a Roman meaning, though on other grounds he was an outspoken antagonist of the Papacy. But Panzani's account contains many improbabilities, and he was very likely to misunderstand, if he did not deliberately misrepresent, the conversations which he had with Mountagu. Better evidence must be produced before we can believe that the Bishop was ready to abandon his old position.

For the moment, indeed, he was the champion of a losing cause. The minds of his generation were not ripe for Anglicanism, which was made still more unpopular by the harshness of the discipline with which it was enforced. But its greatest misfortune was that it happened to be allied with political absolutism. The latter was doomed to perish, but the former survived the Rebellion, reappeared at the Restoration, and, after suffering a temporary eclipse in the Hanoverian period, reasserted itself in the Oxford movement of the nineteenth century. The names of Andrewes, Laud, Overall, and Mountagu are all intimately associated with the earlier movement in the seventeenth century. However imperfect that theology may be, it was at least a great improvement on the hard and narrow school which preceded it, and to Mountagu, more than to any other, belongs the honour of dealing a blow at those Calvinistic doctrines which were almost forced on the Church of England in the Lambeth Articles of 1595, and which had actually become supreme in the minds of Englishmen. It was necessary that men should be emancipated from this yoke before they could adopt some theology which should be at once more reasonable and more historical, and in which it would be possible for later generations of educated Englishmen to find a home. Those who appreciate the important part which Mountagu played in this eventful struggle will be inclined to forgive the extravagances of his language.

CHAPTER IX

DARK DAYS

WHEN King and Parliament came to actual war, it was inevitable that a College with the traditions of King's should, for the most part, embrace the cause of the former. And within a year of the time when the royal standard was raised at Nottingham, members of the College had left their Fellowships or Scholarships to take up arms, while some of those who continued to pursue their peaceful callings had to suffer for their loyalty to Church and King. Such was the case with William Losse, who had been admitted to the College forty years earlier, had gained some distinction as a mathematician, and had been presented to the Vicarage of Weedon Pinckney in Northamptonshire. There, on the afternoon of Sunday, July 2, 1643, he was reading the service, when ten or twelve troopers came from Northampton, entered the church, and ordered the Vicar at once to follow them. Losse begged them to wait till he had finished the service ; to which a trooper answered :

"Patience me no patience, my business is of greater importance than to admit of delay ; come away therefore or I will pull you out by the ears."

The Vicar went with them into the churchyard, and
being told that he must ride with them into Northampton
excused himself, alleging that

"twelve or thirteen horses had been taken from him by
the Parliamentary soldiers, and had left him never a one
able to carry him two miles out of town."

Whereupon one of the troopers swore that he would
carry him behind him ; and "if he did not like that, he
would drag him along with a halter at the horse's tail."
This was too much for the Vicar, who protested

"That he would never be a slave to slaves ; and so rushing
from them with difficulty took sanctuary in the Church,
where he was pursued by one of the Troopers on horseback,
who in that situation was attempting to enter, had not
Mr. Losse with one of the bars of the door resolutely
prevented him, and barred himself in with part of the
Congregation. But not thinking himself sufficiently
secure, by means of a ladder which he drew up after him
he got up to the top of the Belfry."

Meanwhile the troopers succeeded in forcing an entry
into the church, and rode up and down it, "spurring
and switching their horses purposely to endanger the
people." Mrs. Losse and her children were frightened
by this outrageous conduct ; indeed, Mrs. Losse fainted,
and the congregation remonstrated with the troopers,
putting them in mind of the sacredness of the place in
which "they committed these Indecencies" : adding that
they ought to be ashamed to abuse a minister in his
own congregation, who, "besides the reverence due to
his function might challenge some respect from them

being a gentleman of good birth and descent." This last was an ill-timed argument, for one of the troopers broke out with a great oath,

" What do you tell me of birth and descent ? A plague take him and his gentility. I hope within this year to see never a gentleman in England."

After this they all marched to the belfry,

"where when they found they could not come at Mr. Losse, who had taken up the ladder and made the trapdoor fast with the same, they discharged their pistols at him, at least eight or nine times, but by good Providence he avoided their aims; but could not so well the points of their swords; for they wounded him in three several parts of his body and a vein pricked in one of his hands, from which the blood flowed in such abundance on the Troopers underneath him, that they bragged there and in other places that they had dispatched him, and so went their way calling him Rogue, Rascall, Slave, Villain, Dog and Devill; and at their departure protested with many execrations upon themselves that in case they had not murthered him now, which yet they hoped they had, they would return another time, and have him dead or alive."

William Losse offered only a passive resistance to the demands of the Parliamentary party ; other Kingsmen had already taken more active steps. James Fleetwood, was was admitted Scholar in 1622, and was one day to be Provost, left a Shropshire living to become Chaplain in Lord Rivers's regiment, and did such good service at Edge Hill that by the King's command he received the degree of D.D. from the University of Oxford on November 1, 1642. As his kinsmen had chosen the

Parliamentary side, the King may have wished to give a special reward for Fleetwood's loyalty. It may be presumed that his services had been only of a spiritual kind, but the names of a dozen or more Kingsmen are recorded who left their books for the sword. Of these, some, like James Eyre and Charles Howard, lost their lives in battle or siege; the most interesting case being that of Sampson Briggs, who is said to have been a very good scholar and excellent poet. At any rate he wrote an English poem in 1638 on the unhappy loss of Edward King (Milton's Lycidas), drowned on the passage to Ireland. And when Briggs himself fell at the siege of Gloucester, his aged father, the parson of Foulmire, went distracted on hearing the news. Others, however, survived the war. Thus William Fairbrother, who was taken prisoner at Naseby, June 14, 1645, returned to College and became Vice-Provost in 1658. In 1660 he had the satisfaction of entertaining in Hall the soldiers who had just been firing volleys from the roof of the Chapel to celebrate the Restoration. He was still living in 1669, in which year he received the degree of D.C.L. at Oxford on the occasion of the opening of Sheldon's Theatre. William Raven, who had commanded a troop of horse, ended his life as Rector of West Parley in Dorsetshire; and there were other cases of the same kind.

Probably Henry Bard and Arthur Swaine were the two Kingsmen who gained most distinction in the war. Swaine had only been four years at College when he joined the King at Oxford in 1643:

" being a man of extraordinary stout and strong body and

undaunted courage, and every way completely fitted for such an employment. In a short time after his coming thither he was for his eminent service made Colonel of a regiment of Foot and Commissary General for his Majesty's army in the West ; but teaching his servant the postures of the musket at Oxford, by the unadvised going off of the same, he thinking it was not charged and ordering him to level it at him, he was unfortunately slain, and buried in the Cathedral of Christ Church with the general sorrow of the city."

A promising soldier was thus lost to the King. Henry Bard's career was a longer one. He seems to have been of a restless and roving disposition. Even when a Scholar he used his sixty days of absence to visit Paris ; and as soon as he became a M.A. Fellow, he wandered all over the Continent and travelled into Palestine, Arabia and Egypt. On his return he presented a copy of the Koran to the College Library. His enemies said that he had stolen it out of a mosque in Egypt; and that, when told it was not worth more than £20, he " made answer that he was sorry he had ventured his neck for it." He was now to venture his neck for a different cause, and in 1642 he entered the King's service at York, where he soon became a Colonel; his knowledge of French, and perhaps also his " very personable appearance," recommending him to the Queen's favour. He became governor of Camden House in Gloucestershire, and fought his way out of it, when it was no longer tenable, after setting it on fire ; and " entertained the besiegers so that they spilt not so much claret wine in the House as they left blood before it." In March 1644 his reckless courage contributed to the loss of the battle fought near Alresford, and left him wounded and a prisoner.

On his release he went to Oxford, where he received a fresh command as well as an Irish peerage; and as Viscount Bellamont he fought at Naseby. Till 1645, when he married, he remained a Fellow of King's. Some years later he joined Charles II. at Bruges, and was sent by him as Ambassador to the Emperor of Persia, from whom Charles hoped for aid. But "so it was that he being unhappily overtaken in his travels by a whirlwind was choked by the sands in the year 1656."

For those who remained at Cambridge during these years of war there was no lack of excitement. Already some College plate had found its way to the King's quarters; but Oliver Cromwell, who as M.P. for the town of Cambridge naturally took the lead, intercepted the greater part of these supplies; and an attempt made early in August 1642 by one James Docwra to collect a force at King's College, " where y⁶ plate was loaden and readie to be conveyed to y⁶ King," was defeated by the activity of Cromwell, who soon afterwards seized the castle with its magazine. Cambridge was an important outpost of the volunteer army raised by the Eastern Counties Association; and there, in February 1643, a force assembled large enough to deter the Royalist Lord Capel from remaining in the neighbourhood. Within a few weeks, however, most of the volunteers returned to their homes, leaving 1000 men to garrison Cambridge. For the defence of the town it was thought necessary to pull down "five or six fair bridges of stone and timber," and also "to spoil a goodly walk with a new gate pertaining to King's College."

Attempts were also made to extort money from the Heads of Colleges, and the University sent a petition to the House of Lords representing

"how in our Colleges our numbers grow thin, and our revenues short ; how frighted by the neighbouring noise of war our students either fled their gowns, or abandoned their studies."

The Colleges were not, however, empty, for soldiers were billeted in them. The Earl of Manchester, who spent the Christmas of 1643 at Cambridge, supported the Colleges in a petition to Parliament to be freed from the ordinance, which had sequestered all " lands and profits belonging to those Colleges which did convey their plate." These petitions were granted, but the Earl was ordered to make the Colleges " orthodox." As Parliament and the Army had already taken the Covenant, in order to secure the aid of the Scotch, and an ordinance followed on February 5, 1644, directing that it should be taken by every Englishman over the age of eighteen, this meant that Presbyterianism was to be enforced, and the Prayer Book superseded by the Directory. Now came the critical moment for the College Chapel. It was bad enough that bands of soldiers should use it for training and exercise, but it was still worse that William Dowsing, under a Parliamentary order for demolishing idols, images, pictures, &c., which he carried out ruthlessly in the county churches, should lay his sacrilegious hands on the windows.

It appears from Dowsing's diary that this act of vandalism was to have been perpetrated immediately

after Christmas of 1643. How the glass escaped
remains a mystery, especially as Dowsing had authority
from the Earl of Manchester to bring before the latter
any who had opposed his work. Mr. Coneybeare, in
his *History of Cambridgeshire*, adopts a suggestion
made by Professor Willis that Dowsing, who received a
"fee" for each church which he had "purified," may
have been persuaded to take the money and leave the
windows alone. This explanation receives some con-
firmation from an entry in the College Accounts for the
quarter beginning March 25, 1644, "Solut. M^ro
Dowzing 6s. 8d."; but it is difficult to believe that so
small a sum, being the amount to which he was entitled
in all cases of "purification," would have induced
Dowsing to spare so rich a prey. If he received a more
substantial bribe, the transaction was kept out of the
College Accounts. This explanation, however, is more
probable than that which attributes the escape to the
friendship of Cromwell for Whichcote, as Whichcote
did not become Provost of King's till about a year after
the danger had passed away. He was not even a
resident in Cambridge at this time, but was living at
his Somersetshire parish of North Cadbury. If, indeed,
the windows were again threatened at some later date,
the influence of the Provost may very probably have
saved them; but of this there is no evidence. Perhaps
the mystery will seem a little less mysterious, if we
remember Cromwell's position and character. He must
have felt a personal interest in the town and University;
and it was an object with his party to win over one of
the two great Universities; nor had any serious opposition occurred in Cambridge to irritate the minds of his

I

followers. Now to deface the great glory of Cambridge
was hardly the way to conciliate Cambridge men; and
though Cromwell could, on occasions, behave like a
fanatic, as he did when he interrupted the service in
Ely Cathedral and drove out the congregation, yet he
did not allow fanaticism to interfere with policy. It is
on record also that about this time some of the soldiers
defended Trinity Chapel from the rudeness of the rest,
and received a reward from the College for their good
conduct. There is therefore some probability that both
general and soldiers may have been inclined to spare
works of art, which from their very position were
happily protected from anything short of deliberate
violence. The popular legend, which attributes the
preservation of the windows to their having been taken
down and buried in a single night, has neither historical
evidence nor intrinsic probability to entitle it to any
serious attention.

But, if the buildings were spared, the same mercy
was not shown to their inhabitants. Samuel Collins,
at any rate, could not hope to escape. He was Head
of a royal Foundation; he was Regius Professor of a
theology now proscribed; and he was non-resident
rector of a country parish. At Fen Ditton he was denounced for setting up a costly altar; "his superstition
is so great, and his doctrine so impossible to edify";
and it was said that he made feastings on the Sabbath
days. From what we know of his style of oratory, it is
likely enough that he preached over the heads of the
Cambridgeshire peasants; and if it is true that he ex-
communicated some of them for four years for going to
hear sermons elsewhere, it is not likely that his parish-

ioners would exert themselves in his favour. At about the same time he was deprived of his Provostship, but was allowed to retain the sinecure Rectory of Milton. As late as September 4, 1644, he was present as Provost at an admission of two Fellows, and the actual date of his deprivation seems to have been January 9, 1645. As to his Professorship, it is said that he was allowed to discharge the duties without receiving the emoluments of the Living of Somersham, with which it was endowed. This is Fuller's account, who tells us that, " these troublesome times affording more Preachers than Professors, he lost his Church but kept his Chair." And the account is confirmed by the fact that it was not till the year of Dr. Collins's death that another Professor was appointed. He was offered by the King the Bishopric of Bristol in 1646, a time when the position of a Bishop was becoming very precarious ; but he preferred to live on in the town of Cambridge, where the generosity of his successor in the Provostship helped to keep him out of want till 1651, when he died at the age of 75.

The new Provost, Benjamin Whichcote, is said to have protected his Fellows from the necessity of taking the covenant. Five, however, seem to have been ejected at this crisis, the most eminent being Thomas Crouch, who continued to reside in Cambridge as a Fellow-Commoner of Trinity Hall. When after the King's death the Republic was proclaimed, and the members of the College were called upon to take the engagement of October 12, 1649, that they would be true to the new Constitution without a King or House of Lords, a considerable number of Fellows either resigned or were

ejected, among them Henry Molle, the Public Orator,
who lost both office and Fellowship together. The
youngest of the victims must have been Christopher
Wase, who was chosen by Whichcote on his first visit
to Eton in 1645, and admitted a Scholar of King's in
that year. In 1650, the year before the campaign
which ended in the defeat of Worcester, he was accused
of trying to raise men and horses for the King, and was
captured at sea carrying letters from Holland to France.
He then escaped, and served in the Spanish army in
Flanders. A little later we hear of him in Paris, where,
John Evelyn tells us in his Diary,

" he came miserable. From his excellent learning . . .
I bore his charges to England and clad and provided for
him till he should find some better condition ; and he was
worthy of it."

Wase showed his gratitude by writing an elaborate
epitaph on a son of Evelyn's, who died quite young,
and who

> " Libris inhæsit improbo labore
>   Ut sola mors divelleret ;
>   Quid indoles, quid disciplina, quid labor
>   Possent, ab uno disceres."

Wase afterwards became Headmaster of Tunbridge
School, but he ended his days at Oxford, where he was
both a Bedell and Chief Printer to the University.
    The College records show that in the years July 1649
–July 1651 no less than twenty-nine Scholars were
admitted. Possibly some vacancies of old standing
were filled up at this time but the recent ejections

would almost account for the unusual number of admissions. The fact that some of those who served in the King's armies were permitted to return to College and live there as Fellows shews that the Presbyterian party at any rate did not, as a rule, act in an implacable or revengeful spirit. Yet if the studies and discipline of the College did not after all greatly suffer in these troubled times, this must have been chiefly due to the noble character and rare abilities of the usurping Provost.

CHAPTER X

WHICHCOTE AND HIS CONTEMPORARIES

BENJAMIN WHICHCOTE was a member of an old Shropshire family, and became a Fellow of Emmanuel College in 1633, and not long afterwards a Tutor; but at the time of his appointment to the Provostship of King's he was living in Somersetshire as Rector of North Cadbury. He was one of the small but distinguished group of Cambridge Platonists. Bishop Mountagu had asserted the freedom of the human will; Whichcote advocated the rights of human reason. His object was to show that the witness of Reason and Revelation agree, and that there can be no saving faith without a Christlike character. Moreover, he was a champion of toleration. In maintaining these views he parted from the narrow school of theology in which he had been trained, and which his mind had gradually outgrown; and his correspondence with his old Tutor, Anthony Tuckney, Master of Emmanuel, reveals a wide difference between the Puritan and the Platonist.

Whichcote wrote little, except twelve hundred Aphorisms, but he was a great teacher both within his College and outside it. For almost twenty years he lectured every Sunday afternoon to a mixed congregation of townsmen and gownsmen in Trinity Church, and is said thereby to have "contributed more to the forming of the students of the University to a sober sense of religion than any other man in that age." Within his College he encouraged the study of his favourite authors, Plato, Cicero, and Plotinus, and it was probably owing to his influence that two Kingsmen, admitted during his Provostship, Richard Austin and Richard Hunt, gained such distinction as Orientalists that it was said that "The Palme for skill in the oriental languages may well be given to King's College."

Whichcote was accused by his old Tutor, Dr. Tuckney, of exalting the philosophy and virtues of pagans, and also of dabbling in Socinianism and Arminianism. In reply he admits:

" I find the Philosophers that I have read good as farre as they go; and it makes me secretlie blushe before God, when I find eyther my head, heart, or life challenged by them; which, I must confesse, I have often found."

And in one of his Aphorisms he says, "The *Good Nature* of an Heathen is more Godlike than the *furious* zeal of a Christian." While denying that he has any knowledge of Socinian or Arminian literature, he tells Tuckney:

" If a Socinian thinks he can by reason convince of falsehood anything in the Christian religion, and I shew him there is nothing of true reason against aniething of Christian faith. . . . I conceeve, in this case, I deserve as little to be called a Socinian as David, for extorting Goliah's sword out of his hand, and cutting off the master's head with it, did deserve to be esteemed a Philistine."

His toleration was based on a conviction that men must use their reason as much as their eyesight, and

" I will not," he says, " break the certain law of Charity for a doubtful Doctrine " . . . " I dare not blaspheme free and noble spirits in religion, who search after truth with indifference and ingenuitie."

Such men have been, and still are, persecuted; but "I do beleeve that the destroying of this spirit (of persecution) out of the Church is a peece of the Reformation, which God in these times of changes aimes at." " There is nothing more unnatural to religion than contentions about it." He had reached a higher level, and breathed a clearer air, than his old Tutor, to whom he says:

" I cannot returne to that frame of spirit, in the judging and discerning the things of God you seeme to advise me to. I can no more look back than St. Paul, after Christ discovered to him, could returne into his former strayne."

All that we know of Whichcote goes to show that his practice did not fall short of his principles. Even those who differed from him trusted and loved him. Yet neither his own merits nor the intercession of Lord Lauderdale could save him from ejection at the Restoration. Whichcote urged that the appointment of the Provostship was in the King's hands, and that other non-Kingsmen had held the office before him; that he had accepted it unwillingly, and given up for it a valuable living. One of the Senior Fellows, William Godman, though he represented to the King that Whichcote was by Statute incapable of being Provost, yet freely admitted that " his great learning, prudence, and civility

(whereof we of this College have had large experience),"
made him worthy of as great or greater preferment and
dignity; that he was

"an encourager of learning and virtue; that he never
persecuted any of us upon difference of opinion . . . and
that he hath deserved well of the whole Society."

Yet on June 22, 1660, the blow fell, though it was
somewhat softened by the fact that the College conferred on him the Rectory of Milton. Here, though he
had also from time to time the charge of two London
parishes, he "preached constantly, relieved the poor
and had their children educated at his own charge, and
made up differences among the neighbours." He died
in 1683, in the house of his friend Cudworth at
Cambridge.

The Provostship, conferred on Whichcote, had first
been offered to a former Fellow of King's, William
Gouge, who for more than forty years was a noted
preacher at St. Anne's, Blackfriars. He obtained his
Fellowship in 1598, and for some years lectured in
various subjects, including Hebrew. So strict was he in
his conduct and attendance at prayers that he was
known in College as the "Arch-Puritan." In after life
he justified his claim to the title by refusing to read the
Book of Sports and still more by joining a committee formed in 1626 for buying in lay impropriations, in order to maintain a preaching Ministry in
places where "The hungry sheep looked up and were
not fed." This committee was, no doubt, actuated by
a sincere wish to preach the Gospel in neglected
parishes, but it is equally clear that the ministers whom

they appointed, and who held their Lectureships only
so long as their doctrine satisfied their patrons, belonged
to a class disaffected to the discipline, if not to the
doctrine, of the Church of England; and it was a
doubtful gain when the tithes of Presteign in Radnor-
shire, itself very ill provided with clergy, were used to
pay for a Lecturer at St. Antholin's in London. In
1643 Gouge openly adopted Presbyterianism, and was a
prominent member of the Westminster Assembly of
Divines. But he was no republican, and protested
against the King's trial. To the last he was a diligent
student, and spent part of his income in providing for
the education of poor Scholars at the University.

His son Thomas, Scholar of King's in 1625, followed
in his father's steps; and, as a London clergyman,
exerted himself to help the poor by buying hemp and
flax for them to spin; what they spun he took off their
hands, got it wrought into cloth, and sold it as he
could, chiefly to his own friends, bearing the whole loss
himself. The Act of Uniformity in 1662 obliged him
to resign his Living; and his latter years, and what
was left of his property, much of which had been lost in
the Fire of 1666, were devoted to a missionary and
educational crusade in Wales.

The Gouges represent the religious side of Puritanism.
Anthony Ascham, another Kingsman, was a politician
of the same school. Soon after the outbreak of the
Civil War he took the covenant, then sided with the
Independents, and was made Preceptor to James, Duke
of York, on the capture of Oxford in 1646. In
January 1650, when the Parliament had resolved to
conciliate Spain rather than France, Ascham was sent

on a mission to Madrid. Madrid was then full of
English royalists; and Hyde and Lord Cottington, who
represented Charles II. in that capital, remonstrated
with the Spanish authorities for receiving envoys from
a republic which had killed a Christian king. The
Spaniards excused themselves on the plea that Ascham's
visit was only for the purpose of making trade arrangements. Early in June Ascham and his companions
arrived from Seville, and a contemporary tract describes his reception by the favourite, Don Luis de
Haro; and "though this Agent be of a complexion
that the Spaniards do hate (for they paint Judas
always with red hair), yet there hath not been the least
Affront or Indignity offered him yet." Within a week
of their arrival at Madrid, however, Ascham and his
friends were assassinated in their own house by a party
of English royalists; and the Spaniards connived at the
escape of all the murderers except one, who was a
Protestant. When Cromwell broke with Spain in 1655,
this outrage was not forgotten.

The College may be proud both of its Cavaliers and
its Roundheads. It is more difficult to feel sympathy
for a Mr. Facing Bothways, however great his abilities;
and such a man was Edmund Waller. He was left at
an early age heir to a good property in the highlands
of Buckinghamshire, and entered King's as a Fellow-
Commoner in 1621. His wealth was increased by his
first marriage; and, as a young widower of twenty-five,
he aspired to the hand of Lady Dorothea Sidney, whom
he courted in poetry under the name of Saccharissa.
In the Parliaments of 1640 he spoke against granting
supplies before the redress of grievances, and was

employed in managing the prosecution of a Judge who had decided in favour of ship-money. But he opposed the abolition of Episcopacy, urging that the arguments used by the abolitionists would soon be directed against property. So far there was nothing in his public conduct to distinguish him from other moderate reformers. But in 1643 he was concerned in the plot known as "Waller's Conspiracy." In the preceding year he had sent £1000 to the King at Nottingham, and in the negotiations which followed the battle at Edge Hill he visited Charles at Oxford, as one of the Parliamentary Commissioners. It is supposed that during this visit the plot was arranged. Lord Clarendon is confident that Waller and his brother-in-law Tomkins were concerned only in raising a strong party of opposition to the war, and to the taxation by which war was to be supported ; and that the plan of an armed insurrection was known only to Sir Nicholas Crisp, Lord Conway, and their partisans. Later historians, however, do not accept this distinction ; and certainly Waller's conduct, on the discovery of the plot, was that of a man who knew that he deserved death. He saved himself by denouncing his friends and by an abject apology to the House of Commons, from which he was expelled, and he was soon afterwards permitted to leave the country on payment of £10,000. He settled for a time at Rouen, where he married a second wife, who bore him a large family, and who seems to have done nothing to deserve Dr. Johnson's epigram that

" Waller doubtless praised some whom he would have been afraid to marry, and perhaps married one whom he would have been ashamed to praise."

From Rouen he moved to Paris, and eventually obtained leave to return to England, and to live at Hall Barn, near Beaconsfield. It is probable that his escape in 1643 and his return from exile in 1653 were partly due to the fact that he was a nephew of Hampden and cousin of Cromwell. After the Restoration he made two attempts to get the Provostship of Eton. In 1665 it was promised to him by Charles II.; but Lord Clarendon refused to seal the deed on the ground that the office could not be filled by a layman. In 1681 a similar objection was made by the Privy Council. In Parliament, of which he was so constantly a member that it was said "It was no House if Waller was not there," his wit and social qualities made him a great favourite. He lived till 1687. An eminent historian has described him as a type of the loose morals of the Restoration period. That Waller was mean-spirited and unscrupulous, and that his poetry was venal, it would be useless to deny; but the charge of dissolute habits seems to rest on some assertions of Sir Simonds D'Ewes, whose austere Puritanism and rather narrow mind prevent our placing complete confidence in his judgment. It is remarkable that Clarendon, himself a man of strict morality and no friend to Waller, says nothing to confirm these stories. From one of the Restoration vices Waller was certainly free, for he was a confirmed water-drinker, a fault which some of his friends could hardly pardon. Indeed Lord Halifax said, "there was only one man in England he would allow to stay in the room with him unless he drank, and that man was Ned Waller." A man's writings are perhaps no certain index of his character; yet it is remarkable that, if Waller's poems are often prosaic, he hardly wrote a line which can be accused of indelicacy.

Though he was but a third-rate poet, yet his position in English literature, as Mr. Gosse has shown, was of first-rate importance. It is indeed strange that he, rather than his contemporary Milton, should have determined the character of English poetry for more than a century. The "native woodnotes wild" of the Elizabethan writers were now to be superseded by the rhymed couplets which Waller brought into fashion. It was his duty, as Mr. Gosse has said, "to capture and imprison the imagination, to seize English poetry by the wings, and to shut it up in a cage for a hundred and fifty years." And the thoughts, which he himself had to express, were generally of so tame and commonplace a kind that such confinement was not inconvenient. Yet one or two of his songs are charming, and his panegyric of the Protector has been highly praised. It was, at any rate, so superior to what he wrote in welcome of Charles II., that the King made a remark to that effect. "Sir," replied Waller, "we poets never succeed so well in writing truth as in fiction." One thing at least we owe to Waller. If he had not lived and written, we should have lost the most brilliant of Dr. Johnson's biographies.

It is a relief, however, to turn from the time-serving poet to two men whose character and career need no apology. In John Pearson and William Oughtred the College may fairly claim to possess the most eminent theologian and mathematician of their generation in this country. Pearson was fortunate in being brought under the influence of two such men as Sir Henry

Wotton and John Hales while at Eton. As a boy, he is said to have spent all his money on books; and, by stealing hours from the night, to have read most of the Greek and Latin Fathers before he left school. At College he was equally industrious; and

"finding that the fireside diverted the intention of his thoughts and dulled his spirits, he avoided coming near it as much as possible, contented to sit close to his books with a blanket thrown over his shoulders."

The Latin verses which he wrote in 1632, while still an undergraduate, and those which he contributed five years later as a memorial to Henry King, show both scholarship and poetical feeling. In 1640 he was made a Prebendary of Salisbury, and thereupon resigned his Fellowship, though he continued for a time to reside in College as a Fellow-Commoner.

It was at Cambridge that in 1643 he preached before the University a memorable sermon in defence of forms of prayer. The use of the English Prayer Book was already threatened by the Assembly of Divines at Westminster, and Pearson came forward in its defence as Richard Cox had done at Frankfort a century before him. He protests against the men who "instead of the buyers and sellers would whip the very prayers out of the temple, with their new divinity sweeping out all good Christianity," And he asks whether Creeds also are henceforth to be extempore. "Shall we stand up and begin with 'I believe' at a venture?" After this declaration of war, it was only natural that he should be deprived of his Prebend, and of a Rectory which he held in Suffolk. In 1645 he was acting as Chaplain to

Lord Goring's forces at Exeter, and in the following year he was in London engaged in controversy with Roman Catholics. But it was during the later years of the Commonwealth that his best known book was written. The parishioners of St. Clement's, East Cheap, had made him their Lecturer in 1654, and he began a series of sermons which were published in 1659 as an Exposition of the Creed. He does not seem to have been disturbed in these labours, and this may have been because he was now defending doctrines which were, for the most part, the common property of all Christendom.

After the Restoration his preferment was rapid. Within two years he became Master of Jesus, Margaret Professor of Divinity, and Master of Trinity. He took a prominent part in the Savoy Conference of 1661, and the Puritan Divines recognised in him at once their ablest and most conciliatory antagonist. Baxter says that

" he was their true logician and disputant, without whom, as far as I could discern, we should have had nothing but Dr. Gunning's passionate invectives. . . . He disputed accurately, soberly, and calmly, being but once in a passion, breeding in us a great respect for him, and a persuasion that if he had been independent he would have been for peace, and that if all were in his power it would have gone well."

Pearson's later years belong to the history of Trinity College (for he resigned his Mastership of Jesus in 1662). There he lived till he became Bishop of Chester in 1672, and there he wrote his second masterpiece, in defence of the genuineness of the seven letters of Ignatius. Taking advantage of Usher's discoveries, he practically settled the question till it was reopened in the nineteenth century. So great a scholar as Bentley has told us that the "very dust" of Pearson's writings "is gold." Certainly he combined a wide and accurate knowledge with a sober and well-balanced judgment ; and he created a tradition of thoroughness and moderation which has not been forgotten by Cambridge theologians of more modern times.

William Oughtred belongs to an earlier generation than Pearson. He was a boy at Eton in the year of the Spanish Armada, and a Fellow of King's while Elizabeth was still on the throne ; but his principal work, *Clavis Mathematicæ*, or *The Key of the Mathematics new forged and filed*, was not written till 1631, nor much known till some years later. It is a systematic text-book, in Latin, on Algebra and Arithmetic, into which were introduced for the first time the symbols for multiplication and proportion. Although Oughtred was "much courted to reside in Italy, France, and Holland," it was long before he became famous in his own country. He had left the University in 1605, and after 1610 lived at Albury in Surrey, a parish of which he was Rector. There he received a visit from two clever young Cambridge men, one of whom was Seth Ward, afterwards Bishop of Salisbury, and well known as an astronomer. Being interested in the study of mathematics, they came "to be informed of many things in his *Clavis*, which at that time seemed very obscure to them." And, indeed, Oughtred himself, when accused of obscurity, had been content to reply,

K

"non oscitantibus scripsi sed vere Matheseos Candidatis"; but he welcomed two such visitors as these, and had no difficulty in satisfying them. On their return to Cambridge, they proceeded to introduce the book there, and to lecture on it to their pupils.

Oughtred's habits, according to his son's account, were rather irregular and eccentric.

"He did use to lye abed till 11 or 12 o'clock with his doublet on. He studied late at night; on the top of his bed-staffe he had his inkhorn fixt."

Sometimes he "went not to bed for 2 or 3 nights, and would not come down to meals till he had found out the quæsitum." These habits did not impair his health; for at the age of eighty he could handle his instruments as steadily as at that of thirty, a fact which he himself attributed to "temperance and archery." Newton calls him "that very good and judicious man, whose judgment (if any man's) may be safely relyed upon." He was threatened with sequestration in 1645, but escaped by the intervention of powerful friends; and the close of the Commonwealth period found him still at Albury. If, as is said, he died of joy on hearing of the Restoration, his death was not quite sudden, or else the news travelled slowly to Albury; for he lived till June 30, 1660; and the King was proclaimed at Westminster on May 8, though he did not enter London till May 29.

CHAPTER XI

THE OLD ORDER CHANGETH

EVEN in the days of Provost Goad the Fellows had
shown some discontent with their share of the College
revenues. The value of money had fallen, and they
found their statutable allowances insufficient. The
sympathy which was shewn to Edmund Hinde, when he
refused to resign his Fellowship on succeeding to
property worth £5 a year, was probably due to a conviction that the Founder's estimate of wealth had
become antiquated. Meantime the College revenues
were increasing, though it is not easy to explain all the
causes of this increase. It can hardly have been due
to greater productiveness in their landed property, for
the improvements made in farming during the seventeenth century, by the cultivation of turnips and clover
and the folding of sheep, had as yet hardly begun.
Moreover, the custom of granting leases on easy terms
to some favoured Fellows, when they left College, must
have been a constant drain on the revenues. This
practice, however, received a check in 1630, when the
Visitor forbade the granting of leases by way of " Vales,"
unless there was a balance of 1000 marks in the treasury,
and unless an amount equivalent in value to the lease
was given to every Fellow leaving the College and not

beneficed. The discontinuance of this practice would, of course, increase the resources of the College. As the habit of non-residence gradually grew, there must have been a diminution in the cost of commons; and it is probable that during the Civil War and Commonwealth the College was never full. On the other hand, some loss must have been incurred by the difficulty of collecting dues.

When the value of money sank, the amounts demanded in fines and rents rose. Thus the income of the Ruislip Estate, which in 1607 was £52, rose to £213 in 1664; and the whole income of the College, which stood at £1308 in 1583, rose during the next half-century to £2811. There must have been some corresponding increase in the sums paid by the College for commons and service; but as some of the payments due from the College to its own members were fixed by Statute, this change in the value of money also helped to create a surplus, at the expense of the emoluments of individual Fellows.

As early as 1614 a custom began of dividing money at the sealing of leases, out of the fines paid on the renewal of a lease. As a general rule each Fellow received 5s.; but sometimes the share of the different members varied with their degrees or seniority. In 1648 it was agreed that out of every £100 received as fine, £5 should be treated as divisible.

But, besides the fines, some irregular division of other moneys had already been practised by the Seniors, according to their own admission; and on December 8, 1648, the whole College agreed to recognise and adopt this practice, and they fixed the proportion which the different classes of the Society should henceforth receive both of dividend and fines. A few months later, the Provost's salary was raised to £280, and as the Seniors were thought to have surrendered some of their emoluments under the recent settlement, certain fees, which they had been accustomed to receive from manorial courts held in Hampshire and elsewhere, were secured to them and to the Provost for the future.

The amount of money treated as dividend in each year varied greatly ; in the seven years 1648–1654 it averaged £1680; but nothing like this amount was maintained during the rest of the century. One cause of these exceptional receipts may have been the price of wheat, which for a few years was extraordinarily high. A law, passed in Elizabeth's reign, had obliged Colleges to receive one-third of their rents in *kind*, or in the actual money value of the corn and produce specified in the lease. This part of the rent was of course greatly enhanced, when wheat rose to the famine prices of 77s. and 85s. per quarter, and the increased cost of provisions would only partially counterbalance the gain. It is also possible that, in their uncertainty how a new revolution might affect them, the Society became somewhat improvident, and divided more than was consistent with true husbandry. This was certainly the case at Eton, where the Puritan Fellows introduced the custom of charging all extraordinary expenses to capital, and of dividing the surplus income of each year among themselves, a policy which is said to have brought the College within sight of bankruptcy.

The settlement with respect to dividends was of great importance to the College, because henceforth it became an object of ambition to every Kingsman to keep his Fellowship, even if he went permanently out of residence. As yet such non-residence was probably exceptional ; but in 1674 the Junior Fellows objected to their Seniors receiving "Perception" money, which had originally been paid for transacting College business ("ob perci- pienda Collegii negotia "), on the ground that some of the Seniors had been absent from the College for many years. By degrees the old home of poor residents changed into a College of Fellows, some of whom were habitually absentees, and few, strictly speaking, poor. One thing was still wanting to complete the transform- ation. The Statutes enjoined the Provost and Deans to see that all Fellows, except the four who studied medicine and Civil Law, should take Holy Orders within a fixed number of years from their first degree. In course of time this injunction was disregarded, and the Fellows remained laymen, unless they had a special interest in theology, or desired the College or University privileges attached to Divinity degrees, or unless they looked forward to pastoral work, which generally took the form of a College Living.

Every one of these alterations was in direct contra- vention of the Statutes ; there was no ambiguity in the limit of sixty days as the maximum amount of absence from College allowed in each year, nor as to the time when Fellows should become Priests. It might have been reasonable to increase the stipends and allowances specified in the Statutes on the ground that the value of money had altered greatly in the course of two centuries ; but the provisions of the Statutes clearly required that all surplus money should be paid into the common purse and used for the common good of the Society. It is rather remarkable that neither Fellows nor Visitor felt any scruple about these revolutionary proceedings. The revolution may have been salutary and even necessary, but in modern days it would have been effected by a change of Statute. In the seventeenth century it was easier to break Statutes than to amend them.

The settlement of the dividend did not, however, settle all controversies ; for when Bishop Fuller visited the College in September 1674, he found the old quarrels between Seniors and Juniors still rife. It seemed to him that a decision given by Bishop Williams, as Visitor, was partly the cause of this. Williams had introduced a new interpretation of the 46th Statute, and ordered that in transacting business, the places of any absent Seniors should be filled by those next in standing. The episcopal seal had never been affixed to this order, and it had soon been disregarded. The Juniors naturally wished Bishop Fuller to reaffirm it. But he thought the old interpretation was the better one. A case had lately happened which illustrated this. In 1665 the Provost, yielding to the importunity of some of the Fellows, invited the Society to pass a vote for a dividend. The majority of the Seniors present, foreseeing that this would cause a debt of £1200, opposed. All the Juniors and a minority of the Seniors supported the proposal. According to Bishop Williams's " supplementary caution," it would now have been proper for the Provost to summon the thirteen seniors in residence, whether technically Senior Fellows or not, in order to settle the question. This was not done, and no dividend was voted.   As it was not till 1668 that there was enough money for a dividend, and then only owing to a windfall, the College was seen to have had a narrow escape.

The Junior party appeared to be on stronger ground when they objected to the custom by which the Seniors received certain fees derived from the Manorial Courts, as well as a payment ": in loco Ministratorum." Mention has been made in a former chapter of the fact that certain Seniors had Servitors to wait on them. The Servitor received the "diet left at the table," and actually paid the Senior £6 a year for it.   The practice was contrary to the Statutes and had been abolished; yet instead of the old perquisite each Senior now received his £6 directly from the College. The Seniors justified this by enumerating the privileges which they had given up; among these, the fires in the Parlour before dinner and supper in the winter, which had been discontinued in order that fires might be maintained in the Hall, of which the Juniors also had the benefit. In particular, they pointed out that the abolition of Servitors had set free a house called the Pensionary; for which the College now received rent and fines.

Another charge brought by the Juniors was, that the office of Sacrist, ordered by the Statutes, had been dropped.   The Sacrist had care of the vessels belonging to the Chapel, and (so it was alleged) visited the sick. According to the Juniors, for want of a Sacrist the sick "upon their deathbeds have often wanted and in vain desired his assistance, which high and unchristian neglect . . . we humbly submit to your Lordship's pious and prudent consideration." To this the Seniors replied that the Sacrist had never had anything to do with the sick, and that, as a matter of fact, these were well cared for by the Priests living in College.   He had charge of Books, Chalices, Crosses, Reliques, Vestments, Torches, and Tapers; and " considering the change of religion and the few sacred utensils we now have, which are no other than what are daily exposed upon the Communion Table," it seemed quite unnecessary to revive the old office.

The Seniors had no difficulty in making out a list of offences committed by the Juniors, such as the frequenting of alehouses and taverns, not only singly but in great companies, their dining and supping in the parlour, and their insisting on having " flesh " upon fish days. The undergraduate Fellows, soon after their election, were in the habit of entertaining both B.A.s and M.A.s at the taverns :

" to an extravagant expense and an initiation into intemperance.   The like is done by several of the B.A.s and M.A.s on the Founder's Day, having the University Musique with them, so that they come not to Divine Service and do frequently sit up all or the greatest part of the night."

The Provost also having made a complaint as to " excesses in apparel," the Fellows were ordered by the Visitor to wear only black.

The Provost, at this time, was James Fleetwood, who had done good service to the royal cause during the war, and was Chaplain to Prince Charles, so that he was an obvious person to choose for the office ; although John Price, Chaplain and intimate friend of General

Monk, who has left us a curious account of the part
which he himself and his general took in the Restoration, may have thought his claim to a reward as great
as that of Fleetwood.

It must have been a sad day to some of the Fellows,
when Benjamin Whichcote quitted the College, over
which he had ruled so well, and within a few months
the Society shewed their esteem for him by presenting
him to the sinecure Rectory of Milton. There is hardly
a trace of any other ejection. Thomas Crouch was
now readmitted to his Fellowship, but resigned it
immediately in favour of another member of the
Crouch family. Thomas had at first turned his attention to theology, and in 1633 had been admonished by
the Vice-Provost for defending the Invocation of Saints
as Respondent in a Disputation in Chapel, and it seems
that he refused to retract and was discommuned for a
week. He was twice Proctor, and there is a portrait
of him at King's Lodge in his official dress. When
ejected from his Fellowship in 1650 he had found a
home in Trinity Hall. In 1660 he became M.P. for
the University, and was most active in defending the
rights of his constituents. Indeed, in 1674, when the
London printers threatened to interfere with the
privileges of the University Printers, the Vice-Chancellor
of Oxford looked to Crouch as the best champion whom
he could find. He was a benefactor to his College
Library, and contributed liberally to the cost of the
canopies which were placed over the stalls in the Chapel
during the last years of his life, 1675–78. The inscription over his tomb in one of the side Chapels bears no
name, but only the words:

" Aperiet Deus tumulos et educet
Nos de Sepulchris.
Qualis eram Dies istæc cum
Venerit scies."

During the Commonwealth period Roger Palmer
entered King's as a Fellow-Commoner. He was too
young to bear arms in the Civil War, but he freely
hazarded his life in the plots which preceded the
Restoration. His home life was spoiled by the conduct of his wife Barbara, who became a Mistress of
Charles II., and the Irish peerage of Castlemaine,
obtained for him by her influence, was no consolation
for this misfortune. He became a wanderer, first cruis-
ing in the Levant with the Venetian squadron, then
serving in the Duke of York's fleet in the Dutch
war, and afterwards travelling to Syria and Africa.
Apparently he was safer, as well as happier, abroad
than at home; for on his return to England, about
1677, he was denounced by Titus Oates as a Jesuit,
and accused of plotting against the King's life. After
half a year's imprisonment in the Tower, he was tried,
and defended himself so well that even Chief Justice
Scroggs was obliged to acquit him; but his escape was
partly due to the zeal and courage of another Kingsman, John Lytcott, who had been his companion
abroad. Lord Castlemaine was a Roman Catholic,
and as such was chosen by James II., in 1686, to
establish relations with Innocent XI. at Rome. Such
a course did not happen to suit the Pope, who ter-
minated the audience by a violent fit of coughing, and
told Lord Castlemaine that the early hours were best
for travelling. When James fled, Lord Castlemaine

retired to his home in Montgomeryshire, but he was arrested and committed to the Tower again on the capital charge of endeavouring to reconcile the Kingdom to the See of Rome; nor was this his last visit to the Tower. He was a man of letters, as well as of action; for he wrote a memoir of the Dutch war in French, and of the war between Turkey and Venice in English; besides publishing a manly and eloquent vindication of the loyalty of English Roman Catholics. He seems to have deserved a better wife and better fortune than fell to his lot: for he was constantly in trouble, in spite of his abilities and loyalty.

When Fleetwood became Bishop of Worcester in 1675, Sir Thomas Page succeeded him as Provost. He had been Tutor to the virtuous Lord Ossory, the friend of Evelyn, and he afterwards acted as Private Secretary to Lord Ossory's father, the Duke of Ormonde, when the latter was Lord Lieutenant in Ireland. Little is recorded of Page, except that he was a traveller and a linguist, and an amiable and accomplished bachelor, who gave some valuable Communion plate to the College, of which only a silver basket in filigree work now remains. He is said to have died suddenly, on August 8, 1681, in the act of rebuking an irregular Scholar. Of his successor, John Copleston, there is even less to tell. He was born at Lyme, and had the living of Chagford, and he is called " a good Preacher and an honest man." His last act, and, indeed, the only one recorded of him as Provost, was his administering to all his Fellows, in July 1689, the oaths against the right of the Pope to excommunicate Princes, and against Transubstantiation.

His death, in this year, gave the Fellows the opportunity of recovering their right to choose their own
Provost: for resistance to a newly established dynasty
might prove easier than it had been to a Tudor or a
Stuart. The account of what happened is told by a
Mr. Reynolds, who was admitted Scholar of King's in
1689, and was afterwards Fellow of Eton and Canon of
Exeter. Before the Fellows could meet for an election,
one of their number, John Hartcliffe, had posted off to
Court to warn the authorities. The College records
have no mercy for this "false brother"; but he must
have been a man of some note, for he had been Headmaster of Merchant Taylors School, and was afterwards
chosen by Tillotson for a Canonry at Windsor. The
result of his journey was that an order came to Cambridge for the election of Stephen Upman,* Fellow of
Eton. The choice was an unfortunate one, for Upman
had preached in Eton Chapel in favour of the toleration
granted by King James to Roman Catholics as well as
to Protestant Dissenters, and Reynolds adds:

"I who was then in the 6ᵗʰ Form was present at the
sermon; and I remember that the boys could not help
observing in the faces of the Fellows and Masters there
present, scorn in some, and indignation in others."

It was therefore easy for the Kingsmen to represent
Upman as no true Whig. Accordingly a new order
was issued, in favour of Sir Isaac Newton, at that time
M.P. for the University. Against so great and good a
man the only possible objections were that he was an
alien and a layman; and these objections were made.

* See Appendix D.

Once more the Crown sent down a fresh order, this time for the election of John Hartcliffe himself. This was the most unpopular choice of all. No one would appear to receive the *mandamus*, which was left on the Hall table and was thrown over the wall in the night. On September 3 the Fellows met and elected Charles Roderick, then Headmaster of Eton. At the same time they took the precaution of writing to Lord Nottingham, asking him to represent to the King their objections to John Hartcliffe. Still they could hardly hope to escape from a law-suit, and they prepared to meet the expense, by promising to forego their dividends, turn their plate into money, and strike off the " second dish " at dinner.

They did, however, succeed in obtaining an interview, which was held at Hampton Court. Three of the Society went there, and were arguing the case with the Crown lawyers, when there was a sudden hush and a whisper that the Queen was coming through the gallery. One of the Kingsmen, Dr. Layton, being rather deaf and very blind, did not perceive this, and at the critical moment struck the table with his fist, and cried out in a loud voice, " Mr. Attorney General, if we must bear the grievances of former reigns, then is the King in vain come in." Queen Mary was startled by this speech, and the interview was brought to a sudden and not very promising end. However, soon afterwards, the King, on his way to Newmarket, paid a visit to King's College Chapel, attended by the Chancellor, the Duke of Somerset, when he told the College that, at the intercession of his friend the Duke, he gave his consent that the man they had chosen should be their Provost.

On this, Layton, who was prepared beforehand, made a speech of thanks to the King on his knees. Roderick was now " admitted " by " old Gearing, who saving one year had been Vice-Provost for 40 successive years, and had admitted Roderick to his Scholarship."

The battle was won by the College ; and no doubt the right was on their side. But whether it was worth winning is more doubtful. The College had owed much to such aliens as Sir John Cheke and Whichcote. If they could have secured Sir Isaac Newton as their Head, the presence of such a man must have done something to stimulate intellectual life. And before long such a stimulus was sadly wanted. During the eighteenth century the University reached its lowest point, both in numbers and learning. It was hardly possible that King's should escape the torpor of the times ; but most of the Provosts appointed by the College, though estimable and, in some cases, able men, had neither the width of experience nor the force of intellect which were necessary to withstand the depressing influences of the Hanoverian period. It would be rash to assert that a system of unrestricted choice by the Crown would have supplied the College with men of light and leading ; but it is at least a remarkable coincidence that about this time the College ceased to hold the high place in the University which it had consistently maintained throughout the Tudor and Stuart periods,

CHAPTER XII

GIBBS'S BUILDING

CHARLES RODERICK, the new Provost, had been a successful Headmaster of Eton since 1680 ; and this, in spite of an excessive modesty, which had induced him to resign the Rectory of Raynham in Norfolk because he could not face the ordeal of preaching to a country congregation, though he wrote many sermons. Perhaps it was the same bashfulness which prevented him from marrying till late in life, when his sufferings from gout seemed to need the care of a nurse rather than the companionship of a wife. His character is thus described by a contemporary :

> " He labour'd more his worth to hide
> Than others to have their's descri'd ;
> The brightest Preachers that we have
> Do but reflect the light he gave.
> From these great Pupils may be seen
> How great the Tutor must have been."

Another contemporary and less complimentary writer describes Roderick as "an overgrown Pedagog who never mounted a pulpit," and as one of "the five Smoking Heads."

The fact that he was made Dean of Ely in 1708 may

be taken as some evidence that his abilities were of a solid though not of a showy kind.

The two Kingsmen, who accompanied Dr. Layton to the Hampton Court conference, both rose to some eminence. John Newborough succeeded Roderick at Eton. Under his excellent teaching and able management the School flourished greatly, and he was the first person to discover and encourage the talents of Robert Walpole. The third of the party at Hampton Court was William Fleetwood, nephew of Provost Fleetwood, who, unlike Roderick, was so celebrated a London preacher that he was known as "the silver-tongued." Queen Anne was one of his admirers, and spoke of him as " my Bishop"; and she was right in her judgment, for he was much more than a mere preacher. His administration of his diocese (for he became Bishop of St. Asaph in 1708) was exemplary, and he seems in all respects to have been the model Bishop of his days. Yet even he could not keep out of the field of politics. It was the time of the Tory and High Church reaction; and Fleetwood, in publishing some sermons, took the opportunity, in May 1712, to write a preface, in which he attributed the failure of the Tories to obtain satisfactory terms of peace to the political distractions caused by themselves.

"God, for our sins, permitted the spirit of discord to go forth, and by troubling sore the camp, the city; and the country, (and oh ! that it had altogether spared the places sacred to his worship), to spoil for a time this beautiful and pleasing prospect, and give us in its stead I know not what. Our enemies will tell the rest with pleasure."

L

This preface, containing as it did a vindication of William and Mary, and upholding the principles of the Revolution as against the doctrine of Non-Resistance, was so displeasing to the party then in office that it was burned by order of the House of Commons. Persecution, as usual, brought popularity; and the preface was reprinted by Steele in the *Spectator* for May 21, 1712; and thus about 14,000 copies were conveyed into the hands of people that might otherwise have never seen it nor heard of it. The accession of George I. naturally brought Fleetwood into favour again at Court, and in 1714 he became Bishop of Ely. It was a critical moment in the long controversy between Dr. Bentley and his College. The late Bishop of Ely, Dr. Moore, had just drawn up a sentence of ejection against the Master of Trinity; but Fleetwood, who had reason to think ill of the character of some of Dr. Bentley's prosecutors, declared that, if he visited Trinity College at all, it should be to execute impartial justice on all delinquencies, whether of Master or Fellows. As it had been recently decided that the general Visitatorial power belonged to the Crown, Fleetwood's announcement was in fact a refusal to take any action in the case.

When Fleetwood became Bishop of Ely, there was some expectation that another Kingsman might be preferred to him. This was George Stanhope, who had been a Royal Chaplain and Boyle Lecturer, and was since 1704 Dean of Canterbury. He was well known both as a preacher and as a writer of practical theology, and he seems to have thoroughly deserved the respect and affection which were generally felt for him.

It was during Roderick's tenure of the Provostship that the oldest and only surviving son of the great Duke of Marlborough came to King's College as a Fellow-Commoner, and was placed under the care of Francis Hare, of whom more will be said hereafter. Even allowing for the exaggerations, which are probable in such a case, the Marquis of Blandford seems to have been a lad of excellent disposition and no little promise. He was exemplary in conforming to the rules of his College, and in a letter to Lord Godolphin he expresses the warmest approbation both of the studies and discipline of the place. But in the autumn of 1702 there was an alarm of smallpox, and he went for change of air to Newmarket. It was after his return to Cambridge that he was attacked by a malignant form of the disease. His brother-in-law, Francis Godolphin, was a member of the College, and in Cambridge at the time. The Duchess of Marlborough hurried to Cambridge, and sent back to London for medical advice But neither a letter from the Queen to her " dear Mrs. Freeman," nor the despatch of Dr. Haines and Dr. Coladon from the Lord Treasurer's house in a hackney-coach with six horses, could save the poor boy. His father came in time to see him before his death on February 20, 1703, and then returned with a heavy heart to the campaign on the Meuse and Rhine. Lord Blandford's monument in one of the side Chapels, where he lies, attests the affection of his parents rather than their artistic taste.

During Queen Anne's reign party feeling, whether in politics or theology, was at fever heat. Dr. Tudway, Professor of Music and Organist of King's, thinking

that the Ministry was showing too much favour to
Dissenters, allowed himself in public company to make
a bad pun on Queen Anne, and he was deprived for a
time both of his degrees and of all his offices. A few
years later the Lucasian Professor, William Whiston,
was cited to appear before Roderick, then Vice-
Chancellor, at King's Lodge, charged with having
publicly maintained Arian tenets, and was banished
from the University for heresy. It was also a time of
transition in University studies, for Newton's *Principia*
now began to form the subject-matter of exercises in
the schools and afterwards of examination for degrees.
Edward Littleton, who went to King's in 1716,
expressed his disgust at the neglect of classics in a
poetic epistle to his friend Archer:

> "Now, Algebra, Geometry,
> Arithmetic, Astronomy,
> Optics, Chronology, and Statics,
> All tiresome points of Mathematics,
> With twenty harder names than these
> Disturb my brains and break my peace."

And he proceeds to describe how he is learning that
ink is not black, and that a fire possesses no heat.

The records which remain of another Kingsman,
William Batty, throw some further light on the studies
and discipline of the College about this time. In spite
of Littleton's complaints, Batty at any rate did not
give up his classics, and was the first Kingsman who
gained the Craven Scholarship in 1724; not, indeed,
without difficulty, for the Examiners were equally
divided between him and Bentley of Trinity. The

nomination lapsed to Lord Craven, who six months later gave the Scholarship to Batty. Batty by this time had given up all thoughts of it; but, feeling that with this addition he could live on his Fellowship, he proceeded to lay out a fresh course of reading, which included the study of Newton, English and modern history, and some law.

Batty's great rival at Eton had been one Thomas Morell. They came to King's about the same time, where they still continued to torment each other. Morell writes:

" His mother very kindly recommended us to a Chandler at 4s. 6d. per dozen. But, as the candles proved dear even at that price we resented it; and one evening, getting into Battie's room before Canonical hours,* we locked him out and stuck up all the candles we could find in his box, lighted, round the room; and while I thrummed on the spinnet, the rest danced round me in their shirts. Upon Battie's coming and finding what we were at, he fell to storming and swearing, till the old Vice Provost—Dr. Willymott—called out from above, ' Who is that swearing like a common soldier?' 'It is I,' quoth Battie. ' Visit me,' quoth the Vice Provost, which indeed we were all obliged to do next morning, with a distich, according to custom. Mine naturally turned upon ' So fiddled Orpheus and so danced the Brutes '; which having explained to the Vice Provost, he punished me and Sleech with a few lines of Homer and Battie with the whole third book of Milton to get by heart."

* " Canonical hours " lasted from the close of morning chapel to 8 A.M., and from 8 P.M. to 9 P.M. During these periods it was the duty of the Junior of each Chamber to keep the door shut and exclude strangers.

Batty afterwards forsook the study of law for that of medicine, and became a doctor of some eminence. He was already engaged in this profession when, in 1729, he edited *Isocrates*. His criticisms on that author did not satisfy Morell, who wrote an epigram ending with the following lines:

> "Confine yourself to licence given
>   Nor dare beyond your trade,
>   Tho' you are free to kill the living,
>   Yet prythee spare the dead."

After this, it may be hoped that Morell left his old schoolfellow alone.

In 1712 John Adams had succeeded to the Provost-ship; he does not seem to have taken a prominent part in University politics, although he had to make a Latin speech to George I. when that King paid a flying visit to Cambridge on October 6, 1717. The seven years of his Provostship are chiefly noticeable from the fact that a serious effort was now made to enlarge the College buildings.

The old Court had never really sufficed for the wants of the College, and from the earliest days some buildings near the present Porter's Lodge had been set apart as the "Clerks' Lodging" and gone by the name of the "Conductes' Court." More than a century later, in 1571 or 1574, the Hall of St. Austin's Hostel, which stood on ground now occupied by the College Hall, was fitted up as rooms for Fellow-Commoners and styled "the Pensionary"; and in the north-west corner of the old Court itself two chambers for Fellows were gained by building a tower, and so enlarging what had served as a Library till Provost Goad removed the books to the southern side Chapels.

But in the seventeenth century the improvement in the College property and the demand for a higher standard of comfort must have been felt as reasons for attempting something more ambitious; indeed, a MS. account of the "state of King's College relating to their present design of building" remarks that the '

"old unfinished building having been slightly patch'd up at several times has grown more and more inconvenient and more unwholesome, there being but 27 rooms in it for the 70 Fellows and Scholars; some of which rooms are of lath work, 8 more of them ground chambers, and most of them very dark, damp, and unwholesome, being about 2 feet underground."

A letter from Lord Dartmouth to Provost Copleston on March 14, 1686, reminding the latter of "his good Disposition to attempt something towards y° Building of our College," is evidence of the conviction which was gradually forcing itself on the minds of Kingsmen. Lord Dartmouth writes:

"I shou'd think it a great Addition to y° Happiness of my Life to see a Work so necessary for your own Convenience to go Forward in his Majesty's Reign. Begin therefore a Found among yourselves either by cutting down Timber (w°ʰ cannot be dispos'd of to a better use) or what other ways your Prudence shall think best; And if you shall think fitt to lett me know your Proceedings, when this Design shall be reduc'd to some Method and Ripeness, I will not be wanting on my own Part, and to recommend both it and your selves to his Majesty's gracious Patronage."

The writer of this letter, "Honest and faithful George Legge," as James II. called him, had entered King's College from Westminster School, and in 1683 became Baron Dartmouth. He gained great reputation by his services in the Dutch war, and was Admiral in command of the fleet when William crossed the Channel. But, though his own loyalty was above suspicion, and his courage had been shown by driving the Dutch out of his ship when on the point of sinking and by afterwards bringing her safe into harbour, he was unable to strike a blow at the critical moment on behalf of his master, because his Captains had adopted the Orange cause. This failure did not, however, save him from being accused of treasonable practices, and he died in the Tower, 1691. He was very popular with the sailors, who raised something like a riot when they thought that he was being ill-treated in his prison, and could only be pacified by his personal assurance that this was not so. Bishop Burnet says that he was the worthiest nobleman in King James's Court, to whose fortunes he always adhered, though he had opposed the policy which was the cause of the King's downfall. His only son, who rose to be a Secretary of State, was also a Kingsman, and resembled his father in being a moderate Tory and a man of high character. Swift said of him that his only fault was that he "treated his clerks with more civility and good manners than others in his station have done the Queen." The first Lord Dartmouth's advice to the College did not bear fruit during Roderick's life. But John Adams, on succeeding to the Provostship in 1712, exerted himself to the utmost in promoting the project.

The first step was the creation of a Fund. Not long before, a fire had destroyed part of the Hall, a chamber, and some studies; and with a view to rebuilding these it was agreed to sell timber out of Toft Monks Wood in Norfolk, to the value of £500. However, it was found better to cut down the whole wood; and on May 8, 1714, a solemn resolution was adopted and signed by the Provost and eighteen Fellows to the effect that the £2640 arising from the sale of this timber, including what was left after repairing the damage done by the fire, should never be used for any other purpose than the extension of the College buildings. Any other money which should hereafter arise from the sale of timber was, by the same resolution, devoted to the like purpose.

Adams had meanwhile been doing his best to collect subscriptions, and to interest the Queen herself in the project, and he tells the Bursar,

" I have prospect of assistance from private Hands which I did not expect, and do not doubt but I shal see some very good effects of their Promises in a few months, tho' I am often forct to draw back for fear of pressing too far."

Even before the date of the solemn engagement mentioned above, Adams had gone so far as to consult Sir Christopher Wren, and to get plans and models from Hawkesmore, who was one of Wren's pupils. It was proposed not only to complete the Quadrangle to the south of the Chapel, but also to build a Cloister and Bell Tower to the west; to continue the old line of King's Lane to the river, and on one side of it to place a new Provost's Lodge and on the other a brewhouse and stables. The plans also included bridges and gardens.

The Provost suggested certain alterations in the design, which he thought overloaded with ornament; and in particular desired that the studies and bedrooms in the west wing should look towards the river, and not into the east Court, as Hawkesmore intended. Like some other architects, Hawkesmore was inclined to assume that his employers possessed the purse of Fortunatus, and the Provost writes: "The most expensive part will be the Cloyster, but it is ye hardest for Mr. Hawkesmore to part withal."

Adams did not live to see the work begun. But his efforts in the cause continued to the end; and in what seems to be his last letter he refers to a representation which is to be laid before the Visitor, and to an interview with Lord Townshend:

" My Lord received the Vice Provost and myself with all kindness and encouragement; was mightily pleased with some Plans wch I carryd with me and wch I left with Mr Poyntz to shew to Mr Wallpool. The two models are with Mr Hawksmore, who may be heard of at Sir John Vanbrough's, Whitehall. . . . There is no fault in ye best model, but only as to ye Arcade or front over it. His fancy is too luxuriant sometimes, but his judgment very good . . . and if he be not continued as a kind of Surveyor, His Demands will be very Exorbitant for what he has done and not been already payd for."

The letter more than once speaks of the writer's fatigue in consequence of his journey, and his exertions in the cause may have shortened his life. Antony Allen tells us that he died at the end of the year 1719

of an apoplexy a few days before he was to have been
introduced to the King, it having been intimated to
the Society that the King would bestow £200 for the
new building. According to Allen, Adams had in his
younger years contracted heavy debts jointly with
others "embarked in the same cause of prodigality."
Eventually the whole burden "devolved upon the
Doctor, which embarrassed him to that excess that
all his Preferment tho' very considerable was scarce
sufficient to keep him out of Prison." It is added that
he left his wife and children in great want. There
is something very pathetic in the position of a man
devoting himself to raise for the benefit of the College
funds which were sorely needed for his own relief.

From Adams's last letter it seems that the College
already contemplated a change of architect ; and before
January 1723 plans had been obtained of James Gibbs,
and it was determined to begin the west side of the
intended Court, for which Portland stone was used.
According to the new plans the Cloister and other
buildings towards the river were abandoned, but there
was to be an east side corresponding to the one now
to be taken in hand, and a south wing with Hall,
Provost's Lodge, and offices. The west building was
to be adorned with statues ; but the arcades, which had
formed part of Hawkesmore's design, were given up.

It was on March 25, 1724, that the first stone was
actually laid. After hearing a sermon from one of the
Senior Fellows (Gregory Doughty) and an anthem
composed for the occasion by Dr. Tudway, the Vice-
Chancellor, who happened to be Andrew Snape the
new Provost of King's, with the Noblemen, Heads, and

other members of the University, all joined in the
ceremony. One notable figure was missing. Dr. Bentley
had been suspended from his degrees for the last six
years ; and though the Court of King's Bench had
condemned this action of the University, yet the act of
restitution was purposely postponed till March 26, in
order that he might have no part in the ceremony.   If
any of the company present were inclined to be super-
stitious, it may have seemed to them of evil omen that
the greatest Scholar of his times should have no share
in wishing God-speed to a building which was intended
to be a home of sacred and profane learning.   The
stone actually laid was, by tradition, believed to be one
which, more than 250 years before, the workmen had
left half sawn through when they heard of the deposition
of Henry VI.

It was not till 1730 that the building was ready for
wainscoting, and by that time funds had run short.
Mr. Essex was accordingly employed to do only one
half in the first instance ; but a little later it was
decided that the whole building should be fitted up, if
twenty-four Fellows would undertake to pay £5 each in
rent.   They might also underlet their rooms to Fellow-
Commoners for £15.   This arrangement was made, and
in 1753 it was found possible to reduce the rent due
from Fellows.   The College borrowed money from their
neighbours at Corpus and Peterhouse, and also got the
Visitor's leave to sell the old bells.   But what eventually
extinguished the debt was a bequest of Mr. Hungerford,
who left to the College his property of Upavon in Wiltshire.

Cole, writing in 1750, expresses his doubts whether

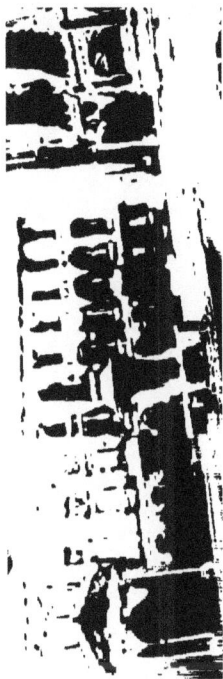

the new building was a real gain to the College. Admitting that the Society was straitened for room, and that the building was a great ornament to the University, he says that these rents were so burdensome that

" ever since I have inhabited the New Building now about 16 years, not half of the Rooms have been let ; but the Fellows chose rather to inhabit the *old* Building, where they pay nothing for their Chambers, and are near the *Hall*, and within Reach of the *Bedmakers* and Servants ; the distance from which makes the New Building very inconvenient ; besides the new Apartments are so sumptuous and grand that it requires more than the narrow Appointment of a Fellow of the College to fit up in such a manner as would become them ; so that upon the whole it has been thought that, if a *Gothic* and less magnificent Building had been erected, it would have suited the *Taste* of the *Chapel* better, been more convenient for the *members*, and there had been a greater *Probability* of seeing the whole Quadrangle *compleated ;* which, as the case now stands, there seems to be a small Prospect of. Dr. Snape in his Life Time gave 250 Pounds towards the Design, which it is supposed in the whole cost 20,000 Pounds."

During the first quarter of the eighteenth century, Cambridge was much occupied with the eccentricities of Dr. Bentley, and the names of two Kingsmen are intimately connected with some circumstances in that memorable career. These were Antony Collins and Francis Hare. Collins had been a friend of Locke, and had already engaged in his first controversy with Dr. Samuel Clarke before he published, in 1713, his *Discourse of Freethinking*, the object of which was to shew that all belief should be based on free inquiry, and that such inquiry would be destructive of orthodox views. The position and character of Collins made him a serious antagonist, for he was said to have an "estate in the country, a library in town, and friends everywhere." In 1715 he settled in Essex, and made himself useful as a country magistrate, besides continuing his controversial writings. Whatever may have been the value of his philosophy, his scholarship was very defective; and Bentley, in an anonymous treatise dedicated "to my very learned and honoured friend F. H., D.D., at London," exposed the mistakes and ignorance of the *Discourse* in a merciless manner. Though the treatise was anonymous, the authorship was no secret; and Hare addressed a pamphlet to Bentley, full of extravagant praise for the labours of the latter, coupled with a suggestion that Bentley should undertake a new critical edition of the Scriptures. Hare had been some years senior to Collins at King's, where he had acted as Tutor to Robert Walpole as well as to the Marquis of Blandford; he had afterwards been Chaplain-General of the army in Flanders, and both a *protégé* and · champion of the Duke of Marlborough. He was now a Fellow of Eton, who managed to combine High Church theology with Whig politics. If he had confined himself to these subjects, he would have escaped a collision with his old friend Bentley; but, unfortunately, in 1724 he produced an edition of Terence with a dissertation on Comic Metres. All that Hare knew of Comic Metres he had learned from Bentley; and he had assumed, without inquiry, that Bentley's labours as Professor of Divinity would prevent him from carrying

out an old intention of editing Terence. But he roused
the wrath of the giant by poaching on his preserves;
and it was not long before Bentley produced a rival
edition, in which he demolished Hare, and spoiled the
sale of his work. Together with the Terence, however,
Bentley published a very inferior edition of Phædrus,
an author on whom he knew Hare to be engaged. This
gave his victim a chance; and in a Latin letter
addressed to Dr. Bland, Headmaster of Eton, Hare
showed his resentment by not only attacking the
Phædrus, but also by a general indictment of Bentley's
learning and character. The inconsistency between the
Epistola Critica of 1727 and what Hare had written in
praise of Bentley fourteen years before was too glaring
not to be noticed, and it is no wonder if Sir Isaac
Newton complained that two divines should " be fight-
ing one another about a play-book."

The quarrel did not interfere with Hare's promotion.
In the same year he became Bishop of St. Asaph, and
a little later Bishop of Ely. In 1736 Sir Robert
Walpole wished him to succeed Archbishop Wake at
Canterbury; but he had lately opposed Government
measures for the relief of Dissenters; and, if Cole's
opinion of him is accurate, that, though he was a man
of sharp and piercing wit and sound practical judgment, he was also of a sour and crabbed disposition, it
can hardly be regretted that his promotion stopped short
at Ely. Certainly his behaviour to Bentley was not
worthy of an Archbishop of Canterbury.

It must have been some help to the College that, at
the time when they were most in need of money for
their great building schemes, two Kingsmen were the

two most powerful Ministers. These were Lord Townshend and Sir Robert Walpole, of whom the former matriculated in 1691, the latter in 1696. Their union was dissolved in 1729 by the resignation of Townshend, who had been outstripped in political life by his colleague and brother-in-law, and who was unwilling to take the lower place. But, in spite of some imperfection of temper, Townshend was as superior to Walpole in character as he was inferior in ability. He was deservedly popular at · Cambridge, among other reasons because it was he who had prompted George I. to present to the University Bishop Moore's Library ; and it is remarkable that it was the Nobleman and Fellow-Commoner who showed an interest in literature and education, while the ex-Scholar, apart from his politics and his pictures, remained a sporting squire of the coarsest type. Robert Walpole, being only the second son of a Norfolk baronet, was a Scholar both at Eton and King's. While an undergraduate he nearly died of smallpox, but was saved by the skill of a Tory physician, Dr. Brady, who remarked to a Fellow of the College, " We must take care to save this young man, or we shall be accused of having purposely neglected him because he is so violent a Whig." Brady seems to have recognised Walpole's abilities, for he said of him : " His singular escape seems to me a sure indication that he is reserved for important purposes."

In 1698, on the death of his elder brother, Robert Walpole became heir to the Houghton property, resigned his Scholarship, and went to live at home. From this time his career becomes part of English history, and it must be left to our historians to decide whether the

benefits of peace and material prosperity, which his
long supremacy secured to his country, were too dearly
purchased by the organised corruption and habitual
discouragement of any disinterested standard of political
conduct, which must also be associated with his name.
It is difficult to trace any connection between his public
career and education, unless it is to be found in his knowledge of Latin, which he used in his conversations with
George I. His mastery of finance could hardly have
been gained at College ; his extraordinary acuteness,
imperturbable temper, and tolerant disposition were
probably no more the result of an Eton and Cambridge
training than were the coarseness and immorality of
his private life. But he was thoroughly loyal to his
old College. When thanked for contributing £500 to
the new building, he said : " I deserve no thanks ; I have
only paid for my board." He was always ready to
promote his old friends, unless they were political
opponents ; and it must be added that they were
generally willing to be promoted. Indeed, it must
have been a surprise to the Minister, when he sent for
Robert Staples, an old Kingsman for whom he had a
great regard, and asked how he could serve him. Staples,
though by no means an old man, and possessed only of
the small country living of Shottesbrook in Berkshire,
replied that he wanted nothing. This must have been
before 1722, when Staples died, having first written as
his own epitaph :

" Pastor immeritus
Qui sui gregisque rationem
Redditurus
Hinc decessit."

M

CHAPTER XIII

WHIGS AND TORIES

FOUR years before the first stone of the new building was laid, Andrew Snape had been elected Provost, in spite of Court influence which was exerted in favour of Dr. Waddington. He was already a well-known man. He had been chaplain to the Chancellor, the Duke of Somerset; he had gone to the jubilee of the University of Frankfort on the Oder as representative of Cambridge theology, and there had read an address to the King of Prussia; and he had also preached before the Electress Sophia. He had become a Chaplain of Queen Anne, and was a popular London preacher. In 1711 he was made Headmaster of Eton, which grew and prospered under him; and it was said that he added the name of a town boy, without his parents' consent, in order to make up the then unparalleled number of 400 boys. But he was soon to become even more famous.

In 1717, Bishop Hoadley preached his celebrated sermon on the Kingdom of Christ, in which he denied that the Church had any power of legislation or discipline, and also objected to fervency in prayer. The sermon is at once a manifesto on behalf of the absolute right of private judgment, and a protest against enthusiasm. Snape was the first to enter the field against him with a *Letter to the Bishop of Bangor*. He ridicules Hoadley's new " Sect of Protestant Quietists," and points out that his principles are fatal to all Churches that have existed from the days of the Apostles downwards, to all Creeds and all Articles. There is no want either of force or dignity in Snape's letter, which rapidly went through seventeen editions. The attack was kept up by Sherlock, Master of Hoadley's own College, St. Catharine Hall ; and William Law, himself probably the most powerful of Hoadley's antagonists, wrote in support of Snape.

At a later stage in the controversy, when writing against M. de la Pillionière, an ex-Jesuit, who was Tutor to the young Hoadleys, Snape indulged in personalities, and accused Hoadley of sophistry and equivocation. But even then both of his opponents spoke of him with respect ; the Bishop saying that he had not expected to receive from Dr. Snape anything that was not humane, gentlemanlike and Christian ; and the private Tutor acknowledging that Snape was, in everybody's judgment, one of the brightest ornaments of what he calls the "Laudean" Church. Other critics were less civil, and made fun of Snape's profession :

> " First, stern Orbilius in the Lists appears,
> Debauch'd in Faction from his Infant years,
> To wage eternal war with Spotless Truth
> And sow sedition in the tender youth.
> The worldly Church in his affections reigns,
> As some men court the Heiress for her gains.

His every period, crabbed and severe,
Smells of the birch and terrifies the ear.
His malice to no Parties is confin'd,
But hates alike all Protestant mankind."

Whatever Snape's hopes of preferment may have been,
his zeal on this occasion cost him his Royal Chaplaincy,
and the most serious result of the controversy was, that
Convocation, when on the point of censuring Hoadley's
sermon, was silenced and suspended for more than a
century. Snape, in private life, is said to have been
" a man of an amiable, sweet, and affable temper, which,
however, was observed to be somewhat ruffled and
soured towards the latter end of his time," partly
because the majority of the College had become Whig,
and partly from attacks of the gout so frequent and
severe that he had to be carried into Chapel in a sedan-
chair and lifted into his stall.   He was also in some
degree a disappointed man, for he attributed to Sir
Robert Walpole's persistent opposition the fact that he
had not reached higher preferment. In his management of the College he was too much in the hands of
one or two Senior Fellows, especially of John Burford.
The Provost made no secret of this, and says in his
will :

" I am so far from being ashamed to have it said of me
that he governed me that I value myself for nothing so
much as having suffered his counsels to have such weight
with me as they had ; of which the Society will reap the
lasting benefit, when the present bickerings shall be
forgot."

The allusion is to the gradual change in the sentiments

of the Fellows under the influence of Mr. Nicholas Harding, a successful barrister and *protégé* of Sir Robert Walpole, who rose to be Clerk of the House of Commons and afterwards M.P. for Eye. It was Harding who was called upon, when Clerk of the House of Commons, to decide a bet between Walpole and Pulteney on the accuracy of a Latin quotation made by the former. The decision was in favour of Pulteney, who, on receiving his guinea, observed that it was the first public money which he had handled for a long time. Burford must have been an ambitious as well as a masterful man, for he actually cherished hopes of succeeding the Duke of Somerset as Chancellor of the University, and the Master of Peterhouse, Dr. Whalley, was for a time at the head of a party formed to promote this wild scheme.

While the new building was in progress, the Provost's attention was distracted by a serious case of discipline. In January 1723, John Dale had been admitted a Scholar. He was evidently one of those students who seem born to vex the souls of Dons. The Headmaster of Eton had said of him that "there was a person gone to King's College that would lampoon the Senior Fellows and make the officers' hearts ake." That Dale was a man of some promise may be inferred from the fact that he was one of the twenty students chosen to be placed under the care of the newly created Regius Professor of Modern History, to be trained for a diplomatic or political career, and, as the choice of these students rested with the King or his Ministers, he was evidently not without interest in official circles.

For some time Dale's delinquencies were of a commonplace type; he was frequently absent from Chapel, Hall, and Lectures, and though he generally pretended sickness or fear of smallpox, yet he was seen on these occasions out in the town or country. It was therefore clear that he made light of College rules. But during his last year, not content with breaking rules, he took to insulting those who had to administer them. Having, on some occasion, been ordered to write and read aloud in Hall an apology to one of the College officers, he produced instead a document which evidently reflected on the Provost and Seniors, and it was with great difficulty that he was induced by his friends to make a submission which saved him from expulsion.

It was some time after this incident that it fell to his turn to deliver in Hall the yearly declamation on the anniversary of Gunpowder Plot. This gave him an opportunity of retaliation which he did not miss. He had, according to custom, shown his exercise to a Fellow, who earnestly advised him to leave out several passages; but Dale would not even consent to correct some faults of Latinity, and when he delivered his speech on November 5, 1725, it was said that the " fury and rage of his gesture, looks, and tone of voice " were indescribable. The speech itself is still extant, and is written in very respectable Latin; the matter chiefly consists of a rather childish attack on Roman Catholicism. He asserts that James I. had done his best to favour Popery, and that there was grave suspicion that his courtiers had something to do with Prince Henry's death; he seems to approve of the rebellion against Charles I., and to exalt dissenters as champions of Protestantism in comparison with the Established

Church. These were the points which, together with
the speaker's manner, gave most offence to the Society,
especially as it was not obscurely hinted that some of
them were no true friends to the Revolution of 1688.
At the end of the month Dale was summoned before a
full meeting of the College, and his attention was called
to the offensive passages; whereupon he made a written
reply "more shuffling, evasive, impudent and contemp-
tuous than any words can set forth." The Provost
warned him that his impracticable temper might cost
him his Fellowship in the following January, and this
would certainly have been the case if a friend had not
interceded, and also persuaded Dale to sign a recanta-
tion. In this document, after confessing that during
his years of probation he had given "just offence in
severall Instances of an untractable and ungovernable
disposition," he ended by promising that

"I will be ready after my admission to my Fellowship to
make such satisfaction for the just offence I have given to
the Society (which I do freely acknowledge I did design to
give) by my late speech as shall be required by the Provost
and proper officers."

On the faith of this promise he was admitted a
Fellow; but when an apology was drawn up for him
to read he refused, defending the various passages to
which objection had been taken. The Provost gave
him seventeen days in which to think better of it and
consult his friends. But he persisted in his refusal, and
was then put out of commons and confined to his
chamber. This action was taken under the 11th
Statute, which requires obedience to the Provost, and

enacts that, if the offender remains obstinate after fifteen days, he shall be expelled. During the fifteen days he must remain a prisoner in his own rooms and provide himself with meals at his own expense. The next day, after sentence had been pronounced, Dale applied for leave to go to Buckden and lay his case before the Visitor. The Provost told him to wait till his application had been considered, but Dale started off at once. This rendered him liable to deprivation under the 58th Statute, which requires members of the Society to submit to all punishments duly imposed, without resorting to appeals or any other methods of postponing punishments, on pain of deprivation ; and he was accordingly deprived of his Fellowship.

It was not likely that Dale would accept this as the conclusion of the matter. He had recourse to the law, and for a time found a refuge in the office of Lord Townshend, then Secretary of State, where he received warm support in his action against the College.

The preliminary proceedings were held at Westminster Hall, where it was settled that the Visitor might receive an appeal from a single Fellow. On the other hand, the College gained a victory in the decision that the Visitor must hear all appeals within the College precincts. Early in March 1726 the Visitor, Bishop Reynolds, came to Cambridge, and the case was argued in the College Hall by lawyers retained on each side. The first day was taken up with the question whether Dale had appealed against his expulsion or against the suspension of commons, and when it was decided that the appeal was against the original punishment, his counsel proceeded to argue that expulsion after this appeal was an attack on the Visitor's jurisdiction.

The sittings continued on the following day from 9 A.M. to 8 P.M., one of Dale's counsel arguing that faults committed during his undergraduateship were condoned by admission to the Fellowship, "osculo pacis"; another, Nicholas Harding, quoting a passage from a sermon preached at St. Mary's by the Provost, which was distorted into a condemnation of the Revolution of 1688. This may have been done either to justify Dale's innuendoes against the loyalty of his College or to bias the Visitor. But counsel chiefly insisted on the argument, that punishment should have been inflicted for "detraction" under the 33rd Statute, which allows suspension of commons for fifteen days, but does not, as in the case of the 11th Statute, result in deprivation of Fellowship, if the offender continues obstinate. The College counsel of course argued that other Statutes were equally applicable to the case, and that, where the particular offence was not specified in the Statutes, the Provost had a general power. At the close of the day's proceedings the Visitor asked for the appellant's bill of costs, a clear indication that he meant to decide in his favour; and accordingly, on the third morning, he gave judgment that Dale's crime, if any, was "detraction," and should have been punished with fifteen days' suspension of commons. The usual wrangle followed about costs, and eventually the sum of £160 was allowed to Dale, whose whole costs amounted to the prodigious amount of £600. The Visitor ended by ordering that, if any person who is punished says that he appeals, the officers shall proceed no further till the case is heard and determined by the Visitor. An account, which professes to come from Batty, the young Fellow appointed to be Dale's companion during the confinement of the latter to his rooms, represents the College case as breaking down, because the Visitor would pay no attention to any promise which Dale had made before admission to his Fellowship, and because the Provost was unable to point to any particular Statute under which Dale was ejected. The 11th Statute seems to be sufficient for the purpose, but perhaps the College counsel mismanaged their case.

Dale's speech of November 5, taken by itself, hardly seems deserving of all the censure which it received ; but we are not able to judge of the offensiveness of the manner which accompanied its delivery, nor was it the first time that he had gone out of his way to insult his Seniors. The College authorities certainly acted weakly in admitting him to his Fellowship before he had apologised ; and there is some reason to believe that their leniency was due to a fear of losing the contributions of the great Whig families to the new building. The bad faith which Dale showed in breaking the conditions on which he had gained his Fellowship was quite inexcusable ; and it is not uncharitable, from all that we know of Bishop Reynolds, to suspect that his decision may have been partly due to other than purely judicial considerations.

The sequel of Dale's story is told in a few words by Antony Allen, viz., that " he lived some years much disturbed in his understanding, and soon died." Batty's account confirms this. According to him, immediately after the Visitor's decision the Provost sent for Dale.

Dale went to the Lodge, expecting a scene and prepared to resent any recriminations. But to his surprise the Provost received him in the most friendly manner, offered him his hand, aud proposed a thorough reconciliation. This was too much for Dale in his excited state, and shortly afterwards Batty found him "in a great perturbation of mind, which at last hurried him into the last degree of insanity."

A new trouble presently arose in the College. William Willymott was in 1729 over fifty years of age and Vice-Provost. He had tried more than one profession and was a Doctor of Civil Law; but, being "a man of a volatile and unsteady complexion," he grew dissatisfied with Doctors' Commons and returned into College, with a view to ordination and a Living. Having been originally a Tory, he now joined the Whig party. His first difficulty was to procure from the College a "Commendamus" to enter Holy Orders; he appealed to the Visitor to know if there was anything to prevent a Doctor of Laws from being ordained or from holding a College benefice, and he obtained a favourable decision. This did not prevent the College from passing him over more than once when Livings were vacant, and on November 4, 1731, they presented a Fellow who was junior to Willymott to the Rectory of Walkern. The choice lay in the first instance with the whole body of Fellows, a majority of whom voted for Willymott, but they were not unanimous, and the duty of presentation then devolved on the Seniors, a bare majority of whom preferred a Mr. Sturgis.

But it was still necessary to affix the College Seal to the Deed of Presentation; and one of the keys was in the keeping of Willymott as Vice-Provost. At 7 P.M. on the same day the Notary Public came to him to say that his key was wanted. He replied that it was lost, and the box must be broken open. This was apparently done; at any rate the Presentation was sealed. As Willymott had already given notice of an appeal, he was perhaps justified in refusing to take part in the sealings, though not in the manner of his refusal. On the other hand, the College were in a great difficulty; for if they had not dared to cut the knot, the Living would soon have lapsed to Bishop Reynolds, who would doubtless have appointed Willymott.

This was no secret, for the question had, even before November 4, been brought to the Visitor's notice by an appeal from eighteen Fellows, chiefly B.A.s, who claimed that a majority of the whole body of Fellows was sufficient for an appointment. Such a view was contrary to the decision of previous Visitors; but it met with sympathy from Bishop Reynolds, who intimated that he was prepared to reverse, or at any rate to reconsider, these decisions; and he went so far as to recommend the appointment of Willymott. This he probably did, either from a belief that Willymott, as Senior, had a right to the Living, or to save himself future trouble; for he may well have hoped that the Seniors would prefer to compromise the matter, and by the appointment of Willymott to escape all question as to their statutable right to present. But in taking this line he somewhat departed from the position of a judge for that of a partisan. And after the meeting of November 4 he did this more openly; for, writing to Willymott from Buckden on November 5, he says that

Mr. Sturgis had come the night before with his Presentation, desiring to be instituted (for Walkern was then in
the diocese of Lincoln), but that he had not only refused
institution, but had given the

"strongest Lecture upon the conduct of the Persons concerned that I ever read in all my time. By which I meant
to express my disapprobation of the proceedings in this
Business, and to give you full time to advise with your
Councell about the operation of any Appeal."

Accordingly, when Willymott on November 15, 1731,
sent in his appeal, he had good reason to expect to
meet with a favourable award. His claim chiefly rested
on what he calls the invariable custom of the College to
present the Senior in standing, but he also raises the
objection that Batty, one of those who made up the
adverse majority, had forfeited his Fellowship by
holding a London Living. The blow to his own
character is what he professes to feel most; for

"if a man be not fitt in Moralls and Learning for a Living,
he is fitt for nothing, and the same reasons that disqualifye
him for a Cure do or ought to expell him from the
College."

The controversy was embittered by the interference
of Nicholas Harding, who on November 11 wrote to
the Visitor a long letter in support of the petition of
the Junior Fellows. This document had contained a
sentence against misapplication of College moneys in
payment of the costs of the Dale case, and had naturally
elicited a protest from the Provost and Seniors, to the
effect that this use of College funds had been voted by

the College and approved by the Visitor eight years ago.
Harding now alleged that other charges *might* have
been brought; the Provost might have been accused of
discouraging those principles of liberty on which the
House of Hanover was established, or of continuing an
unjust and unequal method of dividing the surplus
revenues; or again of permitting the College Tutors to
exact six pounds a year from each Scholar and yet
neglect their duty of reading lecturers; in a word, of
" Partiality, Intollerable Negligence, and Dilapidation."
And he concludes with the remark, "The Provost, I
suppose, flatters himself that the rusty sword which he
has threatn'd to draw upon us will frighten us out of
our wits." Harding must have hoped to represent
Snape as an imitator of Bentley, while he himself
proposed to play the part of a second Serjeant Miller.
No doubt he also wished to prejudice the mind of the
Visitor against the Seniors; and it is to the credit of
the Bishop that he seems to have paid no attention to
Harding, of whom perhaps he had already had enough
in the Dale case.

The Provost and Seniors, in reply to Willymott,
assured the Visitor that they had acted according to
Statute in presenting Sturgis; and that, though they
could quote no case in which a Senior had been rejected
for a Living, there were cases in which the Senior in
standing had abstained from applying, because he knew
he would be rejected. Moreover, there was nothing in
the Statutes to secure to Fellows the right to Livings
in regular rotation; and this doctrine, viz., that the
College had a free choice in the matter, was confirmed
by more than one Visitor in the next century. It was

settled that two counsel should be heard on each side;
but the Provost and Seniors insisted on the hearing
being held in College, and this was very unpalatable to
the Visitor. He could not resist the claim, but he
ordered that the cost of the appeal, or of any hospitality
shown to himself, should not be shared by the Junior
Fellows:

" I, for my part," he writes, "declare that I will not eat
bread any more in College on *any Appeal,* if I am not first
assured, that the bread which is offered me shall not be
paid for by any of the College other than such as are
particularly concerned in the matter of the Appeal on
which I come."

This was rather an unreasonable demand, as was also
the proposal that the Vice-Provost should be the
Bishop's host; for the Provost and Seniors, whether
right or wrong, were acting on behalf of the Society
as a whole; and the Provost replied with dignity:

" As my House is the only place within the College at
present, where you can be lodged with Convenience, I beg
your Lordship will be so good as to accept of the same
Accommodation as before."

It ended, however, in the Visitor's sending two Commissaries to act on his behalf. This was on January 5,
1732; and their decision (of which there is no record)
must have been against Willymott, for in the course of
the year Sturgis became Rector of Walkern. Willymott, however, managed to raise some question in the
Court of King's Bench, and proceedings which had
reference either to the Visitor's right to send Commis-

saries or to some other point in the case were going on as late as November 18.

The next year, 1733, provided Willymott with a fresh grievance. He had, apparently, failed to prove that Batty's Fellowship was vacant ; but Burford had lately succeeded to an estate in Hertfordshire ; and Willymott, in the Provost's absence, could hardly be kept from despatching a messenger to Eton to announce the vacancy and require a Scholar to be sent from Eton to King's. Burford asserted that the debts and other claims on this estate were so heavy that he was out of pocket, and he undertook to resign his Fellowship as soon as he received from the estate the amount specified by the Statutes. The Provost, writing to Willymott from Windsor, where he was in residence as Canon, tells him that if he had not wilfully absented himself from a Congregation, to which he had been summoned, he would have heard Burford's explanation. And then he gives the Vice-Provost a bit of his mind :

" I am persuaded you are still ignorant, wilfully ignorant of the true merits of the Cause. To fly from the Hearing and postpone the affair till you cou'd be Judge, Prosecutor, and Evidence, all in one, is an attempt which I believe no man living but yourself would have ventur'd on ; you have long been used to do rash and unaccountable things, by following your own Head-Strong Humour, and you have hitherto done them with Impunity. You have fals'ly charged myself and others with violation of the Statutes, when you have been a most notorious Violater of them yourself, and I hope the time is not farr off when it will be made to appear to what Degree you have done it."

After this letter, it cannot surprise us to find that at

the annual election in November 1733 a Mr. Parr was elected Vice-Provost instead of Willymott.

But this only added fuel to the fire. Willymott appealed once more, partly on the ground that Burford had no right to vote, partly because Parr was not one of the thirteen Senior Fellows. There are signs in the Visitor's letters that by this time he had become a little tired of Willymott. But he was irritated once more by a refusal on the part of the College authorities to come to Buckden and justify themselves; and, though he advised Willymott to wait for another annual election, he proceeded in June to pronounce the election of the preceding autumn null and void and to order a fresh one. The College met this move by obtaining a Rule from the Court of King's Bench, the result of which was to checkmate the Visitor; and his last letter to Willymott on this subject sums up the situation :

" Buckden, Sept. 11, 1734.

" D WILLYMOTT,

" I have been, ever since ye last election of College officers, fully of opinion, that it was most advisable for you to expect ye re-establishment of the Vice-Provostship at ye next election, which will be in ye beginning of Nov. next. Nevertheless, at your earnest request, I did receive ye Appeal, and Appoint an hearing at my house, which by Universal Consent and Practice is allowed to be y^c place for hearing Appeals, and is, as I am fully persuaded, the only proper place. But, on y^r neglect to Defend that Appointment for hearing ye Appeal, a Prohibition hath issued from the Court of King's Bench : so that I cannot, as I apprehend, hear the matter of that Appeal, in any shape, without ye hazard of a Premunire, as ye matter now

N

stands. But if you shall think fit, to bring, as you propose, a mandamus to have y⁰ Appeal heard, That writ will not only warrant but command me to proceed without danger, and I shall be very far from taking any offence at being provided with so good Armour. As the case, at present, is, It would be not courage, but Foolhardiness to go on. In the mean time you will do me but justice to believe, that I have been, to the Utmost of my power,

                    " Yʳ Faithful Friend,

                              " R. LINCOLN."

No one who reads the Bishop's correspondence can fail to do this amount of justice to him.

Willymott was actually elected Vice-Provost in November 1734. Evidently the College had only wished to inflict a temporary punishment and were not actuated by any rancorous feelings towards him. They were willing enough to let him keep the official position, which they thought due to his seniority. What they were not willing to allow was that, when he had escaped those College and University duties which other Fellows in Holy Orders had performed for years, he should step over the heads of these men into the first vacant Living. However, his turn came at last ; and in 1736 he was presented to the Sinecure Rectory of Milton. When this fell vacant, he was still only in Deacon's orders, and there are some curious letters from Bishop Reynolds, expressing a willingness to give him private ordination on the shortest possible notice, and, of course, without any examination ; but adding that—

"as a Deacon or even a Meer Layman is capable of a Presentation to a Cure of Souls, or a Dignity in the Church,

and such Presentation would be a proper Title for his
ordination ; so certainly a Deacon is capable of a Presentation to a Sinecure."

Cole, who knew Willymott personally, says that he
would afterwards have been glad to give up his Preferment
and resume his Fellowship ; and that at last, " after a
very turbulent and very uneasy life to himself and
others with whom he was concerned, he died at an Inn
in Bedford when on a journey." He was very intimate
with the Cole family, who lived at Babraham, and at
one time would have boarded with them,—

" had not his known Temper deterred any one, who valued
their own Quiet, from accepting him on those Terms ;
however he would come and stay, now and then, when his
facetious and entertaining Company was always acceptable."

One more domestic quarrel is recorded, in which
Provost Snape was a party. He had ordered a certain
brewer to bring in a load of beer and lay it in the
College cellar. This was being done on March 4,
1737 ; but Mr. Bland, the Bursar, " seeing it, took hold
of the horses' heads, and made the Carrmen drive the
Dray out of College." The Provost ordered it to be
readmitted, but Mr. Bland " repeated his opposition,
and declared that he would do the same thing as often
as it should be attempted, and withall told the Butler
that, if it should be taken in and used, it should never
be paid for." The controversy was decided by the
Visitor in the Provost's favour, so that he gained his
last battle. But the subject of the struggle seems
hardly worthy of a man who had won his spurs as a
champion of the Church.

CHAPTER XIV

SOME DETAILS OF COLLEGE LIFE

On Dr. Snape's death in January 1743 a severe contest
for the Provostship took place. William George, the
Eton Headmaster, was supported by the moderate
Whigs and by Sir Robert Walpole; but, besides the
Tory candidate, Chapman, there was another Whig,
Thomas Thackeray, great-grandfather of the novelist, in
the field. Early on Monday, January 17, the Fellows
assembled in Chapel; but it was 2 P.M. on Tuesday
before the election could be completed, and the Fellows
in their surplices were obliged to pass the night within
the building. Fires of charcoal set in braziers helped
to mitigate the cold; but the blankets and brandy, with
which some at least of the Electors had provided themselves, must have been in great request. Eventually,
the sixteen supporters of Thackeray went over to the
side of George, and he was elected Provost.

Like his predecessor, he had been Headmaster of
Eton; but it is said that his abilities were not equal to
the position, and that, when he got into difficulties, his
temper became sour and his manners brutal. Charles
Pratt, then a Fellow of King's, in letters to Sneyd
Davies says:

"1 take it for granted that you have had some relation

of our election, and know that we sat thirty-one hours in the Chapel before we could agree. But perhaps you have not been told another thing, which I assure you is true, that, if you had been qualified, we had certainly made you Provost. . . . The new Provost is the delight of society, and behaves to every one's satisfaction, released from all care, free and jovial. This is very different from his carriage and conduct at Eton. You may see how that perverse disposition, which I call absurdity or blundering ignorance of decorum, will make the same individual odious or entertaining, as the temper in which it acts is in or out of tune. At present, as he has no care, his good nature has returned; so that now his absurdity, which is rather heightened than diminished, gives an agreeable turn to everything he says or does. These men are very unfit for business, which calls for steady abilities and steady resolution; but make very excellent companions in private life, especially when they are tinctured with letters, and have like *him* quick fancies, with a good ear and a powerful memory."

In the critical year 1745 the College had an opportunity of showing its loyalty; and on November 29 the sum of £200 was voted "for his majesty's service in this time of common danger." This act of patriotism was the more praiseworthy from the fact that for three years (1744–46) there was no surplus out of which to vote a dividend. Prudence, however, dictated a second vote, on December 20, that the money should be paid by instalments to the Vice-Chancellor, and in proportion to payments by other subscribers. The purse of the College about this time was freely opened for benevolent or religious purposes. There are votes of money for the S.P.G. and the S.P.C.K., for Exeter Hospital, and for the sufferers from a recent fire at Crediton. Something too was done for the establishment of parish schools.   At the same time the College set apart money arising from the sale of timber to pay off the building debt, and also created another fund for defending lawsuits and increasing the College estates.

Efforts were being made about this time for the improvement of University discipline.   The new Chancellor, the Duke of Newcastle, drew up regulations which were approved by the Senate.   Besides enforcing the wearing of academical dress, they aimed at diminishing the use of coffee-houses and taverns, and the habit of riding and driving ; while such games as tennis and cricket were forbidden between 9 and 12 A.M.

The practice of resorting to coffee-houses was at least as old as 1675.   In the eighteenth century it had become the custom of students after morning chapel to repair to some coffee-house, where

" hours are spent in talking, and less profitable reading of newspapers, of which swarms are continually supplied from London.   The scholars are so greedy after news, which is none of their business, that they neglect all for it; and it is become very rare for any of them to go directly to his chambers after prayers, without doing his suit at the coffee-house ; which is a vast loss of time grown out of a pure novelty, for who can apply close to a subject with his head full of the din of a coffee-house ? "

Roger North, who writes thus, suggests that, since coffee had now become a morning refreshment, it might be provided in College.   One or two exceptional men, such as Horace Walpole at King's and his friend Thomas Gray at Peterhouse, drank nothing but tea ;

and no doubt there were still some old-fashioned people who were content to breakfast at the Buttery-hatch off bread and beer.

Sometimes a mere waste of time was not the only danger to be found in a coffee-house. Bishop Fleetwood's only son, Charles, who became a Scholar of King's in 1711, was, so Cole tells us,

" very near being married to one Mary Paris, who then did, as she now does, keep a Coffee House near the College ; which was prevented by the Interposition of Dr. Green, Master of Benet College and then Vice-Chancellor, who by a Stretch of his Prerogative sent her to the House of Correction and gave timely Notice of the Affair to the Bishop, who put a stop to this inconsiderate Match."

But, though rescued on this occasion by the arbitrary action of the Vice-Chancellor, Charles Fleetwood lived to give his father trouble of another kind. He was already Rector of Barley when the Living of Cottenham fell vacant, and he desired to hold both, as the income of Cottenham would help him to live in comfort at Barley. But it was contrary to the Bishop's rule that any Incumbent should hold two Livings, if one provided a sufficient maintenance ; and the son never forgave the father for refusing to appoint him. The Bishop used to say that he would not wish his enemy a greater curse than "an only favourite and disrespectful son." Evidently Charles Fleetwood brought no credit to an honoured name.

Smoking is not mentioned in the regulations of 1750, and apparently throughout this century it was only practised by Dons in their Combination Rooms. The habits of Kingsmen were probably not very different

from those of other undergraduates, and the College
records of this date furnish instances of Scholars being
punished for keeping horses, or for being " engaged in a
horse-race at Newmarket." Sometimes they did even
worse things; the most serious offence being that of
" keeping up " under pretence of illness and then going
out of College for the day or even for the night also.
There are not many signs of excessive conviviality; but
on December 17, 1771, two Scholars were punished for
"being in Trinity Hall at a most unseasonable hour in
the morning of the 16th instant and making a great
disturbance there." A Scholar named Cooke, in 1767,
who was perhaps ambitious of imitating John Dale,
brought to his Tutor a Latin exercise, which contained
an uncomplimentary description of the Tutor himself:

> " Decipimur specie recti ; sed decipitur quis
>   Hac recti specie ?   Cui Dii tribuere jocantes
>   Exiguum forte imperium parvamque tyrannim :
>   Scilicet hic, regni impatiens sceptroque superbus,
>   Ut falsis olim lætata Monedula pennis,
>   Evehit in cœlum caput, alta voce probrosos
>   Insequitur mores puerorum, abrupta juventæ
>   Inclamat studia ; en ! vacuæ ædes ! "

These and other lines of a still more stinging character
entailed on Cooke a week's imprisonment in his rooms
and hard labour in the shape of extra exercises.
Another Scholar, Jones, in the same year fared still
worse. He had leave out of College on August 11 for
the usual sixty days. On October 7 he wrote to an
undergraduate friend to say that he had been bitten by
a dog suspected of madness, and had gone to Gravesend
for the benefit of sea-bathing. He desired his friend to

get him extension of leave. This was granted on condition that Jones produced a proper certificate from the person under whose care he was. No certificate was sent; and when Jones at last returned, though he had a long story to tell about his accident and how he had been attended by a Mr. Figg, of Ludgate Hill, a specialist in such cases, and even produced what purported to be a certificate from Mr. Figg, further inquiry satisfied the authorities that the whole story was a fabrication, and he was deprived of his Scholarship.

Before this incident occurred the Provostship had passed into the hands of John Sumner, who held it from 1756 to 1772. He, like his two predecessors, had been Headmaster of Eton; he was also a Canon of Windsor and held other Church preferment.

In the latter part of the eighteenth century the College grounds began to assume the appearance with which we are familiar. Avenues or rows of ash-trees, elm or walnut, had been planted in 1580. One reached from the Friars' Gate, the southern entrance to the College, where a Gothic Arch under a tiled penthouse gave admission from Queens' Lane, as far as the west door of the Chapel. A second, at right angles to this, ran across the centre of what is now the Back Lawn to the river, where a stone bridge (replacing an earlier one of wood) was built in 1627. In the north-west corner of this Court were a bowling-green and an inner garden protected by a wall; and within the garden a gallery overhanging the river. On the far side of the Cam the central avenue was continued on a raised causeway till it reached the west ditch at " Field Gate," which was provided with a wooden bridge. To the south of this causeway was a "Grove" or larger garden with a hop-yard, pigeon-house and ponds. This area at one time went by the name of Laundress Yard, and was reserved for the use of the Senior Fellows. To the north lay a meadow, in which the College horses were turned out. Close to the bridge over the Cam, but on the east bank, there was another small garden for the Junior Fellows. One more avenue ran along the north side of the Court, nearly parallel to the new buildings of Clare Hall. In the Front Court also the south and east sides were planted with trees, and the walk which divided the Back Court was continued across the Front Court till it reached the "Clerks' Lodgings," just north of the spot where the Porters' Lodge now stands. The erection of Gibbs's Building had, of course, destroyed one of these avenues; but there seems to have been no other change till the middle of the century, when a walk was made and planted on the west bank of the river, and another along the south side of the Back Court; and the Front Court was also laid down as a lawn.

Next followed a similar treatment of the Back Court, in accordance with a vote of College of April 14, 1772:

" Agreed to proceed in the further improvement of the Chappel yard on the West side of the New Building, by laying down the same with Grass seeds and afterwards feeding it from time to time with sheep as occasion may require in order to get it into good and ornamental condi-tion ; to compleat the Gravelling the Walks round the same as now laid out, and not for the future to put any horses there."

From this period then we may date the existence of the Lawn as we have it, especially as it seems that about the same time the walls which enclosed the bowling-green and inner garden, and a wall which ran along the edge of the river, were removed.

The years 1770 to 1776 were also a period of alteration within the Chapel. The black and white marble squares had been laid down in the Choir in 1702, but the Ante-chapel remained only partially paved. A seasonable gift of £400 from Lord Godolphin enabled the College to complete this work in 1774. At this time, too, the Lectern was banished to the Library in the side Chapel, where it remained till 1854. The legacy of John Hungerford provided funds for a new altar and oak panelling round the east bay of the Chapel, and also for two stone niches on each side of the east window; and a picture ascribed to Daniele da Volterra, the gift of Lord Carlisle, added a little colour to the whole of this work, which was designed by Essex and cost £1650. The style was such as might be expected of the period, and at any rate satisfied Horace Walpole, who writes to Cole on May 22, 1777:

" I dote on Cambridge, and could like to be often there. The beauty of King's College Chapel, now it is restored, penetrated me with a visionary longing to be a monk in it."

A later generation, however, has not scrupled to condemn and undo Essex's work.

It was ten years after this, in 1786, that an alteration was made in the Provost's Lodge. The University were contemplating a new building parallel to the Senate House, and the College accepted the sum of £1150, giving up the north end of the Lodge, " in order to promote the public design of the University." The sum received from the University, but no more than this amount, was to be laid out in making such additions to the Lodge as would compensate the Provost for the loss which he sustained. This consisted of six rooms on the ground floor, four bedrooms and the Audit Room, and two staircases. To make up for this loss the " Brick Building," which stood at the south end of the Lodge, was now made part of it. This building dated from 1692; the ground floor served as a school, and the upper storeys had provided rooms for Fellow-Commoners till they found a home in Gibbs's Building. There must always have been some school-room for the Choristers, and one such had certainly stood on this site before 1692; but the school seems gradually to have grown in importance. Some Fellow of the College usually acted as Master; and other Cambridge boys, besides the King's Choristers, received their education here. One of these was James Essex, the architect. It may have been convenient that the school should be near the " Clerks' Lodging " or " Conducts' Court "; but there seems something incongruous in the close proximity of Fellow-Commoners to Choristers, though it was an advantage that the former should be within easy access of the Provost's Lodge.

The building contemplated by the University was soon given up, and in 1797–98 a new passage was made from Trumpington Street to the north-east corner of the Chapel, dividing the two properties; the University binding themselves not to build on it nor to open it for horse or carriage traffic.

The change in the Lodge took place while William Cooke was Provost. He, too, had been Headmaster of Eton, but only for three years, when ill-health obliged him to resign and retire to the Vicarage of Sturminster Marshall. It was said that the boys, at any rate, did not regret him. Cole's account of him is far from flattering : " Made Master of the Schole, for which not being found equal, he was made Fellow of the College to let him down gently ; and to get rid of his Imperti- nence, Insolence, and other unamiable Qualities, he was strongly recommended to be Provost of King's, on Dr. Sumner's death. It is not the first time that a man's unsocial and bad disposition has been the occasion of his advancement. I know the College would be delighted to kick him up higher, so that they might get rid of a formal important Pedant, who will be a Schoolmaster in whatever station of life his fortune may advance him to." This is not complimentary, but it is mild, compared with the language used by the same writer about Cooke, when smarting under what he considered a grievance.

According to Cole's story, Cooke, soon after his election in 1772, was instrumental in raising the rent of a cottage at Milton in which Cole lived, and on which he had spent £600. The injured tenant can find no words bad enough for this "scoundrel" of a Provost, and for "Paddon, a dirty wretch of a Bursar, very suitable to him."

It is likely enough that Cooke was a bit of a pedant, and he may have thought it his duty to treat the College tenants with justice rather than generosity. But the only College vote which deals with the Milton case (November 20, 1776), " To seal a lease of Milton Farm to the Rev. Mr. Cole for twenty years from April 5 last under the same rent as the former," does not bear out Cole's complaints, and it was passed unanimously at a meeting of the Provost and thirteen Fellows. Perhaps the rent, though nominally due before, had not been exacted till a lease was granted, in consideration of the tenant's outlay on the premises.

It is to the credit of the Provost that he seems to have lived in harmony with his Fellows, and that he raised no difficulties to the alteration of his Lodge, which must have caused him at least temporary discomfort. And it must be added that during his tenure of office there was a marked improvement in the discipline of the undergraduates. One bad case, indeed, is recorded a few months after his appointment. A Scholar, named Stanhope, who had obtained leave of absence for the purpose of paying a visit to his mother, never went near her, but took the opportunity to

"drive through the town of Eton in an open carriage, having with him a person of suspicious Fame and Character, and there taking up into his Carriage one of the Scholars of Eton and Carrying him away from School without leave obtained of the Master, and otherwise behaving in a very unbecoming manner to the Ill Example of the Scholars there."

Stanhope was severely punished, and there is no other record of misconduct for more than twenty years. It is reasonable to infer that, if Provost Cooke had the manners of a Schoolmaster, he also possessed the Schoolmaster's art of keeping order. In one respect he was unlike all other Provosts, for he had received his earliest schooling at Harrow; but he makes no mention of this in the epitaph which he himself composed, and in which he attributed all his successes in life to his training in the two Foundations of King Henry.

It is interesting to notice the readiness with which the College of those days contributed towards national objects. In 1776 twenty guineas were given to relieve the distress caused to the clergy in North America by the revolt of the Colonies; and when the French Revolution drove some of the Priests into exile, fifty guineas were voted, in 1792, to " the French clergy now in this Kingdom." The war which broke out in 1793 induced the College to open its purse again, and grant £21 to " provide Cloathing for the Troops on the Continent," and £105 towards the augmentation of the Militia; and on November 10, 1797, £10 10s. was voted

" for the relief of the Widows and Orphans of the Seamen who fell in the late Action between Admiral Duncan's Squadron and the Dutch Fleet."

An extensive purchase of Livings was made in 1781, when the College acquired, for the sum of £2000, the Advowsons of Kingston, Richmond, Kew, Petersham, East Molesey and Thames Ditton. A legacy from a Mr. Bullock provided more than half the purchase-money, and the rest was borrowed from their own Timber and Chest Funds.

The last year of Dr. Cooke's life was marked by an unfortunate loss. The Provost, on returning to College towards the end of October 1796, found that the whole of his Plate, which had been deposited in the Treasury of the old Court, had been abstracted, although the doors were still locked and there was no sign of violence having been used. No time was lost in taking a review of the College Plate and in making over to the Provost what could be spared. Much of the old Plate was also now sold, and new and more necessary articles either purchased or given by former members of the College.

CHAPTER XV

SOME EMINENT KINGSMEN

WHEN the College preferred George to Thackeray as their Provost they lost a man of some real distinction. It was said that, when Thomas Thackeray preached at St. Mary's the church was crowded both to see and to hear him, for he and his wife, a Miss Woodward, were reputed to be the handsomest pair ever seen; and the portrait of Thackeray in King's Lodge shows that this report was not altogether without foundation. According to Cole, he was of a most humane and candid disposition, and generally beloved. His defence of Whig or Latitudinarian principles cost him his Eton Mastership; but a vacancy in the Headmastership of Harrow, in 1746, gave him a new opportunity. A former Fellow of King's, Thomas Bryan, had held the post for forty years, and had done much to raise the School. But since 1731 a disastrous period had followed, and it was Thackeray who now restored the School to the position to which Bryan had brought it, and paved the way for a period of still greater prosperity. At 53 years of age he was rather old to undertake such a task; but, with a family of more than a dozen children, it was necessary for him to exert himself to the utmost. When he resigned, it was expected that he would be made a Bishop, for he had for the last seven years been Archdeacon of Surrey. Hoadley, then Bishop of Winchester, had given him this office, telling him that he could perform its duties in the Easter holidays of each year. No further preferment, however, followed, for Thackeray died suddenly in London, in September 1760.

A few years after this an unusual scene took place in the College Chapel. On May 4, 1763, nine colours taken at Manila by Sir William Draper, a former Fellow of the College, were carried in procession by the Scholars, accompanied by the Fellows, the organ playing, and the Choir preceding and singing hymns. The offer of these Flags was first made in a letter from Draper to one of the Fellows :

PALL MALL, *April* 18.
" DEAR BURFORD

"Many thanks to you for your obliging Epistle. I have got some Spanish Colours taken at Manila for the Chapel. And His Majesty has been pleased to consent that they shall be sent to your College and hung up there. So if you have no objection to see your old Friend's Trophies over your head, I will send them down. Love to Glyn.

"I am
"y^r aff. Friend
"Upon recollection I believe   "WILL. DRAPER."
I ought to address the College
in Form : if so let me know it."

The Provost, however, who was now John Sumner, did not wait for a more formal address, but wrote on April 20 :

" DEAR SIR

"Your L^r to Mr Burford, acquainting him with y^r Intention of sending the Spanish Colours taken at Manila

o

for y^r Chapel He this morning communicated to Me; and I immediately desired a Meeting of all the Members resident in College, that they might receive the same satisfaction with myself, in having your Design imparted to them; and be informed of His Majesty's goodness in granting His royal permission for that Purpose. We were rejoicing indeed in the general Joy of the Nation, upon so glorious a Conquest being atchieved; and were flattering ourselves with something like a secret Pride, that so important an acquisition had been made by one of our own Body; when it appeared that you too in the midst of your Triumph were as Mindful of Us: and while we were indulging ourselves in the pleasing Thoughts of bearing a relation to the Commander, and having some Share in the honour of his success; you have realized, Sir, our imaginary Glory, and made us actually the Depositaries of your Trophies."

There is a good deal more, for the length, as well as the style, of the Doctor of Divinity contrasts with that of the practical soldier.

The Colours were placed on each side of the altar rails; and Latin orations were delivered by two Fellows, one of whom, Mr. Burford, was Public Orator. These were followed by Evening Service and a Thanksgiving anthem. It has to be confessed, with shame, that the Colours, which afterwards found a home in the organ loft, have for many years been allowed to moulder away in obscurity in one of the side chapels.

Draper had entered the army early enough to be present at Culloden. He had afterwards served with some distinction in India, and his capture of the works of Manila by assault was a considerable feat of arms. The citadel still remained to be taken, and the Archbishop, who was also Governor, proposed to capitulate

and so save the inhabitants from plunder. Draper
consented to accept as ransom bills for two million
dollars on the Treasury at Madrid. These were afterwards repudiated by the Spanish Government; and
when, in 1769, Draper defended the Marquis of Granby
against the attacks of Junius, Junius turned on Draper
and accused him of having been bribed by the red
riband of the Bath to abandon the claims of his troops
to the Manila ransom. It was true that Draper had at
last ceased to press on the Government the duty of
forcing the Spaniards to pay their debts; but this was
because he had been assured that a war with Spain was
out of the question; and to have declined an honour to
which he was thoroughly entitled, because his colleague,
Admiral Cornish, and the soldiers and sailors were
defrauded of their rights, would have been Quixotic
rather than sensible. Besides, he had already shown
his disinterestedness by refusing, when at Manila, to
accept from the Archbishop a large bribe if he would
abate the amount demanded for a ransom. Draper's
brother Kingsman, Christopher Anstey, defended him in
the following lines :

"But alas ! to his fortune, his interest blind,
   How blamed by the *sensible* part of mankind !
   In a land so remote, in that barbarous ground,
   When victory spread her glad ensign around,
   To sheath the fell sword, in a ransom engage !
   So unlike many other great chiefs of the age—
   To feel for the helpless ! to hear the fond prayer
   Of widows and orphans,—to *conquer* and *spare* !
   From foolish compassion to hazard that gain,
   Which others by fair, lawful plunder obtain."

The author of these lines became a Fellow of King's in

1745, and in 1748 as Senior Bachelor he was called upon to make a Latin declamation in the Public Schools. Whether this was an innovation or not is uncertain; Anstey, at any rate, considered it an infringement on the College rights, and began his speech with words which seemed to ridicule the University authorities. The Vice-Chancellor suspended him from his degree, and required him to make a fresh declamation, when he introduced an ironical apology. Tradition says that he began this second speech with the words, "Doctores sine doctrinâ, Magistri Artium sine Artibus, Baccalaurei baculo potius quam lauro digni," but there is no trace of such words in the author's MS.

In this second speech he admitted that his manner might have given offence.

"Haud inficiar me rei oratoriæ adeo non peritum esse ut plurimos vestrum viderem qui vix a risu temperarent cum tragica quadam cervicis jactatione Roscii partes non Ciceronis agere viderer. Quapropter vir doctissimus, qui huic exercitationi præfuit, ipso etiam in oratiunculæ meæ vestibulo importunitatem coercuit, veritus fortasse pro singulari sua humanitate ne severiorum virorum iracundiam commoverem."

This second speech failed to give satisfaction, and he was again suspended. There was an appeal to Delegates, who confirmed the sentence in spite of the efforts of the Kingsmen. Anstey's son says that this was the last Latin declamation pronounced by a Bachelor of King's in the Schools. If so, Anstey gained his end, but at the cost of his own M.A. degree; for he writes of

"Granta, sweet Granta, where studious of ease
Seven years did I sleep and then lost my degrees."

But he remained a Fellow till 1754, when he succeeded to a property at Trumpington, married, and led
the life of a country gentleman.   His classical studies
were not wholly abandoned, for together with a brother
Kingsman, Roberts, afterwards Provost of Eton, he
made the first Latin version of Gray's Elegy, and at a
somewhat later date he spent much time in preparing
his own sons for Eton.   A bilious fever led to his
visiting Bath, and in 1766 appeared the letters in rhyme
called the *New Bath Guide or Memoirs of the Blunder-
head family.*   The book became fashionable at once;
and Horace Walpole says, "So much wit, humour, fun
and poetry, so much originality, never met together
before.   Then the man has a better ear than Dryden or
Handel."   Parts of it, however, would not be tolerated
at the present day; for he seems to have considered
that he might say anything against doctors or Metho-
dists.   Even in those times objections were raised; and
he replied to them in the following lines, which also
contain a reference to his improvements at Trumpington, and his farming troubles :—

" May this drowsy current, (as oft he is wont),
    O'erflow all my hay, may my dogs never hunt,
    And O ! may some dæmon, those plagues to complete,
    Give me *taste* to *improve* an old family seat,
    By *lawning* a hundred good acres of wheat !
    Such ills be my portion, and others much worse,
    If slander or calumny poison my verse ;
    If ever my well-behaved Muse shall appear
    Indecently droll, unpolitely severe ! "

But indecent, and it may be added profane, drollery
was just what his Muse did sometimes indulge in.   In

spite of this fault, he was a man of upright character, benevolent, and public spirited ; a good father and a warm-hearted friend. Whether he ever forgave Cambridge for stopping his M.A. degree seems doubtful. The complimentary lines, which he wrote in 1767, sound more ironical than serious :—

  " 'Tis thine, Sacred Science ! new charms to display ;
    How much I rejoice thou hast chosen thy seat
    In Granta's delightful and quiet retreat!
    Where men of such piety, learning and sense,
    Distribute thy gifts at so small an expense,
    And season the minds of well-disciplined youth
    With patriot maxims of wisdom and truth ;
    Regardless of changes in Church or in State,
    They ne'er court the favour or smiles of the great ;
    For candour, for softness of manners renowned,
    Shed the blessings of peace and contentment around ;
    And far from malignity, faction and noise,
    With dignity seek philosophical joys."

A still more distinguished Kingsman, seven years junior to Anstey, was Charles Pratt. For eight or nine years he remained a briefless barrister, and he was so much dispirited that he was on the point of returning to College, and perhaps of taking Holy Orders. Even to Antony Allen, who finished his catalogue of Kingsmen in 1750, Pratt was known only as a promising young pleader, who had just ventured to marry and resign his Fellowship. But two years later he became famous by his defence of the right of juries to determine questions of law as well as of fact in libel cases. Throughout his career he was a champion of liberty, and perhaps a little too much inclined to pose as such; whether as Lord Chief Justice he was condemning arbitrary arrests, or arguing in the House of Lords as Lord Camden against the American Stamp Act. He rose to be Lord Chancellor in 1760. His success was partly due to his own talents and exertions, and partly to the support of his old friend and schoolfellow, the elder William Pitt, from whom he may have learned his somewhat theatrical manner. In his later days he made the mistake of remaining in a Cabinet with men whose policy he condemned; and it has been said of him that " he was unfit to stand alone, and on the eclipse of Chatham he sank into insignificance." Yet after Chatham's death he had the satisfaction of giving strong and valuable support to Chatham's son in his early political struggles, as well as of helping to pass a Libel Law, which secured to juries the rights for which he had contended forty years earlier. Another Kingsman, who gained distinction in public life, was Thomas Orde, who became Lord Bolton in 1797. As a Scholar of King's he was chiefly remarkable for his artistic tastes, which, no doubt, were the cause of his subsequent friendship with Romney. He used to caricature well-known Cambridge figures, of the lower class, and give the profits of his etchings to his victims. But he found more serious occupation at the Bar and in Parliament; he rose to be Under-Secretary to Lord Shelburne in 1782, but declined to continue in office under Pitt. It was in Ireland, however, as Chief Secretary to the Duke cf Rutland, 1784–1787, that he gained most fame, for his efforts to carry out a commercial union between England and Ireland and also to establish a comprehensive scheme of education for Ireland. To judge by Romney's portrait, Orde was a handsome man. Indeed, it is said that he owed his first success in life to his good looks and good manners. For when the Duke of Bolton happened to pay a visit to Cambridge, Orde, then a young scholar at King's, was chosen to act as his guide, and he made a favourable impression on the Duke. It is certain that he afterwards married the Duke's daughter, and succeeded to the name and estates of the Powletts.

No Kingsman, during the eighteenth century, after Andrew Snape, seems to have been particularly successful as Headmaster of Eton; but what Thomas Thackeray had accomplished at Harrow, that and even more Thomas James did for Rugby. As a boy at Eton, he had been distinguished for excellence in Latin and Greek composition; and at King's he had twice gained the Members' Prize for a Latin Essay. It was in 1778 that he went to Rugby and reformed the school after the Eton model, raising it from 60 to 245 boys, and earning from a recent historian of the school the title of the "creator of Rugby as it now is." On his resignation the Trustees begged Mr. Pitt to give him perferment, and he was made a Prebendary of Worcester and Rector of Harvington. The Trustees also showed their confidence in the College, which had sent them such a man, by electing as his successor another Kingsman, Henry Ingles. James did not forget his old College, but founded there annual prizes for Latin Declamations.

With all the influence of a long-established Cathedral Choir, it might have been expected that King's College would have become a school of music; and the names of some composers, including that of Provost Hacomblen, are recorded within the first century after the foundation. But, although in the Elizabethan age,

Fellows of King's are said to have cultivated the art, there seems little trace in later days of any great musician ; unless we may except Ralph Thicknesse, who in 1742, being at that time the favourite candidate for the Provostship, suddenly fell down dead, when playing a composition of his own, as first violin, in a concert at Bath. During the last half of the eighteenth century the Professor of Music was a Kingsman, J. Randall ; and it was his duty to set to music Gray's Ode for the Installation of the Duke of Grafton as Chancellor in 1768. The poet had his own views about music, and for three months Randall was in constant attendance, endeavouring to comply with the author's taste by adapting the music to the Italian style. But when he came to the chorus, Gray said : "I have now done ; make as much noise as you please."

One name, however, certainly deserves to be recorded. It is that of Joah Bates, who had studied under an organist at Rochdale, before he went to Eton in 1756, and who found encouragement to persevere in his musical studies from Mr. Graham, one of the Eton masters. For a short time after leaving school he was a Pensioner of Christ's College, and he gained the Craven University Scholarship two months before he was admitted to his Scholarship at King's. Afterwards he became a Fellow and Tutor ; and one of his pupils was a son of the profligate Lord Sandwich, who at least did one good action in making Bates his private secretary and giving him a berth in the Post Office. While still an undergraduate, Bates had conducted a performance of the Messiah at his own native town, Halifax ; and this is said to have been the first occasion on which an oratorio was performed north of the Trent. In

1776 he became Conductor of the Concerts of Ancient Music; and in 1783, in conjunction with Lord Fitzwilliam and Sir Watkin Williams Wynn, he brought about the Commemoration of Handel at Westminster Abbey, and acted as Conductor on that memorable occasion. Though a scholar and musician, he seems to have been a bad financier; and an unfortunate investment nearly ruined him, so that his later life was saddened by poverty. He died in 1799.

All Cambridge residents, during the latter part of the eighteenth century, must have known by sight Dr. Robert Glynn, who began lecturing at Cambridge on medicine and anatomy in 1751, and after practising for a short time at Richmond returned to Cambridge and lived in College, where he might generally be seen walking after dusk under Gibbs's Building, or along the south face of Clare Hall. He usually wore a scarlet cloak and three-cornered hat, with pattens in rainy weather; and was the most active, eccentric, and benevolent of doctors. He gave gratuitous advice to the inhabitants of the Fens, where there was a great deal of fever and ague; and he would never take a fee from a Cornishman (for he was himself born near Bodmin), nor a clergyman. Horace Walpole called him "an old doting physician," but that was because he believed in the genuineness of Chatterton's poems. Lord Chatham spoke of him as "one of the cheerful and witty sons of Apollo"; and the younger Pitt, whom he had attended in 1773, offered him the Professorship of Physic in 1793. Probably Glynn felt himself too old for such a post. But he was for some time the leading physician of Cambridge, and his treatment had a certain originality, for he always (so it is said) began with a blister, though he would never resort to bleeding. His habits were odd.   He had no fixed hour for meals, but there was generally a cold shoulder of mutton standing in his rooms ; and he gave undergraduate tea-parties of a thoroughly unconventional kind.   When Charles Simeon had to preach his first sermon at St. Mary's (it was on Advent Sunday, December 3, 1786), Dr. Glynn called on Simeon the day before, and begged him to come to his rooms and read over his sermon.   For, as he told Simeon, he would have a critical and prejudiced audience next day.   Simeon was glad to accept the invitation, for friends were scarce in those days.   The Doctor heard the sermon, corrected and improved it, and concluded :

" Now, Sir, as I am called out, and cannot be at St. Mary's, I am glad I can say I have read the Sermon, and shall be your advocate wherever I go."

No account of prominent Kingsmen of these times would be complete without some reference to Horace Walpole, who entered the College as a Fellow Commoner in 1734.   He does not seem to have taken kindly to University life, and speaks of Oxford and Cambridge as " two barbarous towns, o'errun with rusticity and mathematics."

" We have not," he writes, " the least poetry here ; for I can't call verses on the 5th of November and 30th of January by that name, more than four lines on a chapter in the New Testament is an Epigram."

If, like his friend Gray, he had spent some part of his long life as a College resident, how valuable (though probably uncomplimentary) would his picture of College life have been !   His character had nothing heroic

about it; it was hardly even serious; and he had none
of his father's solidity.   But he was the prince of letter
writers, and ahead of his age in some of his opinions as
well as his tastes.   For it must be remembered to his
credit that he spoke with loathing of the Slave Trade;
and to him, at least in some degree, we owe the revival
of a taste for Gothic Art and Romantic Literature.
Strawberry Hill was, indeed, but a gingerbread kind of
castle ; but it led the way to something better.   And if
the *Castle of Otranto* is no masterpiece, yet without
it we might have had no *Ivanhoe* and no *Kenilworth*.

William Cole, when doubting what to do with his
collection of MSS. said that

"to give them to King's College would be to throw them
into a horse-pond; the members of that Society being
generally so conceited of their Latin and Greek that all
other studies were barbarous."

If the eight Fellows who have been described in this
chapter were at all representative specimens of the
Society, Cole's criticism must have been unjust.   Two
of them were, indeed, schoolmasters; but one was a
lawyer, one a doctor, one a politician, one a soldier, one
a musician, and one a poet.   There is, however, a third
schoolmaster, whose name deserves to be recorded, that
of John Foster.   As Headmaster of Eton, indeed, he
was singularly unsuccessful, being in too great a hurry
to raise the standard of education and discipline.   But
he was a man of real learning.   His *Essay on Accent
and Quantity*, published in 1761, is an elaborate defence
of Greek accentuation and an explanation of the true
relations of accent and quantity in Greek, Latin, and
English.   Not only is it a work of great research, but it

shews also that in dealing with literary problems he possessed the judgment which he lacked in his treatment of boys; and its publication was seasonable, at a time when the Oxford Press was beginning to print Greek texts without any accents. Had Foster been a Cambridge Professor, instead of being Headmaster of a Public School, he might have made a name for himself and done something to stimulate a love of learning in others.

This list of distinguished men does not, however, contain any Theologian; for there seems to have been no Kingsman, in the most important of all studies, who can be compared to the men of an earlier generation, to such men as Snape, Fleetwood, Hare, or Stanhope. Simeon had hardly yet become prominent; Sneyd Davies, though an Archdeacon, was more of a poet than a Theologian; and Jack Young (brother of the well-known Arthur Young), Fellow of Eton and Prebendary of Worcester, who was killed out hunting when trying a newly purchased horse with the King's hounds in 1786, though a man of high character, unspoiled by his friendship with the Duke of Grafton, and marked out for higher preferment by Archbishop Cornwallis, can hardly claim a place in any list of Divines.

This was, perhaps, the inevitable result of that decay of interest in Theology which is characteristic of the Hanoverian period. But something may have been due to the fact that no pressure seems to have been put on the Fellows to study Theology. Throughout the eighteenth century "diversions" continue to be recorded; but they are all to Medicine, or Law, or Astronomy. The Statute requiring the bulk of the Society to study Divinity and take Holy Orders remained, indeed; but no Provost seems to have made an effort to enforce it.

CHAPTER XVI

THE AGE OF SIMEON

CHARLES SIMEON's life at King's covers a period of fifty-seven years, and during a great part of that time he was the most notable man in the College. He was admitted a Scholar in January 1779, and attended lectures on Aristotle's Ethics and Pearson on the Creed. The former course was especially needed, for though he was already a good Latin scholar, he had learned but little Greek at Eton. Cooke was then Provost, and in Simeon's first term sent him word that in three weeks' time there would be a celebration of the Holy Communion in Chapel and that he must take part in it. Such was the College rule, which, no doubt, often hardened men into formalism ; but in Simeon's case it was the beginning of a real religious life ; and though he complains of the irreverence with which the Chapel services were performed, yet he found in them, as an Undergraduate, the spiritual food which he needed. Not content with his own conversion, he collected a small congregation of bedmakers in his rooms ; and when he was at home, he persuaded his brothers and the servants to join in family prayers. Such was the humble beginning of a life-long ministry. Within a few years he was acting as a volunteer curate at St. Edward's, where his preaching attracted such crowds that the overworked clerk hailed the Vicar's return with joy, saying, " Oh, sir, I am so glad you are come: now we shall have some room ! " A year later Simeon began the great work of his life as Minister of Trinity Church, where more than a century earlier, another Kingsman, Provost Whichcote, had exercised so wide and wholesome an influence.

Within his own College Simeon found but little sympathy, and was quite surprised when a brother Fellow ventured to walk with him for a quarter of an hour on the grass plot before Clare Hall. Perhaps he exaggerated the antagonism which others felt; at any rate, he held College office from 1788 to 1798, and for two years was Vice-Provost. A friend, writing to him in 1789, observes that his influence in the College was evidently increasing, and that the Provost was inclined to co-operate with him in reforming the College. In 1791, when, with Dr. Glynn's help he had, as Vice-Provost, sent out of residence a Fellow senior to himself for scandalous conduct, Provost Cooke wrote that " yourself and Dr. Glynn will ever have my hearty thanks for your prudent and spirited conduct." A reference has already been made to his first sermon at St. Mary's. There was a crowd of Undergraduates, many of whom evidently meant to disturb and annoy the preacher. However, he very soon had complete command of his audience; although the prejudices of the time were shewn, when he remained for some time on his knees after the benediction, by one man saying to another, " Just look at that hypocrite ! what a time he goes on praying ! " On the other hand, as two men were leaving the church, one said to the other, " Well, Simeon is no fool, however ! " " Fool ! " replied his companion, " did you ever hear such a sermon before ? "

In order to secure more time for prayer and study, Simeon formed the habit of rising at 4 A.M.; not, however, without an effort, but he paid a fine of 2s. 6d. to his bedmaker if he failed to get up; and when that proved an insufficient stimulus, he determined, if he was late again, to walk down to the Cam and throw a guinea into the water; and on one occasion he actually did this. One other habit he had, which no doubt found more sympathy with his neighbours. He was very fond of riding; and when George Corrie entered the University in 1813 with a letter of introduction to Simeon, the writer said, "When you call, he will probably be either in the stable with his horses, or by the sick-beds of his parishioners." He might have inherited a considerable fortune from his brother Edward, who died in 1814, but he declined to receive more than a legacy of £15,000, the interest of which he devoted towards charitable objects which his brother had supported; and, after making this disposition of his money, he considered himself justified in retaining his Fellowship, the loss of which would have seemed to him a desertion of the post of duty. Two years before this he had settled in the rooms in which he eventually died.

The second Provost of Simeon's time was Humphrey Sumner, son of John Sumner, the former Provost. Humphrey was Rector of Dunton in Essex, at the time of his promotion in 1797; and he received the thanks of the College in the following year for resigning this living. Apparently it was a novelty for a Provost to be contented with the emoluments and duties of a single office. Sumner, however, may have had special reasons for resigning, as he was a victim to gout, and so deaf that he never knew whether he was speaking in a high or low tone. Ben Drury, an impertinent young fellow of his own College, used to make the most uncomplimentary remarks to him in the manner of a person conversing on ordinary topics; and the Provost, quite unconscious of what was really said, received these remarks with the blandest courtesy. One of the Scholars, Scrope Davies, treated the Provost no better. A game hamper was found one morning hung on the handle of the Lodge door, directed to the Provost with "Mr. Scrope Davies's compliments." In those days, when game could not be bought, such a present was particularly acceptable; but the hamper, when opened, was found to contain a dead cat and even less attractive objects. Of course Scrope Davies was convened; but he coolly maintained that, if he had sent the hamper, his own name was the last which he would have chosen to attach to it; and so he escaped.

There is some reason to think that the first years of Sumner's Provostship were marked by a deterioration in discipline. *The Public Advertiser* for July 19, 1798, quotes from "a Morning Paper the following statement of the origin of the existing disputes between the Provost and Scholars of King's College, Cambridge."

"A number of Tradesmen in the town of Cambridge represented to the Provost of King's College that debts to a considerable amount had been incurred by the Scholars for various articles both of luxury and necessity, and that they were anxious these debts should be liquidated. The Provost consulted the Vice-Provost, Bursars, and Fellows on the subject, when it was unanimously agreed, as an act of justice, that a part of the boys' emoluments should be appropriated towards the payment. This resolution so

P

irritated them, that they pulled up the pavement and broke all the windows in the Old Court, destroyed the Convention Bell, and committed various other acts of violence. The Provost, in consequence, ordered them to be detained in College during the whole of the vacation, or until they gave up the first aggressors. The latter they refused. Dr. Goodall, of Eton, happening to be there, represented to the Scholars the heinousness of the offence, and advised them to repair every injury, and afterwards go in a body to the Provost, express their contrition, and solicit forgiveness ; which they very reluctantly did. The Provost told them he should take one fortnight to consider of it, and here the matter rests for the present. Yesterday the fortnight expired, when the boys expected to be liberated."

There is no allusion to this affair in the College records, and perhaps the story is mythical. But there were certainly some very troublesome Undergraduates in residence at this time ; and one Scholar had to be placed in temporary confinement as a lunatic. Yet at this very time there was in residence a Scholar, John Bird Sumner, who lived to be the one Archbishop of Canterbury educated at King's College. He gained some distinction at the University, and afterwards made a name for himself as a writer of Evangelical Theology. As Bishop of Chester, 1828–48, he was most energetic in providing more churches and schools in his diocese ; as Archbishop, though appointed by the Duke of Wellington, he supported the Whigs on the questions of Roman Catholic Emancipation and Parliamentary Reform ; and he also took the side of "comprehension" in the Hampden and Gorham controversies. The fiery Bishop Phillpotts protested against the Archbishop's "heresy"; and it was not till Sumner lay dying in 1862 that the charge was withdrawn. The portrait of the Archbishop by Eddis, in the College Hall, represents a benevolent and dignified gentleman ; but there is not much sign of intellectual force, or of statesmanlike firmness. Bishop Wilberforce described a speech of Sumner's as "like himself, good, gentle, loving, and weak."

J. B. Sumner had become a Fellow in 1801 ; and five years afterwards there arrived at King's a group of Scholars who reflected no less credit on their College. For in 1806 Thomas Rennell, Stratford Canning, and John Lonsdale were admitted; and, a little later, Edward Craven Hawtrey and John Patteson. Canning's stay, as a Scholar, was short, as he joined the diplomatic service in 1807 ; he then became a Fellow-Commoner hoping to come back and keep the terms necessary for a degree. A letter from Rennell tells him that the Provost and one or two of the Fellows were anxious to keep him if possible :

"as for the rest of the College, they know little and care less about the matter. The Scholars gaped a little on being told that you were gone into 'foreign parts' ; but even that, as well as every other idea, is now totally defaced from their minds, and they grunt on in their ancient piggish apathy."

Eventually, in 1812, Canning received a M.A. degree, by royal mandate. He describes his undergraduate life as one

"of pleasant monotony, in which an easy amount of study was mingled with healthy exercise and social enjoyments suited to the character of the place and its youthful occupants. I had friends or at least acquaintances in other Colleges besides my own ; but I had nothing to do with

horses, carriages, or boats.   Lectures and rare compositions
were the only demands upon our time."

He volunteered to study Mathematics, and nearly gave
them up in despair.   But he belonged to what he calls
a "spouting club," in which Lord Palmerston had made
his first flight of oratory.

His bedmaker, Mrs. Harradine, called him a nice
"still stiddy man," and John Lonsdale, who left Eton a
few months later, writes to him in the warmest terms,
and quotes Goodall, the Headmaster, as saying that no
boy ever left the school with so good a character from
all persons and all ages.   This quiet exterior concealed
a will of iron.   In 1810 he was left alone at Constanti-
nople, with no ambassador to guide him and no instruc-
tions from home, to re-establish English influence and
to make a peace between Russia and the Porte.   The
skill and courage with which he accomplished both
these purposes, and finally, May 28, 1812, brought
about the Treaty of Bucharest, thereby setting free a
Russian army to act against Napoleon at the critical
moment, are astonishing in so young a man.   Canning's
achievements in diplomacy at the age of twenty-four
may well be compared with Pitt's Premiership at the
same age.   The Duke of Wellington called it the
"most important service that ever fell to the lot of any
individual to perform."   He, indeed, attributed it to his
own brother, who was then Foreign Minister.   In
reality the Foreign Office just then was "fast asleep"
under Lord Wellesley, and the most important despatch
which Canning received from him related to some
classical MSS. supposed to be concealed in the Seraglio.
The fate of nations was left to the care of the Cambridge
Undergraduate.   The influence which Stratford Canning

exercised over the Porte at the time of the Crimean
War was perhaps more complete, but it did not achieve
greater results, and is not so wonderful in a fully
accredited Ambassador as it was in an inexperienced
Attaché. A portrait of him, as Lord Stratford de
Redcliffe, when he was nearly ninety years old, painted
by H. Herkomer and now in the College Hall, gives
some notion of the handsome countenance and piercing
eye which no doubt helped to impress the Oriental mind.

John Lonsdale came from Eton with a great reputation as a Latin Scholar, which he maintained at
Cambridge by gaining a University Scholarship. Indeed, the Latin verses, which he wrote when a boy of
fifteen, might excite the envy of a generation with whom
the composition of original Latin verse has become
almost a lost art. But he was more than a scholar.
Gunning, who at any rate had a long experience on
which to found his judgment, says of Lonsdale that he

" kept his exercises in the Divinity School in a manner
superior to any other person I ever listened to. He discovered a fallacy in an argument quicker than any other
man I ever met, discussed each syllogism on its own merits,
and when he arrived at the end he disposed of the argument in the fewest possible words, but so completely that
the opponent felt himself incapable of rejoining."

In the last year of his life the same quality of intellectual
thoroughness was noticed by a gentleman who, having
heard the Bishop's address to the Church Congress at
Wolverhampton, observed, " That's all ; there is nothing
more to be said."

Lonsdale became Rector of St. George's, Bloomsbury,
and Preacher at Lincoln's Inn. In 1840 the Fellows of
Eton elected him as their Provost ; but, finding that

his friend Hodgson was the nominee of the Crown, he retired. Three years later, he became Bishop of Lichfield, where he won the reputation of being the best Bishop that the diocese had ever had; being a model of justice, kindness, humility, and shrewd sense. He belonged to no party, but managed to keep peace in a stormy time, and to do a great work in his diocese in the way of Church extension. When the see of Canterbury was vacant in 1848, it was believed that Lonsdale would be Archbishop Howley's successor. But Lord John Russell was bent on putting down Puseyism, and thought he could do this by appointing a thorough-going Evangelical. Had Sir Robert Peel still been in power, a different choice would probably have been made. Lonsdale, however, if a High Churchman at all, was one of a very moderate type. His relations with Nonconformists may be inferred from the fact that the Independent Minister of Eccleshall, where the Episcopal Palace then was, not only attended the Bishop's funeral, but also put his own Chapel into mourning. It may be doubted whether a better scholar than Lonsdale, or a more faultless character, was ever trained in King Henry's two Foundations. Certainly the year 1806, which saw two such men as Canning and Lonsdale admitted to the College, was an "annus mirabilis" for King's.

Thomas Rennell, of the same year, was also a man of brilliant promise as a scholar and theologian, but he died at the age of thirty-seven. Gunning, however, who had kept an Act against him in 1822, on "the necessity of a connection between Church and State," was of opinion that "though he abounded in eloquence yet in reasoning he was very defective." But he does not hesitate to call him a man of undoubted talents and prodigious acquirements.

Francis Hodgson was some years senior to this remarkable trio, and acted as Tutor, 1808–14. When Provost Sumner offered him the post, he found that he was expected to lecture on Pearson and Locke. For the latter he wished to substitute some literary topic; observing that his own Tutor, Lloyd, who had studied Locke deeply, had failed to make his lectures either interesting or intelligible. However, he had to give way. Hodgson's opinion of his own College was not very favourable:

"Our having all been at the same school certainly deadened emulation by placing us at that rank in Cambridge, in which we relatively stood at Eton. Neither had we any public honours to contend for; and ambition too often expired in indolence."

He himself was far from indolent either in mind or body. His spare time was spent in writing reviews and poetry, besides an annual examination at Rugby. More than once he walked from Cambridge to London, and thought nothing of walking from London to Eton. What would he not have accomplished with a bicycle! His advice to Lonsdale, not to reside at King's, is given in a poetic form:

> " But haste to life ! no glorious scope
>   Can in these walls be found ;
>   The grave of disappointed Hope,
>   Ambition's early bound.
>   Here indolence with baneful frost
>   Shall nip the vernal bloom,
>   Here shame shall mourn o'er glory lost,
>   And Vice await its doom."

Perhaps Juvenal, whom he had already translated in 1807, inspired him with a somewhat pessimistic view of his neighbours.

During his residence as Tutor he became an intimate friend of Lord Byron, and tried to win him back from scepticism. Harness gives an account of a visit to Newstead in 1811, when conversations were held which, after fifty years, he could not recall " without a deep feeling of admiration for the judicious zeal and affectionate earnestness which Dr. Hodgson evinced in his advocacy of the truth." At a later time he tried to reconcile Byron with his wife ; he was more successful in preventing a duel between his friend and Moore.

Contemporary with Hodgson at King's was Harry Drury, for forty-one years a Harrow master, great both as a teacher and ruler of boys; and in 1820 having ninety pupils out of the 250 then in the school. Lord Byron had been his pupil, and was attached to him. Drury was a collector of Greek books and MSS., and "a great walker with an utter contempt for an umbrella."

In 1809 a controversy of some importance arose at King's. There had been a disagreement between the College and the tenant of their tithes at Prescot in Lancashire, the result of which was that no fine was paid and money for dividends ran short. Accordingly in November 1808, a vote had been passed to borrow £9000 stock from the Chest Fund, which could only be used for defending law suits or enlarging the College property. A former Fellow, Henry Dampier, acting with the concurrence of another old Kingsman, Sir J. Mansfield, Chief Justice of the Common Pleas, appealed to the Visitor against the action of the

College; and the Visitor (Bishop Tomline) decided
that the Fellows must refund the four dividends which
they had received, and restore to the Chest Fund both
principal and interest. In the course of his appeal
Mr. Dampier took occasion to object to the policy
which he attributed to the College of getting rid of
beneficial leases and copyholds.

" I have heard from good authority that this is but the
beginning of an extensive system : that by this sort of
Loan all the estates of the College are to be brought into
hand and let at a Rack Rent. I very much doubt whether
the projectors of this plan are aware of the vigilance and
attention necessary to look after a large and dispersed
Real property so let. The attention of the Fellows would
be diverted to pursuits very different from those for which
the College was founded and is supported."

But the College were wiser in this particular than
Mr. Dampier. Finding that their copyhold estates let
on lives were valued at £12,000 a year but only brought
in £2000, they determined in 1812 that, where two out
of three lives had dropped, no renewal should be
granted ; and thus they began a reform which is hardly
yet completed.

There was also a prospect of increased revenue from
another cause. As early as 1798 the College had offered
easy terms to their tenants at Grantchester and Coton,
if they would bear the cost of obtaining an Act of
Parliament for "dividing and allotting the open and
commonable fields, commonable land and waste grounds
within the parishes of Grantchester and Coton." Other
enclosures had since then taken place, including the one
which altered the whole character of the land lying

immediately to the west of Cambridge, and ultimately
provided Fellows of Colleges with gardens, and Undergraduates with cricket grounds.

It was left, however, to a later generation to deal
with the beneficial leases. That system, which made
the tenant almost joint owner with the landlord, was
not ill suited to a time when College circuits could only
be made on horseback; especially if, as was the case
with King's College, a large proportion of the property
lay at a distance of 100 or even 200 miles. The coming
of railways made it possible for Colleges to undertake
the responsibilities and receive the profits of a modern
landowner; and, though backward in their educational
policy, King's was one of the foremost Colleges to venture on financial reform. The change could not be
made without some temporary sacrifice; although an
Act of Parliament enabled the College to borrow money
in lieu of the fines which they had surrendered, and the
discovery on their eastern counties estates of a fossil
called Coprolites, which made a valuable manure, helped
to furnish them with capital for carrying out improvements only too sure to be necessary on the expiry of a
long beneficial lease. It would seem that for the last
two centuries the College had managed its estates
wisely; at least if we may judge by the steady increase
of dividends, and by the large sums always forthcoming
to be spent on repairs and on additions to the College
buildings. In two respects the College must always
have been an easy landlord. Game preserving did not
diminish the farmer's profits; and if a right of sporting
was nominally reserved to the College, this amounted
to little more than an occasional friendly visit to the
tenant. At other times the farmer probably shot or

trapped as he pleased. Nor is there any record of the
College attempting to influence the politics of the
tenants. The College, if not always an improving, has
never been an interfering landlord.

In the last year of Provost Sumner's life, 1813, the
College embarked on two adventures, neither of which
turned out successful. They petitioned the Lords of
the Treasury to grant them a " close " at Grantchester,
which had belonged to a man named Kidman. Kidman
had formerly robbed the College of " many hundred
pounds of plate and medals," and so was enabled to
purchase the property, which he now forfeited for
felony. The College, as Lords of the Manor, claimed
a right to the forfeiture, under an Act passed in the
reign of Henry VI. At the same time they complained
that since 1700 they had been defrauded of two tuns of
Gascony wine, which Henry VI. had granted annually,
and instead of which a compensation in money had
afterwards been paid. My Lords referred them to the
Law Courts to make good their claims ; and nothing
more seems to have been attempted.

Towards the end of the same year they raised an
objection to the custom by which Fellows of Eton held
Livings. This was contrary to the Eton Statutes and
to the oath taken by Fellows that they would not make
use of any dispensation exempting them from observance
of the Statutes. Such a dispensation had been granted
by Queen Elizabeth in 1566,

" because we certainly perceive the price meet for maintenance of hospitality and living to be far greater at this
day, than in former times, and that it is not inconvenient
for you to have some cures abroad, where you may both
teach and inform our subjects in their duties to God and us."

The controversy went on for some time, till the
Visitor decided, on April 8, 1816, that the oath taken
by the Eton Fellows did not debar them from profiting
by Elizabeth's dispensation. The apparent impertinence
of one College interfering with the practice of another
is to be explained by the intimate connection between
the two. The Kingsmen held that they had a claim
on the Eton Fellowships, and were injured by any
diminution in the number of vacancies, and the succession was certain to be more rapid, if on taking a
Living every Fellow of Eton vacated his Fellowship.
Nor was this their first protest. As early as 1636 they
had preferred complaints before Archbishop Laud, that
aliens were admitted to Eton Fellowships, that the
Statutable number of Fellowships was not maintained,
and that the Scholars were stinted in food and clothing
in order that the revenues might be divided among a
few Fellows. Laud did something to satisfy the Kingsmen, by deciding that five out of seven Fellowships
should be reserved for members of their College, and
this settlement was confirmed after the Restoration.

A case of a different kind had been referred to the
Visitor ten years before the appeal against Eton. A
clerical Fellow, named Bearblock, had long lived in
Essex with some one who passed as his wife and was
treated as such by their neighbours. At last his right
to a Fellowship was challenged, and he was ejected. The
Visitor had to decide whether unanimity was necessary
for this purpose. He decided that it was not, and at
the same time administed a severe rebuke to the
single Fellow who had ventured to maintain that Bearblock's case was not provided for by the Statutes. More
than thirty years later, two similar cases occurred. A

Mr. Cliffe Hatch, who had lived first at Brecknock and then at Worplesdon in Surrey, was deprived of his Fellowship; the accuser in this case being Sir F. Wetherall, who claimed the vacancy for his grandson, a boy at Eton.

In the case of Mr. Hunt, a resident Fellow, it was decided by a majority at a small meeting, that there were not sufficient grounds for summoning him before the College. It seems probable that the Fellows were determined not to condemn a man, who had lived among them for many years, and had made himself useful as a Bursar of the College.

CHAPTER XVII

THE END OF OLD COURT

On Sumner's death, Thomas Rennell, Dean of Winchester, father of the Scholar of 1806, was a candidate for the Provostship, and wrote to ask for Hodgson's support, March 26, 1814 :—

"I fear you will think me very presumptuous, in placing myself before you as candidate for the succession to the Provostship. But as I thought I discerned, when I had the happiness of seeing you, that a large portion of the milk of human kindness was combined with your high talents and attainments, I trust that whatever may be the part you take in this contest you will receive with candour my application for your support. I can only add that, if by the kindness of my friends I should succeed, my residence upon my post would be constant."

The applicant had a great reputation as a scholar and preacher, and in 1794 had preached a Commencement Sermon on the French Revolution before Pitt, which had gained him the Mastership of the Temple. It seems strange that a Dean of Winchester should condescend to apply for the Headship of a College, and also that he should think it necessary to promise that he would reside. But as yet, perhaps, it could not be taken for granted that Sumner's example, in resigning his Living, would be followed by his successors.

The electors, however, preferred George Thackeray, a member of a family well known at Eton and King's. His grandfather, Thomas, had been a strong candidate for the Provostship in 1743, and it was thought that his uncle, Elias Thackeray, might have been elected instead of Cooke in 1772 if he had offered himself as a candidate. The father of George Thackeray was a doctor at Windsor, who died young, and the son would never have become even a Scholar at King's if George III. had not persuaded an old Fellow who resided at Windsor to resign in time to create a vacancy just before the election of 1797.

Thackeray soon returned to Eton as a Master, and in a few more years became Lower Master as well as Chaplain in Ordinary to the King. Elected Provost at the early age of thirty-seven, he might reasonably have been expected to become a prominent figure in the University, but his activity was much impaired by bad health. He had met with an accident at a cricket match when he was an undergraduate, the ball hitting his side and injuring him so much that he was not expected to recover, and the effect on his health was permanent. Indeed, a tradition, preserved by the oldest Kingsman now living, Mr. Tucker, says that the Fellows were anxious to elect Ben Drury, a popular but improvident Eton Master, but the vacancy came too soon. Drury was too young, or there was some other difficulty at the moment, and in electing Thackeray they thought they were putting in some one who could not live more than a few years. However, as Mr. Tucker writes: "That was in 1815. I saw him placidly looking into the shops in the main street of Cheltenham in 1845— and Provost still."

Besides want of health, another misfortune which helped to depress his spirits was the loss of his wife, who died in 1818, leaving him an only daughter. The daughter was born in a house in Wimpole Street, where Mrs. Thackeray was attended by Sir Richard Croft, whose mind was unhinged by his recent failure in the case of Princess Charlotte; and it was in this house that the unfortunate surgeon shot himself, perhaps from a presentiment that a second failure was imminent.

Provost Thackeray's favourite pursuits were the study of Shakespeare and of Natural History; but he also knew by heart whole poems of Walter Scott; and those who were admitted to the hospitality of the Lodge, where his sister-in-law, Miss Cottin, lived and acted as mistress, found the Provost a master of the art of conversation. The well-known scholar, Dr. Parr, was a frequent visitor, and observed: "There are two things, Mr. Provost, that I always enjoy here—roast pig, and the drive to the Gogmagog Hills in your coach and four."

Like most of his family, he was a handsome man, and he seems to have concealed under a rather stiff manner a really kind heart, for it is said that, if a young Fellow was out of health and needed change of air, the Provost would supply him with the necessary funds.

The habits of those days, however, did not encourage much intercourse between Heads and Undergraduates, and an old Kingsman writes:

"We seldom saw him excepting when he occasionally appeared in Chapel on a week day, and when the news spread rapidly through the rooms that white ties were indispensable. We appeared at the Lodge after examinations, but there was very little sympathy between the

Head and the junior members, or consciousness on our side that we were cared for—certainly there was no hospitality shewn."

Another old Kingsman describes his first experience of a visit at the Lodge, at the end of Term, when prizes in books or in money for regular attendance at Chapel were awarded to some; and he himself received a reprimand for mispronouncing the name "Tychicus" in reading a lesson for the first time. There is no doubt that Thackeray could be severe on occasion. Once in a dispute at a meeting, when a Bursar was rude enough to say to him, "Ah! Pontius Pilate was a Provost," he replied, "True, Mr. H., and Judas Iscariot was a Bursar." His cousin, the novelist, went to call on him in 1850, and found him "perfectly healthy, handsome, stupid and happy, and he isn't a bit changed in twenty years." But, at seventy-three years of age, a man has some right to be stupid, and, as he died within a few months, perhaps there was some mistake about the health.

The election to the Provostship in 1814 was not the only occasion on which the houses of Thackeray and Rennell were opposed to each other. Martin Thackeray, a cousin of the Provost, had been elected annually to some College office from 1815 to 1826, and in this last year was made Vice-Provost. A junior Fellow, George Rennell, in the following autumn appealed to the Visitor and complained " that so much College money bestowed in so many appointments on one individual could not be contemplated by the Founder "; and that younger members had been discouraged from residing in College and becoming serviceable to its interests by this " heaping office and emolument on certain individuals as

Q

private friendship, interest, or caprice afford a cause or direct the will of the Provost." Whereupon, at a meeting on November 7, 1827, the nine Seniors present declared that "the Reflection cast upon the Provost was utterly without foundation," and expressed their regret that the Visitor, in his answer to the appeal, had ignored, instead of censuring, " so highly objectionable a clause." * In November of the following year, 1828, a strenuous effort was made to oust Martin Thackeray from the Vice-Provostship, and when that failed, to prevent Charles Simeon, who was a warm supporter of Martin Thackeray, from being elected Dean. There were frequent adjournments, and the list of officers was not completed till January 31, 1829.

Martin Thackeray is highly praised by Gunning, who tells us that Thackeray was a great advocate for those reforms in the examination of the Eton boys, " which were for a long period strenuously resisted by the Provost, by Goodall, and by Keate." Thackeray was more successful in reforms within his own province. Before his time, when Fellows had friends to visit, they used to give a round of dinners of the most expensive kind; but

" he introduced such a system of neatness and elegance at the table over which he presided, that the Fellows took their friends into Hall, and then adjourned to their own rooms for wine and dessert."

It was not that he himself cared for good living, for he always dined off mutton and rice pudding. Gunning tells us that at a contested election for the county

* Mr. Tucker's reminiscences represent George Rennell's character in a more favourable light. See p. 248.

Thackeray refused to canvass, on behalf of a friend, for the vote of a tradesman largely employed by the College, thinking it unfair to put any pressure on him. He was, in short, a very highminded man, impatient of what he thought to be abuses, and somewhat intolerant of men who adopted a low standard. He could appreciate Simeon, but most of the Seniors seemed to him men " with little disposition to do anything for the Founder, who had done so much for them."

In 1817 the Butt Close controversy was re-opened by the College proposing to resume possession of the part of the Close hitherto let to Clare College. However, it was eventually arranged that Clare should become proprietors of the part which they occupied, and should surrender to King's not only a piece of ground at the north-west corner of the Chapel, but also the White Horse Inn and other houses between King's Lane and the Bull Hotel; and this settlement was ratified by Act of Parliament.

During the next few years various alterations were made in the College buildings and grounds. Iron gates were put up at the west door of the Chapel, and under the north and south Porches; the old Clock and Penthouse at the north-east corner were removed, and a plantation was made on the south side of the College field across the Cam. The College stables were also removed to their present position. Even more conspicuous an alteration than these was the building of a new bridge. A surveyor having reported that the old one was likely to fall into the river, it was determined, September 30, 1818, that a new bridge of stone should be placed in a line with the south walk, and the old walk across the " Quarters " changed into two " mounds," and some of the trees cut down. At the same time ivy and trees were planted under Clare wall. The cost of these improvements was naturally more than had been anticipated; and Simeon generously gave £700 to help the College. Whether the College really needed the help is doubtful. In 1817 they gave up their feast on March 25, " owing to the present distressed state of the country," and contributed 40 guineas for the relief of the poor; and in the years which follow there are frequent instances of abatements of rent owing to agricultural distress; but in 1818 they were able to vote no less than 11 dividends—*i.e.*, to each senior £330, and £220 to each M.A. Fellow ; and ten years later it was ordered that all Tenants, who failed to pay their rent and fines within three months after they became due, should be charged 5 per cent., a penalty which it certainly would not be possible to exact at the present day. Moreover, they were about to embark on the largest building operation known since the foundation of the College. There may sometimes have been difficulty about the actual specie needed for immediate use ; and on December 14, 1825, the College accepted an offer from Simeon to bring down from London £750 in cash and notes from Messrs. Hoare for the ensuing quarterage. It does not appear whether Simeon travelled by coach, or whether he rode from town with the money packed in his saddle-bags.

The year 1822 is an important epoch in the history of the College buildings. The old Court no longer satisfied the requirements of the age. It must have been gloomy and sunless, as Elias Thackeray complained in 1790, when he had to write an epigram for some slight College offence :

" Mirarisne, meæ si tardum forte Camœnæ
　　Ingenium, et votis absit Apollo meis ?
Unde etenim has veniat nobis ille æquus in ædes,
　　Quas numquam roseo conspicit ore, Deus ? "

The habits too of those who lived in the old Court
were more picturesque than academical. Mr. Tucker,
who afterwards held the College Rectory of Dunton in
Essex and is still living, has left us a graphic account of
his own experiences in 1822–25. In his time the upper
floor was no longer used except for lumber-rooms; a
Freshman began life on the ground floor and was afterwards promoted to the floor above, where the rooms
were larger and better lighted, besides being panelled in
oak. One article of furniture is said to have passed on
from tenant to tenant—viz., the curtains, which changed
their colour under the dyer's hands, as well as their
price, but remained as fixtures for all time.

It was the duty of the Scholar who lived immediately
above the Freshman to take him in hand and initiate
him in his duties. For a week or more the "Nib"
hardly dared to go out of sight of his "Chum." Tucker
describes the ample repast given him, by way of
welcome, by his chum, John Wilder; and those who
knew the late Vice-Provost of Eton in after days will
readily believe that the hospitality was unstinted.

The Court itself was

" wholly unpaved, rough-gravelled, and rather grotesque
under its ancient and modern look ; with its bricklayer's
white-sided schools; tiled Hall, and red-bricked wall,
screening the lower side of the modern kitchens. The
Hall was moderate in size and of no style, panelled and
painted, with a central stove. It had five tables; four for

dining, the fifth for hats and caps. Always very popular and deservedly on Feast Days."

"Most of us," Mr. Tucker writes, "had dogs. Dogs and King's were in a manner identical. None of us ever went a single step out of College in cap or gown. Dog, top-hat, and walking-stick. Why not? we had nothing to do beyond a Greek or English Lecture at 11,—not always that; and at no time over long. It was little more than a distraction. To be sure we had Chapel at 8,—our great grievance,—as no Chapels were allowed us; and it was so monotonous to get up every morning at 8. The authorities had no doubt felt this, and had provided a relief. It was in the form of a Latin epigram of four lines, in which utter grief was usually expressed at the power of sleep, and the regret which must be felt by the Dean at our absence. The same epigram was sufficient for the whole three years of residence. In the fervour of a first Term I had composed two,—which were submitted alternately with the regularity of a loom.

"It may be seen, as I have already said, that taking it as a whole we had a good deal of leisure; and that after the strain of Lecture we had only to think of our constitutions in the Madingly, Grantchester, Gogmagog and other roads; or quietly to saunter into Deighton's, and look at his books; or to read the morning papers in the Union until lunch time between 1 and 2. Stilton was nearly universal in the book-case cupboard, supplemented with ale and bread from the Buttery. Some preferred a chop in the Kitchen, hardly off the gridiron with potato from the steam,—which, considering that Hall was at 4, presumed an unusual vitality.

"But these are trifles. In the summer of my first year, Maturin, afterwards Vicar of Ringwood, organised an instrumental Band of Kingsmen and others. Some dozen or so of players with Band instruments, formed a circle in the midst of Old Court, Maturin, a very fair violinist, stood at their head as conductor and leader. The programme chiefly from overtures. Bishop's Guy Mannering was a favourite, and if I remember rightly Rossini's William Tell. They rehearsed in Maturin's rooms, and played in the Court remarkably well. No one was invited; but the strains were full and sonorous,—waving afar; and many came within the iron gates to listen. Vice Provost, Deans and Tutors took not the slightest notice;—perhaps they were musical."

It so happened that just about this time a real musical genius was a member of the Society. This was William Sterndale Bennett, who from 1824–26 was a King's Chorister, but at the early age of ten was transplanted to the London Academy of Music.

Old Court, however, was, as Mr. Tucker tell us,

" not always harmonious. Very noisy sometimes; roughish games after a sort, with lots of small College loafers intermixed; not always best behaved; mostly old oppidans with much freedom of speech among themselves. Occasionally a casement from the Schools would open, and a voice protest; ' Non possumus procedere propter '—that ' Propter' would be the last word heard. Apologies were loudly shouted back in the doggiest of Latin,—and the window would shut with a snap."

The Lectures which Mr. Tucker had to attend were either English or Greek. The former were given by the Vice-Provost, and consisted of "Locke on the Understanding." They do not seem to have been taken very seriously by the Scholars; and the Lecturer did little more than read half sentences from the author and then ask one of his class for the conclusion of the sentence.

More interest was taken in a Lecture on Aristophanes given by Richard Byam, a great favourite; each of the class took the part of one of the "dramatis personæ" and construed in turn. On Sunday evenings at 6 P.M. the Vice-Provost lectured on the Greek Testament; but the preparation for this consisted in a wine party after Hall; and the results were not satisfactory.

There was one among the Fellows who wished to raise the standard of the teaching. This was George Rennell.

" On the vacancy of a Tutorship he applied for it. But unhappily he was a 'persona ingrata' to the Provost. The Provost hated change, and set his face firmly against any; and Rennell had been a reformer in a small way, of course an unsuccessful one. But he was not only a competent aspirant to the honour, but an only one. There was not a single resident at that time in the College whom the Provost could appoint; and turning a deaf ear to Rennell he proposed to substitute an out-College man.

" Rennell appealed to our Visitor, Kaye, Bishop of Lincoln and Master of Christ's. It was a novel application of the Visitor's powers; but a week's appeal to the Statutes might reasonably have been thought sufficient for a decision. Month after month passed. Rennell re-appealed. He was not to be foiled by delay. To no purpose. Oracle dumb. At last the climax came.

" The Bishop and the Provost were on most friendly terms, and the former accepted an invitation to dinner. One of his Fellows remonstrated with him for going while the Appeal was on as an indecency. The answer rumoured at the time was :—'I don't see why I should lose a good dinner because of the Appeal.' At all events the Bishop dined; and very soon afterwards the Appeal was dismissed; and an out-College Tutor appointed. One may feel for

Rennell; but the change as a principle was of infinite advantage to King's."

Although Mr. Tucker represents himself and his contemporaries as rather an idle set, yet he and a brother Kingsman, Best, gave up some time to the study of French, German, and Italian; the only available teacher of German being a young tobacconist in the Petty Cury. In fact, they were ready to learn whatever Cambridge was not prepared to teach.

It is evident from Mr. Tucker's account that some of the resident Fellows did not set a good example to their juniors. One of this class was Edward Pote, who though in full orders had long ceased from any clerical duties.

" He was to be seen throughout the year in strong, stout, white Russia ducks—mostly a little frayed at the heel; but—coat, always black, which had a degree of merit at a time when every one else had swallow-tailed coats of blue, green, olive, or various shades of brown with gilt buttons. He was a constant attendant in Hall except on shooting days, when he dined in his rooms. Never once in Chapel in my time, but invariable in the Old Court ' Combi.' He was a good shot; a thorough sportsman over King's lands and farms, and occasionally, like the Highlander, a little ' over the Border.' But he was a thoroughly fair sportsman, and a true lover of animals, as his outer room testified. There was in that neither carpet nor curtains; low, green Venetian blinds, as they were then called, shut in the windows. There was his dog, a setter, naturally enough in one corner. Then there were his magpie, or his jay—in short a petty menagerie of various kinds. The effect was such that a visitor made his way across to the inner room, or sanctum, as quickly as possible. That inner sanctum had a book case of cherished books ; a gridiron, and other culinary accompaniments for shooting days when too late for the Hall, under the Market-ministration of his Bed-maker.

"The writer not unfrequently went out shooting with him. One day as we were out two or three miles from Cambridge on unpreserved ground, he said to me, 'We must go a little to the right to such-and-such a church, as I have promised to take a funeral there at 3 o'clock.' We reached it in time, and stopped at the outer gate. 'Keep the dog and my gun,' quoth he. He leaned the gun by the gate ; tucked up his trousers into shorts ; went in ; performed the funeral ; came forth ; took up his gun ; patted doggie on the head, and we went on as before, shooting our way home."

Mr. Tucker also describes excursions to balls at Huntingdon and Bury, made in gig or tandem. Some former Scholar had managed to possess himself of a surreptitious key, which was always lent to the ball-goers. But even this seems to have been almost an unnecessary precaution ; for Mr. Tucker says, "We happily had no 'gates'; or if late arrivals were chronicled we never heard of it; no notice was taken." Perhaps a return to College at 4 or 5 A.M. would have been too much even for the tolerant Dons of those days.

Mr. Tucker has also something to say about wine parties and whist clubs ; and altogether the contrast between the actual life of his contemporaries and that prescribed in the Statutes is a glaring one, even when due allowance has been made for the inevitable change of habits in the course of three centuries and more. Nor is it surprising if the authorities thought it high time to transplant the Undergraduates, and give them the benefit of new surroundings. Accordingly architects were invited by advertisement to furnish plans and elevations for a new building ; and prizes of £300, £200, and £100 were offered for a competition which was to be anonymous. Only a week before the prizes were awarded the College decided to give the preference to a Gothic plan. On March 25, 1823, the first prize was awarded to Mr. William Wilkins, whose plan was then submitted to a Committee of Architects, two of them being Wyatt and Nash, and was altered in accordance with their suggestions. It was a year more before the contract with Stannard, a Norwich builder, was settled ; the estimate was £73,000, but the whole cost eventually amounted to £100,000. The stone used came from Ketton in Rutlandshire.

At the same time the Provost was empowered, after the building was erected, to make a contract for "Gothicizing" Gibbs's Building according to Wilkins's plan, and then for adding cloisters behind the screen. The original dimensions of the Court had to be somewhat curtailed, because the College failed to acquire Mr. Cory's house, which stood on the site now covered by Scott's Building. The College had done their best to come to terms with Mr. Cory ; and the latter had actually accepted an offer, which he afterwards repudiated. Leave was, however, obtained to divert the course of King's Lane, which formerly entered Trumpington Street, to the north of Mr. Cory's house. It was intended that at each end of the Screen there should be a gateway : that on the south to admit carriages, and the one on the north to be a dummy. This kind of mathematical symmetry was characteristic of Mr. Wilkins's

Gothic; and there were to have been two oriel windows
in the Hall, in addition to the two galleries and two
lanterns. The new kitchen, and therefore probably the
new Hall, was used for the first time on February 27,
1828.

Though the College failed in their dealings with Mr.
Cory, they were more successful with the University, to
whom, after a good deal of bargaining, they sold the old
Court for £12,000. This would not have gone far
towards paying their new bill; and, as a matter of fact,
it was applied for the purchase of landed property;
but a large sum was by this time accummulated in the
Chest Fund, and something was added by the sale of
trees, walls, and the gateway on the south of the
College. In January 1828, when the new buildings
were finished, the old Provost's Lodge was also pulled
down, and the materials sold.

The Lodge had undergone so many alterations,
especially in 1786, that it must have lost much of its
original character. Mr. Tucker describes it as a
"largish, dark-red brick, tiled house; many windows
broad; unsightly, but not uncommon. It had nothing
noticeable about it; it was like many old houses
scattered over the country;—mostly turned nowadays
into schools; conveying on the whole a strong idea of
dulness. As one looked at it and fancied, the idea
would come of darkish passages, and wide wooden
carved staircases. Nor would the looker's idea be far
wrong. The rooms to which we were at any time
admitted were low, large, and panelled. If I remember
right, it was separated from the Lawn by a low garden
wall and hedge, which ran down the whole side towards
the Lane, enclosing, as it went, the little bits of yards

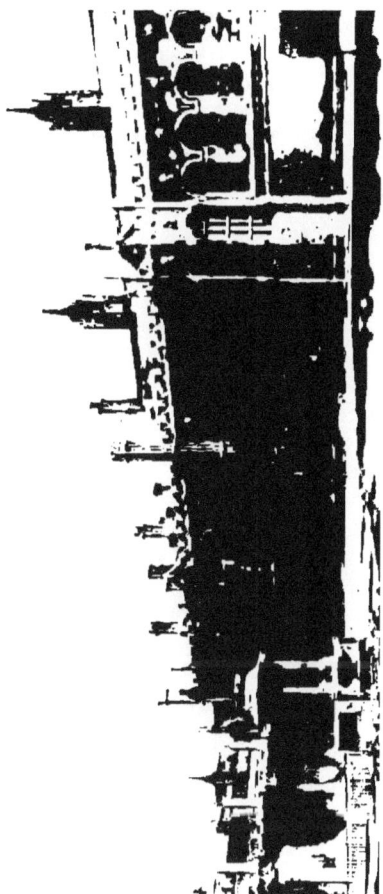

and gardens of the street cottages." Most of this must already have been swept away to make room for the Screen and Porter's Lodge.

The adoption of Wilkins's plan naturally led to the completion of the easternmost window on the south side of the Chapel, the lower half of which had been left a blank wall, in order that the eastern wing of the projected building might abut against it. In 1830 it was glazed in accordance with Mr. Hedgeland's design, the old glass being moved from the upper to the lower part of the window. At nearly the same time Lord de Dunstanville gave glass to fill the oriel window in the Hall.

The attention paid to material improvements had perhaps diminished that which discipline demanded. At any rate, for some years after the building was finished, the younger members of the College seem to have been even more disorderly than before. Early one summer morning half a dozen scholars broke into the old and now deserted Court, and lighted fires, to feed which they used wood from the old Combination Room. A little later, a Scholar and a young Fellow were in disgrace for intruding into a Meeting House in Green Street on a Sunday evening, and trying to provoke laughter in the congregation. One of them made matters worse by escaping from the Proctor without giving his name. The next year a Scholar named Price was actually deprived of his Scholarship, a very rare occurrence; but, besides knocking down and insulting a tradesman who had called to get his bill paid, he had been guilty of habitual misconduct. A man of older standing, Lionel Buller, elected a Fellow in 1821, began in 1832 to behave in so outrageous a manner as to make his sanity a matter of doubt. Ten years later, he was in prison for debt, having borrowed £300 (half of it in wine and brandy) on the security of his Fellowship; finally he was accused of fraud and perjury in 1848. The case came before the Master of the Rolls, who condemned Buller's conduct so severely that the College had no hesitation in depriving him of his Fellowship.

From these scenes it is a relief to turn to the closing days of Simeon. In his early life he had proved the truth of the proverb " Bene facere et male audire regium est "; but opposition had gradually died down. He had long had a devoted band of Undergraduate followers, larger (according to Bishop Charles Wordsworth) than that which followed Newman, and for a longer time. In 1831 as many as 120 Freshmen were introduced to him. It was more difficult to conciliate official opinion; yet even this had been done. In 1826 he received a visit from three Bishops, and he observes :

" In former years I should as soon have expected a visit from three crowned heads as from three persons wearing a mitre ; not because there was any want of condescension in them, but because my religious character affixed a stigma to my name."

And Lord Macaulay told his sister that Simeon's influence and authority extended to the most remote corners of England, and that his real sway over the Church was far greater than that of any Primate. Yet within his own College the old prejudice never quite disappeared. When Tucker was an Undergraduate, Simeon used to dine in the Bursars' parlour

with Leycester and Hinde. Hinde and Simeon did
not speak to each other. Leycester was Moderator.
Mr. Tucker, who tells us this, adds:

" I never once saw Simeon in our Chapel.   He was among
us—not of us; and during the six years I was at King's, he
never made a single convert or disciple."

He says, however, that Simeon's " manner was singularly
gentle; and he invariably received the greatest respect
from us."

The visits to Simeon's rooms, at the top of Gibbs's
Building, were almost looked upon as pilgrimages, and
the iron rail, fixed into the wall opposite the banisters
to help Simeon, which went by the name of the " Saint's
Rest," must have been useful to many other elderly
men on the way up or down these stairs.   In these
rooms, after a short illness, Simeon died.   He was
buried in the Ante Chapel on November 24, 1836.

Rowland Williams, who had just been admitted a
Scholar, tells us that:

" about 800 gownsmen, old and young, followed in procession, though the day was cold and wet.   As we entered
Chapel, the opening Anthem had a beautiful effect; our
Provost also read beautifully, and never perhaps were more
tears shed for a man by those in no way related to him."

The history has already reached a period within the
memory of men still living; Mr. Tucker is a witness to
the state of things during the third decade of the
century, and some reminiscences of the College, 1833
to 1836, are furnished by Bishop Abraham, a man
" quem nemo non parum amat, etiam si plus amare non
potest."

"We had," he writes, "two hours of Lectures every day, one hour for Classics and one for Mathematics. Our Tutor for both was the Rev. F. Isaacson, Fellow of St. John's, a *firstrate* Tutor in Classics and quite good enough for us in Algebra etc. As an *accurate* scholar he was, to my mind, unrivalled. Probably Shilleto was more of a genius; but Provost Goodford's great reputation for *reliable accuracy* was, I think, gained rather from Isaacson the College Tutor than from Shilleto his coach. The Divinity Lecturer was the Revd. Sir George Craufurd, a devout and refined gentleman, much respected by us all. I need hardly say that the great resource of all was cricket.* We were too few and too poor for boating. But cricket kept us from loafing in the summer; and occasional rides on horseback, or driving a trap, were our only resources in the way of amusement in the winter.

"Considering the lack of any incentive for study and distinction in the College or the University, it was fortunate that men had brought from Eton to Cambridge *independent tastes and resources;* and on looking back to my Undergraduate and B.A. Terms, the thing that strikes me most is the *versatility* of the men I knew there."

In illustration of this versatility, Bishop Abraham mentions W. W. Harvey, the editor of Irenæus; R. Barrett, a man of great learning and a skilful chess player, in spite of his being nearly blind; C. A. Wilkinson; Robert Latham, a pioneer in philology and also a physician; John Hibbert,

* At this time most of the cricketers of Cambridge came from a few great schools, Eton supplying a large proportion of them. Not long before Bishop Abraham's time, King's and University was an annual match; and in 1820 and 1821, the scores for which years happen to be preserved, each side in turn won a close match by one wicket.

"a philanthropist on a large scale, who used to open his grounds to the poor, and occasionally entertained them by hundreds, to the astonishment of the police ; for he maintained perfect order by means of his simple large-heartedness and joyous welcome to all ; "

lastly, George Williams,

"who was, I cannot deny, the boy of least intellectual mark at Eton, but who became, mainly by the encouragement and example of the good Charles Simeon, a man of very considerable literary eminence and personal influence for good."

It is impossible to compare the Bishop's account with that of Mr. Tucker without feeling that Wilkins's Building, or some other cause, had done something to change the tone of the College. Yet it will be seen from the next chapter that the old leaven had not entirely disappeared.

CHAPTER XVIII

THE CLOSE OF THE OLD REGIME

THE College does not seem to have indulged in any extravagant outburst of loyalty at the accession of Queen Victoria; but, in order to keep Coronation Day in June 1838, the College Tinman was ordered to provide the necessary lamps for a Crown and for the Queen's initials; and £10 was voted towards a dinner to be given to the poor. The scale on which these rejoicings were held contrasts with the sum of £500 voted in 1864 for the reception of the newly-married Prince and Princess of Wales. Greater liberality, however, was shown in helping Eton College with their new buildings, which have done so much for the improvement in the condition of the Collegers; the sum of £500 being voted on November 25, 1841, for that purpose. In August 1843 there was an extraordinary hailstorm in the Cambridge district, which did great damage to the crops; and in the following spring £300 was divided among the tenants who had suffered. Nor did the horrors of the Irish famine pass unnoticed, but a vote of £100 was passed for the " remote parishes of Ireland and Scotland."

During all these years the attention of the College was much occupied with the development of their property. In 1832–33 they purchased for £12,000 the estate of Troy on the Colne in Hertfordshire; and a few years later they added to their Grantchester property. The money for this last purchase came, in part, from the gifts of Mr. Davidson, one of the most munificent of our private benefactors; and in part from a bequest from Dr. Barnes, formerly Vice-Provost, whose appointment to be Master of Peterhouse was a surprise both to himself and to the members of his second College, but who never forgot what he called "the dear place of his education."

The Tithe Commutation Act of 1836 gave the College and their agents plenty of work in settling the amounts to be paid in future in the parishes in which they were interested, either as owners or payers of tithe. Railway legislation too was already in full progress; and it was no easy matter to decide whether this novelty should be welcomed or opposed; more often than not, the College seems to have resisted the invasion of their estates by the steam-engine. The tendency to enclose waste or open land had by no means ceased; and the College was ready enough to promote the policy of converting down into arable land, while the price of corn still remained high. Moreover, they had experienced the difficulty of keeping a firm hold on the land over which they had manorial rights. In parts of the country, especially in Dorsetshire, squatters had built themselves cottages and occupied plots of ground without any recognition of the landlord's right. Such appropriations were generally converted into legal tenures at the next manorial court held in the district, and the regular College circuits no doubt helped to prevent any permanent alienation of property; but to promote enclosures may have seemed the best way to stop encroachments.

At home a beginning had already been made to provide a new and larger garden, which should replace the one formerly enjoyed by the Fellows on the east side of the Cam. The enclosure of St. Giles's parish had given the College ground to the west of the road which runs through the "Backs"; and in October 1836 it was resolved that the nearest of these fields should be

"planted, and a walk made through the plantation; the interior to be secured by an iron fence and enjoyed by the Provost rent free : The Walk to be accessible to the Provost and his family, and also to Fellows by keys not transferable."

The Provost consented, on condition of three acres being left as pasture. The Fellows thus gained the privilege of walking round a shrubbery, and contemplating the four horses which drew the Provost's coach, as they grazed within the iron fence. But this did not satisfy them for long; and on March 20, 1851, Provost Okes having "consented to commute the Close now assigned to him for some other as soon as one becomes vacant," the original field was to be "laid out as a pleasure ground for the Fellows of the College." The field assigned to the Provost, as compensation for this loss, now forms part of the College cricket ground. Considerable skill was shown by the Bursar, Mr. Bumpsted, in laying out the Fellows' garden; and perhaps the only fault to be found in it is its remoteness from the College buildings, and the fact that it is practically inaccessible after dark.

The Chapel also called for a good deal of expenditure. The windows had often undergone some repair, but

more thorough attempt was now made to mend and
secure them, and Mr. Hedgeland was commissioned to
undertake the work, which went on at intervals for
about seven years. At last, in 1849, it was discovered
that Mr. Hedgeland was introducing new glass and
destroying the character of the windows, and his proceedings were stopped.

Ten years later the Organ had its turn; being
reconstructed by Hill at a cost of nearly £1000.
About the same amount had been spent on it at the
beginning of the century, the organ builder chiefly
employed at that time being Avery. It was in 1859
that the angels were placed on the organ case. Smaller
figures of a similar kind had formerly stood there, but
had been removed to make way for pinnacles.

But the roof of the Chapel now called for attention ;
and a report of Sir G. G. Scott's in 1860 showed that
both timber and lead must be renewed. It took several
years to complete the necessary repairs, which included
the addition of tie-rods, and the cost was £2715.

It was long since the College had given any trouble
to their Visitor; but the intervention of Bishop Kaye
was called for, in 1838, by a case which had occurred at
the Eton election. The Founder's Statutes did not
limit the number of boys to be examined for Scholarships at King's; but since 1660 it had been the custom
to admit to examination only the thirteen seniors in
standing, and twelve of these had in each year been
placed on the Indentures. As every boy who reached
the age of eighteen without being in this list had to
leave Eton, it might easily happen that a boy who
entered College rather late would fail to have any
opportunity of standing for a Scholarship ; especially

in days when the position of the boys during their
school career was seldom or never altered by the test of
examination. This was actually the case with William
Hardisty, who was excluded from the election trials in
July 1837 because he was not among the first thirteen
Collegers. The Visitor decided that Hardisty, though
already eighteen years of age, should be examined in
1838. He does not seem to have laid down any general
rule for the future ; but about this time the practice of
admitting to examination every boy who had reached his
seventeenth year must have begun. In the earlier years
of the century the examination had been a mere form.
No one was plucked, and there was no changing of
places. But in 1819 a rumour spread among the boys
that all this was to be altered, and two years later the
rumour was found to be true. The fact was that one
of the Posers, John Lucius Dampier, a barrister, had
determined to put an end to what he rightly thought
to be a scandal; and he had the support of his colleague
John Tomkyns. The latter was a man of varied experience, for he had served in the Peninsular War, he was
afterwards a barrister, and finally he held a College
Living. If, as we are assured on good authority, boys
had sometimes got to King's who never did a verse or a
theme of their own while at Eton, and who could not
construe ten lines of Virgil without a dictionary,
Dampier's reforms did not come too soon.

Some light is thrown on undergraduate life at King's
during the later years of Provost Thackeray by the
letters of two distinguished Kingsmen, Rowland
Williams and William Johnson. Williams was five
or six years senior to Johnson, being admitted Scholar
on November 11, 1836, just before Simeon's death.

He was not wholly satisfied with the state of things which he found there, and writes home :

"My greatest difficulty at King's will be to keep up religious feelings. A certain party in the College is such as to throw everything into extremes, and it is difficult to avoid being either a fanatic or a profligate."

Evidently Simeon had failed to create a school in which the more intellectual men could feel themselves at home; and seven years later Johnson had to go outside his own College to find men " much more thoughtful than the team of King's Scholars" in which he "ran"; men whose conversation was really useful and stimulating, though he felt it to be perilous from the " untheological and in plain truth irreligious opinions" which were prevalent among them.

In his picture of College life Rowland Williams has a good deal to say about wine parties. At first he determined to go to them, but not to stay beyond 6 P.M. (the hour of dinner being then 4.30 P.M.), except when he gave a party himself, which would not be more than three times in the Term. " A reading man," he says, "is allowed to leave after the first hour." However, he very soon found that it was not so easy to leave early, and made up his mind to do without wine, or at any rate not to frequent King's parties. He was evidently a hard worker, but no recluse :

" I am learning Hebrew," he writes to his father, " according to your wish ; we have Mathematical Lectures twice a week, four days in Classics. The Lectures and Chapels cut up the time like mincemeat. Our examinations cannot be much stricter than they have been for some years, but we are now to have *degree* Examinations in addition to others. I read every day till one or sometimes two o'clock ; take my aspen stick of huge bulk, and begin moving for upwards of an hour out of Cambridge as fast as I can. I then move back. I dine at 4.30 P.M., read at 6, get generally three hours of the rest of the evening.

"We have had four or five days' skating. There is such a difficulty in varying the monotonous walking that any novelty of a kind such as this is quite an event."

The next winter, when under examination in the Senate House, he recognises a fellow skater :

" I found with a mixture of horror and amusement that three days before I had been playing at hockey on the ice with the Vice Chancellor !! to say nothing of talking to him just as if he had been an Eton fellow."

By degrees Williams's life became less monotonous, for his friend Essington says :

" We played fives when we were undergraduates, and went to the Union together, where Rowland was a leading speaker on the Conservative side ; and as Fellows we used (of course quite by chance) to fall in with Mr. Allix's harriers in the fen country by Little Wilbraham, or the Cambridgeshire at Madingley or Babraham. On these occasions he soon left us behind, and every one except the rider regarded with apprehension the heels of the brown thorough-bred, which Rowland Williams was fond of praising, though he seemed to us to be a stubborn and dangerous stallion."

The year 1838 saw the beginning of King's boating, and Williams shared the office of steerer with John Hawtrey. The Provost did not approve of it, and threatened impositions whenever the boat interfered with attendance at Chapel. But a more serious diffi-

culty must have arisen, when, in February 1844, the
number of Scholars actually sank to four, two having
been elected in 1841 and two in 1842, but none since
that year.   However, in April 1845, a boat was manned
after a fashion, and Johnson, who himself rowed, describes its success :

" We have achieved a complete conquest over the unkind
prejudices of our elders in the College, who at first threw
some cold and not very clean water on the project of the
revival of the boat club. . . . We had to start last but one,
because we had so recently entered. . . . In about 200
yards one might infer from the noises that we were close
upon the quarters of the Emmanuel boat. Going round a
corner, with not light enough to steer by, we found our
oars digging into the sedge, and the boat going one-sided ;
one or two lookers-on holloaing to our steerer (a very young
and marvellously coolheaded being) to steer out. Luckily
he disobeyed, and persisted in making for their *inside ;* so
in a few strokes more we were bumping them most deci-
sively, and stopped and hoisted our flag, having not had
enough work to give us a breathing—the Emmanuel eight
looking sulky at being caught so early by a six-oar."

Rowland Williams gained the Battie Scholarship in
1838, and writes home that :

" my dignity is manifoldly increased by my becoming for
seven years the owner of an estate, or landed property, or
in other words of a little farm with a tenant too ! ! ! who
signs himself ' your umbal servant J. J.' "

He was ordained in October 1842, and it is satisfactory to learn that :

" there were six Kingsmen, all of whom satisfied the Bishop
[of Lincoln] in their first day's examination, so as to make

it unnecessary to keep us longer. He told us that no set of men came to him so well prepared; and his Chaplain, Mr. Jeremie, said they *now* did as well as they *once* did badly."

Williams had already begun work as Classical Tutor at King's, and two years later was pointed out to a Freshman as the only great Aristotelian lecturer in Cambridge. He held this post till 1850, and would probably have continued to reside if he had succeeded in gaining the Public Oratorship in 1848, when Bateson was elected. As it was, he consoled himself with knowing that, leaving King's and St. John's out of account, he had received most votes; and he accepted the posts of Vice-Principal and Hebrew Professor at Lampeter College. It is unnecessary to pursue his later career, which was full of theological controversy, culminating in a prosecution before the Court of Arches and an appeal to the Privy Council in 1863 and 1864. Even before this last crisis his published writings had brought him into collision with more than one Bishop. But there was another side to his life. From 1859 till his death in 1870 he was Vicar of Broadchalke, a Wiltshire country parish, which had long suffered from a non-resident Vicar. Williams made himself the friend as well as the pastor of his parishioners, and his devotion was repaid by their gratitude and affection. Possibly his reputation for combativeness may have increased their respect for him. On one occasion when the Provost and Bursar, on a College circuit, were on the road between Salisbury and Broadchalke, their driver pointed to the distant figure of the Vicar riding over the downs, and said: "That's him as tackled the Bishop." Williams was a man not quite happy unless he was "tackling" somebody or something. But his wars were all waged on what to the Wiltshire peasants was foreign ground. Within his own parish there was peace.

William Johnson was the first Kingsman to gain the Chancellor's prize for an English poem; he was rather shocked at beating Maine, but observes that, when the exercise was forgotten, it would be pleasant to have his name in a list which contained those of Macaulay, Praed, and Tennyson; and he lived to publish a small volume of poetry, which fully justified the verdict of the University Examiners. In 1844 he became Craven Scholar.

"I really believe," he writes, "that no one is disappointed, *i.e.*, no one but Thring has not some other chance of high distinction, and he was told by one who could tell him only to expect the second place. I have by one small and one large supper, at great but unavoidable expense, got over that part of the consequences of my election, which my acquaintance here expect as their due."

He valued his own success chiefly because it set him free for wider reading; and when invited by the Headmaster of Eton, in 1845, to take a Mastership, he says:

"If Hawtrey would but let me alone a little while longer, I would come to his great verse-mill almost a learned man, instead of a smatterer. But see if I don't make the smaller fry at Eton write me holiday essays about St. Louis or Simon de Montfort or Charlemagne."

His first experience of the noise of 200 boys and four Masters in the Upper School at Eton was a little discouraging.

"I found myself bellowing to forty-five book-bearing bipeds, of whom I found one to be an intelligent being and expect to discover more."

But those who know Eton know that his force and originality soon made him the foremost of Eton Tutors. To be a pupil of Johnson was, in itself, almost a testimonial.

The Headmaster of whom Johnson speaks was one of a long line of Kingsmen, who in succession held that office. Edward Barnard had formed the one exception in the eighteenth century ; and since 1802 the courtly Goodall, the strenuous Keate, the accomplished Hawtrey had all been Fellows of King's ; and they were to be followed by Goodford, most indefatigable and, in spite of appearances, most wide awake of Headmasters, and by Balston, to know whom produced the same beneficial effect on manners which, according to the well-worn couplet, is gained by a thorough training in "ingenuæ artes." And, of these, Hawtrey had the longest connection with King's, for he held a College Living till after he became Provost of Eton. Even as an Undergraduate he had shown his genuine love of books. In a letter which he wrote when Provost of Eton, in 1857, he recalls an incident of the year 1807 :

"In the first week of my Scholarship at King's, having then a monomania for Oriental Philology, I explored the old King's Library in that portion of it, which contained the Hebrew Bibles. I found it stated in the list of Books, which used then to be pasted on each case (a very good custom), that there was in that case a copy of the Complutensian Polyglot, a book which I had never seen. I looked in vain for it, and supposed that some unknown Hebraist among the Seniors was consulting it. I was, until my own rooms were fit to receive me, a guest of the Provost (Sumner), and on the same evening I told him of my search and of its result."

It turned out, however, that it must have been stolen ; and that very evening Hawtrey had resolved, if ever he could do so, to fill up the place with another copy. And now, fifty years later, he tells Provost Okes that his intention was fulfilled. He had become possessed of a copy; only he wished to keep the six volumes till his death. He seems, in 1857, to have dreaded the results of the Commission ; for he inscribed in the first volume a note that it was

" μνημόσυνον amicabilis concordiæ inter regalia hæc Collegia nondum dissolutæ et, ut ex animo sperat, nullis factiosorum hominum simultatibus dissolvendæ."

But perhaps he had in his mind a snub which he had himself received from the College in 1827. He had been appointed College Preacher for March 25 of that year; and he had sent an excuse, apparently at the last moment, pleading, no doubt, his engagements as an Eton Master. Thereupon the College resolved :

" That Mr. Gee be directed to write to Mr. Hawtrey a Letter expressive of the dissatisfaction of the College on account of his non attendance to preach in the Chapel and inform him that his excuse is deemed inadmissible ; inasmuch as his absence from College is altogether an indulgence and the duties which he considers to be imposed on him by any other engagement cannot be allowed to interfere with the paramount duty which he owes to his own College. That Mr. Hawtrey pay as a fine £6 6s., and that he be appointed Preacher on the 25th March, 1828."

In the sequel, however, he was excused from preaching; and he seems to have made his peace by a present of maps to the College Library.

Edward Thring, of whom Johnson speaks as a disappointed candidate for the Craven Scholarship, had to content himself with the Porson Prize. But, if his undergraduate career was not brilliant, he has the rare distinction of being the maker of a great public school. His life at Uppingham from 1853 to 1887 has lately been described by Mr. G. R. Parkin, and we are now better able to measure the greatness of his work there; the difficulties with which he had to contend in an obstructive body of Trustees, and in the debt which he had contracted in order to carry out his theories. For he was determined to prove that it is possible, even in an English public school, to do full justice to each individual boy, and to train the character and the intellect, such as it is, even of the most stupid and backward.

Thring's first appearance, as Fellow, at a College meeting was on May 29, 1846, when the Society had been alarmed by a strange rumour. The Visitor had written to say that the new Bishop of Oxford, Samuel Wilberforce, desired to obtain a clause in an Act of Parliament, which would transfer the Visitorship of King's College from Lincoln to Oxford. This roused the Kingsmen to declare that they had sworn obedience to the Bishop of Lincoln, and could not break their oath; moreover, that it was highly objectionable that a Bishop of Oxford should exercise jurisdiction over any College in Cambridge. Bishop Wilberforce soon wrote to assure them that he had never " entertained the faintest wish to occupy the post of Visitor in King's

College." His eloquent addresses had already gained him a position of influence at Eton; and he may have hoped that, as he did the work of a Bishop there, so he might enjoy the honour of being Visitor of the great school which now lay within his own diocese. It was not so likely that he would be anxious to act as umpire in the quarrels of a distant College belonging to the rival University.

Yet seven years later, on the death of Bishop Kaye, Bishop Wilberforce again raised the same question; and in a letter addressed to the Provost of Eton argued that, Eton being within his own diocese, he was now actual and legal Visitor of that College. About King's College he spoke with less confidence; but he was of opinion that this College also had been transferred, together with Eton, from the diocese of Lincoln to that of Oxford, and was therefore now under his care. Sir John Patteson, who was consulted, suggested a method of settling the question as far as Eton was concerned. As to King's College, he held that nothing short of an Act of Parliament could transfer the Visitorship of that College from Lincoln to Oxford. Bishop Wilberforce acquiesced in this view; and the Statutes of 1882 have once more declared the Bishop of Lincoln to be Visitor of King's College.

CHAPTER XIX

REFORM

THE establishment of the Classical Tripos in 1824 had made it clear to some members of the Society that their exemption from University examinations was a restriction rather than a privilege. An anonymous pamphlet, which bears no date, but which is shown by internal evidence to have been written by a Kingsman, or possibly by a knot of Kingsmen, about 1837, argues that this exemption was contrary to the Founder's intention ; and that the growth of the University, together with the encouragement given to classical studies by the establishment of a Tripos, had increased the competition for the University Scholarships, thereby diminishing the probability that Kingsmen would come to the front. In point of fact, since 1827 no Kingsman had gained a University Scholarship. The force of this last argument was somewhat weakened by the success of Rowland Williams and Edward Balston in 1838 and 1839; and nothing came of a protest which, though powerful, was premature. Nearly ten years later, in 1846 and 1848, Edward Thring circulated two pamphlets on the same subject. These are written in a lighter vein than that of the anonymous author, but the general line of argument is the same. Thring points to the example set by the members of New

College, who had already surrendered their corresponding privilege at Oxford; and, like the earlier writer, he is at pains to remove an objection which evidently weighed with the College authorities, viz., that the mathematical test required by the University would force Kingsmen to devote their time to a subject which was to them distasteful and almost degrading.

But the Provost had set his face against the movement; and it was not till his death in the autumn of 1850 that anything could be done. The appointment ⌐of Richard Okes, Lower Master of Eton, to the Provostship in November of that year, gave the opportunity, which had been secured to Eton ten years earlier, when Francis Hodgson became Provost. Reform was now possible; and when Okes, accompanied by Harry Dupuis, who had been supported by a minority of the Fellows in the recent election to the Provostship, went to London to be instituted by the Visitor, Bishop Kaye took the opportunity to impress on the new Provost the duty of facing this question. Ten years before, so he said, he had received a petition from Fellows of the College asking him to intervene. The petition was informal, and he could do nothing; but he had looked into the subject and satisfied himself that the practice of the College had no real warrant in the Statutes. The advice fell on willing ears. Even as a boy Okes had heard something of the same kind. For, just after he had been elected an Eton Scholar, he met an old Fellow of Trinity in the streets of Cambridge, a friend of his own father's, who said to him:

" Now you have begun your career; you'll become a Fellow of King's in time and, I hope, Provost. If you do, mind that you get rid of the exemption from Degree examinations."

s

A meeting of Seniors and Officers on March 25, 1851, agreed to surrender the old privilege and to lay the question before the whole body of Fellows on the following first of May. In the interval the Provost circulated a memorandum, in which he pointed out that the privilege rested on no solid basis, and that the University might at any time *refuse* the B.A. degree to a Kingsman ; in which case the Visitor would certainly reject any appeal made to him. He did not fail to add that the true interests of education in the College called for this change.

On May 1 it was unanimously agreed

" that the present practice of claiming for the undergraduates of this College the degree of B.A. in the Senate House without passing the Examinations required by the University be abandoned."

Some of the 34 Fellows present must have stared at one another in surprise that no one was found to defend the old monopoly, and that the impossible was at last accomplished with such ease. The document of surrender was sealed and sent to the Vice-Chancellor, Dr. Corrie, Master of Jesus. He does not seem to have acted in a hurry, for it was not till November 26 that a Syndicate was appointed, whose report was confirmed by the Senate on February 18, 1852. By this final settlement every one admitted to a King's Scholarship after May 1, 1851, was obliged to pass a Degree Examination. For Scholars of older standing the Examination was optional.

This auspicious opening of the new Provostship was somewhat overclouded by a controversy in the autumn of 1854, when at the annual election of officers the Provost used his veto to prevent the election of a Vice-

Provost and Bursar supported by a small majority of the Fellows. The disappointed party did not accept their defeat without sending a batch of petitions and appeals to the Visitor. There was nothing against the character of these two candidates; but the physical infirmities of one were such as made the Provost's objection reasonable; and in the case of the other, who had been chosen as Bursar, the Provost doubted his financial capacity, and considered the fact that he had long been a non-resident to be a disqualification. The appeal which seems to have given the Visitor most trouble was one sent by a B.A. Fellow, Charles Caldecott James, now Rector of Wortham, who was the first Kingsman to take advantage of the recent settlement, and had gained a high place in the Classical Tripos of 1853. The point which he urged was that the election of Bursars was invalid, because one of the Deans who happened not to be a Senior Fellow had not been summoned to take part in the election. It was difficult to deny that the Statutes conferred this right on the Deans; but long custom had confined it, in the first instance, to the actual Seniors; the probability being that the Founder had never contemplated the election of a Junior to the office of Dean. The Visitor admitted the difficulty, but declined to interfere, on the ground that a Bill was already before Parliament which would enable the Colleges to amend their own Statutes.

The presence of the Dean at the meeting of Seniors would have made no practical difference on this occasion; and the Provost had only exercised what was his undoubted prerogative. Yet the dissatisfaction which naturally follows the use of a veto, together with the detection of a flaw in the Statutes, which made it difficult to interpret them consistently, probably helped to prepare the minds of the Fellows for a second revolution, which was soon to follow.

Meanwhile the new stimulus to industry was producing a silent and gradual change in the habits of the College; but it must be remembered that, even in the case of those who came under the new rule, the election to a Fellowship preceded the Tripos Examination, and a high place in the Tripos list was therefore of less importance to a Kingsman than to members of other Colleges. William Green, now Rector of Hepworth, was the first Scholar obliged to pass a Degree Examination, and he set a good example by being bracketed second Classic in 1855. Of course, when he began residence, he found among his older contemporaries some who did not imitate Charles James in volunteering for a Tripos; and he tells us that, though the College Lectures were good, yet

"a room filled with undergraduates of three different years, who had no University Examination to work up to, and though intelligent were of very various tastes, was hard to deal with. Attendance was pretty strictly enforced : we had two Lectures on every day but one, and one on that day. But for attention—that was a different matter. Mathematics in King's before 1851, one might describe as an Unknown quantity, small, that might be neglected. Hardly any of us had received any mathematical teaching at Eton. No Lecturer could have done much with such a class. Our Lecturer had before him a set of youths knowing next to nothing of the subject, and not caring to learn anything."

Mr. Green describes the social life of his days as that

of a family rather than a College, without much intercourse with men of other Colleges.

" As a rule we worked, played, dined and wined together,
with little admixture of non-Etonian. Pleasantly and
sociably; and probably the absence of stimulus to work
made some of us more convivial than was good for our own
persons or our fathers' purses. But King's parties were
very seldom large, uproarious, or rowdy. The Junior
Combination was an established institution; it met after
Hall (which was at 5 P.M.) every evening, if there was a
quorum of three; turn by turn each Scholar was host.
Now and then a Scholar entertained friends in his room at
a ' wine.' More evenings than not, a Scholar went either
to Junior Combination or to a friend's wine. No doubt
more wine was drunk than need have been ; some nonsense
was talked, but some sense likewise. To much I look back
as not only pleasant, but far from unprofitable. Symposia
were at times even Platonic and literary. . . . I sometimes
think there is among undergraduates more trifling and
childishness, less manliness than forty years since. Students
are over-guided, and so fail to get the self-reliance won by
those who had to work out their own success."

Mr. Green has also a good word to say for the Dons
of his time.

" As Fellow during 1855–1857 I was thrown more with
my seniors, with some who were considerably older. I
met them in the Combination Room continually. No
doubt Eton Masterships drained away some of our best
men ; and others of energy sought fields of work elsewhere,
in the Church, Law, Literature. But with regard to those
who remained in College, I think harsh judgments have
been formed. There were among them men of learning,
taste, and culture; there were men who helped and

encouraged the younger generation ; there were men who conscientiously and diligently managed the College estates and business.   Even some, whom we youngsters in our conceit put down as old fogies, had done some useful work in times past.   The family life, if narrowing, was pleasant. Enlargement and cosmopolitanism are not attained without some sacrifices.   Loosening of bonds there must be, and some liked the bonds and close union."

The Provost, like his predecessor Thackeray, had the misfortune to lose his wife not many years after his election.   Notwithstanding this grievous loss he continued to shew towards his own Scholars a hospitality which in those days was not expected of a College Head.   And these meetings at the Lodge must be reckoned among the humanising influences which helped to train more than one generation of Kingsmen.

In July 1856 an Act of Parliament was passed, and Commissioners were appointed, for promoting reforms in the University and Colleges of Cambridge.   The Commissioners began by laying down certain principles of reform, on some of which, as the sequel shewed, they were not prepared to insist.   The next four or five years were occupied by the efforts of the Colleges to reform themselves, and the new Statutes for King's College did not finally become law till the spring of 1861.   Great pains were taken to ascertain the views of each individual Fellow, and by repeated discussions to arrive at the matured judgment of the majority.   There were two important subjects in which a radical change was made.   The Provost had hitherto possessed the sole power of initiating legislation, and also an absolute veto. He now lost both initiative and veto ; the latter not without a struggle, for the Committee who made the first draft of the new Statutes had desired to preserve it. The Seniors too were deprived of their old monopoly of government; but they retained a larger dividend and the right to dine at a separate table. These privileges, however, were not continued to persons admitted to the College under the new Statutes. All legislative power passed into the hands of the M.A. Fellows, including, of course, those who had taken a higher degree; and the B.A. Fellows lost even the small share of government which they had enjoyed under the old Statutes.

Still more striking, at least to the outer world, was the change in the constitution of the Society itself. Instead of a body of seventy Etonians, in which the proportion of Fellows to Scholars fluctuated as the number of deaths, marriages, and vacancies in Livings varied, there was to be a fixed number of forty-six Fellows and forty-eight Scholars. All obligation to take Holy Orders was removed, but the Fellows of the future were not to enjoy the emoluments of a Senior Fellowship. Of the Scholarships twenty-four were reserved for Eton, and the rest thrown open. Care was taken that both in emoluments and in the length of tenure the Eton Scholarships should be of such a value as to be attractive to the best scholars at Eton, although the certainty of succession to a Fellowship had disappeared. It was at first intended that the College might, if they pleased, elect any Members of the University to Fellowships. But Eton College protested strongly against this provision, as inflicting an unnecessary injury on Eton boys. They also objected on the same grounds to any diminution in the number of Fellowships; but on this point their protest was unsuccessful; and, indeed, the finances of the College were somewhat strained to furnish as many as forty-six Fellowships, when provision had been made for the increase in the value and number of the Scholarships.

The alterations in the government and constitution of the Society proposed by the College were acceptable to the Commissioners, who complimented the members of King's on their liberality; but in two or three respects the College were not to be won over by compliments to the Commissioners' views. They would not hear of terminable Fellowships, and all that they could consent to do in favour of matrimony was to allow a married Fellow a year of grace: a privilege which had hitherto been confined to Fellows taking a College Living, in whose case it was more appropriate, since after marriage there is no " locus pœnitentiæ."

Such was the settlement, not destined to last very long, but of great importance in the history of the College. It was inevitable that questions should arise about vested interests; and in the first place it had to be settled what rights should be secured to existing Scholars and to Eton boys already on the Indentures for King's. An appeal to the Visitor resulted in his ordering that all vacancies in the Fellowships occurring before the July election of 1861 should be treated as actual vacancies in the old body of seventy and be filled by the admission of Collegers from Eton. To one boy this made the difference of his becoming a Scholar of King's, instead of going to Oxford, where he had already matriculated; and his services to the College in after years have certainly repaid any debt which he owed for this benefit. In the case of another boy, it produced the curious result that he was twice admitted to his

King's Scholarship, first under the new system in
October 1861, and then, after the Visitor's award, under
the old system in February 1862.

The Statutes, as originally drafted, had made no
special provision for those who held Scholarships at the
time when the Statutes became law. The Scholars
presented a petition to the Privy Council, and an
amended Statute secured to them and also to the two
Scholars mentioned above the old privilege of succeeding
to a Fellowship after three years of probation. Everything, in fact, was eventually arranged so as to prevent
the period of transition from bearing hardly on individuals.

CHAPTER XX

" A little flock we were in Henry's hall
　*　　　*　　　*　　　*　　　*
Hardly the circle widened, till one day
The guarded gate swung open wide to all."

BEFORE the College could fairly start on its new
career, it was necessary to reduce the number of Fellowships to forty-six, and to fill up the whole number
of twenty-four Eton Scholarships. It was easily arranged
that every alternate vacancy in the Fellowships should
be allowed to lapse ; but the question of the number of
Eton Scholarships to be offered in each year furnished
not unfrequently a battlefield to the two parties in the
College.　There were those who were anxious, possibly
over-anxious, to hasten the time when Open Scholarships
could be offered; and others who were constantly
haunted by fears lest their dividends should be reduced
by a forward policy.　The controversy is of too recent
a date to be told in detail; but it may be said generally
that the College owes much to the patrotism of its non-
resident Fellows, who, sometimes at great inconvenience,
attended the meetings at which critical questions were
to be settled.　Among these none were more prominent
than William Johnson, whose spirited counsels and
fearlessness of speech were often invaluable; while, of
the residents, Henry Bradshaw, who became University
Librarian in 1867, possessing as he did in great measure

the confidence of both parties, was able to maintain
views which would have been most unpalatable if they
had been advanced by some hot-headed junior.

The life of Henry Bradshaw has been well and fully
told by a former Tutor of King's, G. W. Prothero, who
was afterwards Professor of History at Edinburgh. In
his own department of knowledge Bradshaw was
perhaps the foremost man of his day; and, in addition
to this, he did more than any other resident to influence
the character and form the habits of many generations
of young Kingsmen. Though his scholarship did not
secure him a high degree, yet his originality and
devotion to letters soon raised him far higher than any
Tripos could have done; and in particular his knowledge of the first half-century of printing, and of early
printed books, was probably unrivalled. But this was
not all. If any one wished to know the age or history
of a MS., he was the person to consult, and he was
seldom consulted in vain. The binding of a book or its
title-page seemed to tell him more than the contents of
it did to an ordinary reader. He was tolerant of everything except affectation; and if it was a characteristic
of the Kingsmen of his day to covet wisdom more than
the reputation of being wise, and to be more afraid of
becoming prigs than of remaining Philistines, this was
in no small degree due to Bradshaw's influence. In
spite of his shyness and indifference to the out-door
pursuits of Undergraduates, there was a charm in him
which to most young men was irresistible. Nor was it
by any means only the most studious or the most
virtuous who were attracted within that circle, where
you might talk confidentially to your host, or read
silently at the same table; a circle, which was some-

times conversational, sometimes musical, but always homelike. Rather brusque in his manners and occasionally downright and even personal in his remarks, he had a fund of unselfish sympathy which seemed inexhaustible. And this unselfishness was as characteristic of his official as of his private life. Other men wrote books; he supplied them with the materials. The College happily possesses a portrait of him by H. Herkomer, R.A., who, while engaged on another work at Cambridge, happened to be Bradshaw's guest. He could not fail to appreciate his host, and for his own satisfaction made a sketch of what was certainly a noble head. In after days he gave it to the College, where it now hangs in the Hall. It was right that the portrait of such a man should have been a labour of love, and that it should be a free gift from one of Bradshaw's many friends.

It was not till 1873 that an Open Scholarship was offered; and in the same year a non-Etonian was for the first time elected to a Fellowship. The liberality of William Johnson had enabled the College to elect two Exhibitioners in 1865. Even this step had met with some opposition; and it was quite an epoch in the College history when Mr. Witt, now a Q.C., carried a resolution to the effect:

" That Mr. Johnson's offer be accepted with the thank: of the College; that the first Examination be held a Easter 1865, and that Pensioners be admitted in Octobe 1865."

The decision to admit Pensioners entailed the necessit of fixing a standard; and care was taken that only candidates for Honours should enter the College. A yet there was no Tutor; and so unused had the Societ

become to such an officer that some of the Fellows
wished the duties of a Tutor to be performed by one of
the Deans. But on November 28, 1865, it was decided
that a Tutor should be appointed. The appointment
rested with a small Board, called the Educational
Council, and here the consent of the Provost was still
necessary. William Ralph Churton became the first
Tutor under the new system; and though he held the
office only two years, yet much of the work inseparable
from a new start fell on his shoulders. The number of
Lecturers, the amount of fees, the Examinations to be
passed, were among the subjects with which he had to
deal; and it required all his patience and all his
unselfishness to disarm opposition, and to secure a fair
field for the new venture. Progress was very slow.
Perhaps the public could not believe that King's was
really open, especially as no Scholarships were offered;
perhaps there was some dread of Eton exclusiveness, or
some fear of an examination which professed to aim at a
high standard.

Before 1873 the largest number of Freshmen in any
one year was nine. In 1876 the number rose to twenty,
and in 1879 it reached thirty. Ten years later, in
1889, there were about ninety Undergraduates, exclusive
of Questionists. The largest entries hitherto have been
in the years 1894 and 1897, when forty-five and forty-
eight men were admitted to the College.

The prospect of Pensioners also awoke the desire for
additional buildings, and the first practical measure
adopted was the purchase of Mr. Cory's house from his
executors. This house stood between King's Lane and
the south-east corner of Wilkins's Building, and was
bought in November 1869 for £4000. The next year

a loan of £6000 was sanctioned, and on May 30, 1871, a design submitted by Sir G. G. Scott, for a range of building fronting Trumpington Street and abutting on Wilkins's Building, was approved. Part of the money used for this addition came from the residue of a legacy bequeathed by a Senior Fellow, Walter Chetwynd, for a similar purpose. The College gained twelve sets of rooms for Undergraduates; the town lost a picturesque building by the demolition of Mr. Cory's house, but the street was improved by the addition of space and light. Scott's Building, as seen from Bene't Street, presents rather an imposing appearance, besides possessing the rare merit of having two niches which are not empty.

Five years later some small houses in King's Lane were converted into College rooms; and about the same time a more ambitious scheme began to occupy the attention of the College. A proposal for buying the Bull Hotel had been mooted in 1870; in 1876 it was seriously prosecuted. At the same time a rival plan of extension, by substituting a range of building for Wilkins's Screen and completing the east side of the Court, was pushed forward; and in February 1877 it was resolved to invite three architects to send in designs for a building the cost of which should not exceed £35,000. Designs were accordingly furnished by Sir G. G. Scott, Mr. Street, and Mr. Burges; they still remain castles in the air, for neither of the two plans contemplated by the College was destined to be accomplished. The negotiations for the purchase of the Bull were stopped by the veto of the Copyhold Commissioners; and when it came to the critical point, the majority which had hitherto supported the plan for

SCOTT'S BUILDING (FROM BENET STREET)

building on the Screen site disappeared. This was in June 1878. One more effort was possible. The Universities Act of 1877 encouraged the union of Colleges; and in the winter of 1879 King's College made overtures to their neighbour St. Catherine. This was almost a counsel of despair; and though the conferences held by representatives of both Colleges seemed at one time to promise a favourable result, yet eventually the smaller Foundation shrank from a union which looked too much like an absorption.

The College finances were by this time in a less flourishing condition; however, in the autumn of 1883, Mr. Fawcett was commissioned to build a Lecture Room and a few sets of chambers opposite Scott's Building, and on the west side of the Chetwynd Court. It is remarkable how long the College had managed to exist without Lecture Rooms. In early days the Chapel and Hall had served the purpose; and even as late as the nineteenth century Fellows had lectured in their own rooms. It can hardly be said that Wilkins had provided a Lecture Room, though he built a room, long, narrow, and dark, in which lectures were in fact delivered. But it was not meant for this purpose, and was called by Wilkins a "Muniment Room." From time to time one or more sets of rooms were either fitted up temporarily, or permanently converted into Lecture Rooms; some people taught in Hall, and some in the College Library. At last in the Chetwynd Court a room was actually built for the purpose; and on the evening of October 13, 1885, Dr. Westcott, one of the great and good men whom the College had fortunately been able to secure as Professorial Fellows, delivered an inaugural Lecture on Provost Whichcote. Since that time one more Lecture Room has been added by the appropriation of the back drawing-room of the Provost's Lodge, which had in Dr. Thackeray's days been used by the College as its Audit Room; and about the same time, in 1889 and the following years, an important extension of the College was accomplished, when two wings of a three-sided Court designed by Mr. Bodley, and built of Lincolnshire stone, were erected on what had been the kitchen garden of the Lodge. The College thereby acquired forty-six sets of rooms at a cost of nearly £30,000. The result is so attractive both to those who occupy the building and to those who 'view it from the outside, that it is doubtful whether a future generation will have the courage to add a third wing, and run the risk of spoiling the two which already exist.

On April 22, 1879, there was a great gathering of old Kingsmen to celebrate the completion of two works of art within the College. Ten years earlier, F. E. Stacey, a former Fellow, had offered to fill the west window of the Chapel with stained glass. The offer was accepted, but the first design brought before the College was not approved, so that Messrs. Clayton and Bell could not begin their work before 1873. The opportunity was a grand one; and both Mr. Stacey and the College felt the importance of giving the artists time to exert themselves to the utmost.

Our benefactor, Mr. Davidson, among his many donations to the College, had in 1826 given £700 for a "statue of the Founder and a handsome fountain." By the end of 1872 this sum had grown to £3360, an amount considered sufficient for the purpose; and in the following November it was resolved to have a

From a Photograph by]

BODLEY'S BUILDING (LOOKING SOUTH)

[J. Palmer Clarke, Cambridge

" bronze figure upon a base out of which a fountain or conduit should flow," to be placed in the centre of the East Lawn. Some members of the College wished Mr. Foley to be the sculptor, but the majority preferred Mr. Armstead. A letter from him to the Bursar, May 10, 1877, describes the progress of his work. He had made alterations in the figure of the Founder, who was now represented as "gently offering the charter"; and, upon a suggestion of Provost Okes, he had changed a pavement, which was ill suited for the reception of water, into an outer basin. Two reliefs of an Eton Colleger and a Fellow of King's had disappeared; and the two large figures of Philosophy and Religion were already on view at the Royal Academy. Unfortunately Portland stone was used, instead of granite, for the basin; and the action of frost and water has been fatal to this part of the work, as well as to the base of the main structure.

For the festival service in Chapel on this occasion the Choir was reinforced by a few men's voices; but no such aid was necessary for the boys, who were now much more efficient than had been the case with choristers of former years. As long ago as June 11, 1862, attention had been called to the unsatisfactory state of the Musical Service, and the Precentor and Organist had been desired to exert themselves for its improvement; but one great difficulty lay in the fact that the Lay Clerks did double duty, singing both at Trinity and at King's. Mr. Brocklebank, who moved in the matter, had always taken a keen interest both in the history of the Chapel and in the conduct of the Services. But his time was engrossed with Bursarial duties, and it was impossible even for him to be everywhere and to see to everything.

T

So things went on much as before till 1869, when another effort was made, and a Committee reported on the reforms which were necessary. The report was agreed to, but it remained a dead letter till 1871, when the determination of Trinity College to have a separate staff of Lay Clerks forced the hands of the College, who happened also, just at this time, to have elected a more energetic set of officers. Things were now set on a better footing, and other reforms followed in 1876–78. The Organist was pensioned, the stipend of his successor, appointed in June 1876, was raised; the real power and responsibility, which had hitherto been divided between Organist, Precentor, and the Provost himself, was definitely conferred on the Deans; and, most important of all, a Choir School was built. The Statutes of 1862 had ordered that the Choristers should be boarded and lodged, as well as taught, and the conviction had gradually forced itself on the College, that the old system of recruiting the Choir from Cambridge boys of the lower classes produced a result which was not satisfactory either musically or morally. Accordingly a School House for a resident Master and sixteen boys was built, and ready for occupation in the autumn of 1878. Fortunately the finances of the College were still in a condition which justified a spirited policy, and no experiment has hitherto been more successful than this. The boys are drawn from a higher class than formerly, and come from all parts of England, and they receive a classical education, at very small cost to their parents, till their voices break, or till they are of an age to go to a public school. Besides the musical gain to the College, something is thus done towards restoring the advantages of a liberal education to a class which the

Founder meant to benefit, but which is apt to be left behind in an age of unrestricted competition.

Private liberality, a few years later, enabled the College to establish some Choral Scholarships, and volunteers from among the Undergraduates are also not unfrequently introduced into the Choir. This addition of an undergraduate element has at once strengthened and refined the singing, while it helps to give the Services a more devotional and less professional character. The result of all these reforms has been that the Musical Services of King's College Chapel are now reckoned as among the best in the kingdom. Much of this improvement is due to the ability and devotion of the present Organist; something, also, to the fact that in 1888 about £1400 was spent on the enlargement and improvement of the organ, £500 of this amount being the gift of the Fellows themselves.

One other department must be mentioned in which the College showed considerable activity. The Duke of Cleveland's Commission in 1873 had inquired into the property of Colleges; and it was understood that this would be followed by a second Commission for a further reform of their Statutes. At King's a Committee was appointed on February 23, 1872, to suggest alterations which would be beneficial to the College. During the next five years there was much discussion, both in printed papers and at College meetings; so that, when the Universities Act of 1877 was passed and the Commissioners appointed, the Society was ready with a scheme, and had practically made up its mind that Fellowships should be terminable and also tenable after marriage, the two points which had been stoutly resisted fifteen or twenty years earlier. A third

point had also been partly conceded ; for in the spring
of 1876 conferences had been held with representatives
of Trinity College, St. John's College having declined
to join in the proceedings, in order to fix the amount
of the contribution to be made to the University and
the principle on which it should be levied ; and the two
Colleges had agreed that five per cent. of the distribut-
able income should be paid as a tax, and another five
per cent. applied in augmenting professorial stipends.
The Colleges did not, indeed, bid high enough to satisfy
the Parliamentary Commissioners ; nor did they hit
upon the plan of Professorial Fellowships, which was
afterwards adopted ; but these preliminary attempts at
legislation had at least made the Fellows of King's
familiar with the problems which the Statutes of 1882
endeavoured to solve.

Perhaps the most important result of the new code
to the College is the greatly increased number of resident Fellows. They had begun to grow when, as a
consequence of the Code of 1861, Pensioners were
slowly attracted to the College. But the possibility
of marrying and of making either College or University
work a life-long profession, carrying with it a Fellowship for life, has greatly accelerated the tendency.
Those who are now the Seniors of the Society can
recall a time when not more than seven or eight Fellows
were in constant residence ; and even of this number
some appeared to have little or nothing to do. Now,
there are at least twenty-five Fellows in residence, most
of them fully employed either in College or University
work, though perhaps not fully paid for their employment. Agricultural depression has sadly diminished
the College income ; and the increase in the tuition

fees, though supplemented out of the College purse,
does not provide stipends sufficient to console Tutors,
Deans, and Lecturers for the loss of their dividends.
Happily competent men have been forthcoming, willing
to devote their best energies to College work without
any regard to a stipend " of nicely calculated less or
more."

With this increase in the number of residents it is
only natural that the College should exercise greater
influence in the counsels of the University, and be well
represented on the Boards and Syndicates ; and this
has proved to be the case. The highly democratic
nature of the College constitution introduced in 1861
has probably helped to train successive generations of
Kingsmen in the peculiarly English faculty of getting
through business without any great waste of time or
temper; of seeing and keeping to the point ; and of
expressing their opinions shortly and clearly. Yet it
may be doubted whether even now King's has regained
the place which it held in Elizabethan and even in
Stuart times, when the great Foundation, which now
eclipses its neighbours, had not yet reached its maturity,
and some rivals had only just entered the field.

At the present time the College list shews about 120
Undergraduates and more than thirty Bachelors or
Advanced Students in actual residence. With such a
body of young students and with the increased staff of
Fellows, it is hardly possible that the College should
relapse into what was sometimes its old condition, that
of a family party, comfortable, indeed, but inclined to
be sleepy and self-indulgent, and not wholly free from
family quarrels.

But the problems of the next century will probably

not bear much resemblance to those with which our predecessors were familiar. Or, if the foes are old, they will wear new faces. It remains to be seen whether the Kingsmen of the future will be equal to their opportunities; whether they will have the insight to detect the dangers of their own days, and the faith and courage necessary to surmount them.

APPENDICES

A.—EXEMPTIONS FROM DEGREE EXAMINATIONS

DEAN PEACOCK, in his well-known book on the Statutes of the University published in 1841, maintains that the practice by which Kingsmen then received the B.A. degree without examination, rested on no authority; but he does not explain how the abuse, for such he evidently considers it to be, crept in.

The examination for the B.A. degree, in the fifteenth century, was of the following character. Students, after completing their quadriennium and keeping two "responsions" and two "opponencies," became questionists, and were examined by the Proctors and others in the Schools during the week before Lent. Those who were approved were admitted "ad respondendum quæstioni"; and this "question," taken out of the *Prior Analytics* of Aristotle, was proposed in the Schools by the "Father" of each candidate. The questionist then became an "incepting bachelor" or "determiner." As such he was obliged "stare in quadragesima," and to determine one or more questions in a strictly logical form. This process lasted till the Thursday before Palm Sunday, when he became a complete B.A.

No exemption seems to be contemplated in the original College Statutes of 1443. In the 26th Statute stress is laid on the necessity that a Scholar or Fellow should keep the full years required by the University. He is then to be examined by his College authorities, and if found fit by them, to become a B.A. ("statum baccalaureatus assumat.") So far there is nothing inconsistent with the custom by which the University accepted the College examination in lieu of its own. But the 27th Statute, which makes special provision for Scholars too poor to pay the expenses incidental to a B.A. degree, allows 13s. 4d. for those who are about "respondere ad quæstionem," and the same sum to those "determinaturis." And if this Statute could be interpreted as using the technical terms merely in order to fix the dates at which the fee should be paid, there is no such ambiguity about the 31st Statute. This Statute orders that those who are about to "determine" in Arts must rehearse within the College, at least three times between October 9 and the first Sunday in Lent, the subject of their approaching disputation in the Schools ("disputabunt materiam quam proponunt disputare in Quadragesima proxima tunc sequente.")

It is hardly possible to resist the conclusion that the framers of these Statutes, and especially of the 31st, intended Kingsmen to take their degrees in the usual way.

A little later Henry VI. obtained Bulls from the Pope exempting his College from the jurisdiction of the Chancellor. After some demur the University, in 1448, granted a "Concession" to the College, admitting their separate jurisdiction. In this Concession, however, it is expressly stated that in matters which affect education ("propositum studii scholastici"), viz., in hearing and giving lectures, in disputations and the obligation "respondendi ad quæstionem," &c., Kingsmen should obey the University Statutes like other Scholars.

The final document, dealing with the question of jurisdiction, is the composition made between the University and King's College in 1456. In this it is provided that no member of King's, who is about to take any degree, shall be obliged to take any oath contrary to the Composition, "Sed quod æqua gaudeant libertate et capacitate quoad gradus et officia suscipienda sicut cœteri ejusdem Universitatis magistri et Scholares." In other words, the existence of a separate jurisdiction was not to be made an excuse for refusing a Kingsman his degree. But this document throws no fresh light on the question *how* a Kingsman became entitled to a B.A. degree.

Matthew Stokys, Esquire Bedell, who wrote an account of University ceremonies in the sixteenth century, tells us that on Ash Wednesday the Bedells collected the "determiners," and brought them to St. Mary's Church before 8 A.M. "Last of all the Bedells shall fetche the Determiners of the Kyng's Colledge unto St. Maryes Churche." That the members of King's College were fetched last, immediately before the Vice-Chancellor, was evidently a compliment; but could they be called "determiners," merely because they had reached the standing of those who were actually going to "determine" on that day at St. Mary's?

All this evidence points in the same direction. Yet, on the other hand, there is the great improbability that the exemption would have been granted at any date later than the reign of Henry VI. The

University, although they disliked surrendering the Chancellor's jurisdiction, were much gratified by the foundation of King's College. This appears both from their language in the " Concession," and also from the precedence granted to Kingsmen. Their feelings of gratitude and loyalty may have induced them, in view of the ample provision made for education by the College, and in consideration of the fact that the previous training at Eton was a security that no one would be admitted to a King's Scholarship who had not acquired the rudiments of learning, to dispense with any further test in the case of Kingsmen ; but it is hardly conceivable that they should grant such a dispensation after Henry's deposition or death. Mr. J. W. Clark, whose judgment on such a question is superior to that of any living writer, is of opinion that from such motives as these the University actually did allow the members of the newly founded College to receive the B.A. degree, without insisting on the usual requirements.

The later history of the College throws no light on this question ; for the Latin Declamation, which Christopher Anstey in the eighteenth century was called upon to deliver in the Schools, was not one of the preliminaries for a B.A. degree, but an exercise for the M.A. degree, which had fallen into disuse, and which Dr. Paris, an energetic Vice-Chancellor, was attempting to enforce on Bachelors.

Nor is much help to be got from the parallel case of New College ; for here, too, the facts are uncertain. The common account is that the Founder obtained a charter entitling his Fellows of New College to an examination in his own College, instead of one in the University Schools, for their B.A. degree. The Statutes of New College, like our own, seem to contemplate no such privilege. One of them expressly forbids members of New College to supplicate for graces to shorten the time of residence ; and Mr. Rashdall, the historian of Oxford, thinks that this rule, which was really a restriction, gradually became an exemption ; i.e., that, being forbidden to apply for an indulgence which afterwards became universal, New College men eventually got their degrees without any application at all. This is, of course, only a conjecture ; what is certain is, that in 1607 the right of the College to the privilege was challenged by the University, but confirmed by Archbishop Bancroft as Chancellor. At any rate Mr. Rashdall's explanation will not account for the exemption of Kingsmen.

If the records of our own University had preserved the names and Colleges of those who in the fifteenth century performed the exercises for a B.A. degree, we should at least have known whether the Kingsmen of the earliest days enjoyed any exemption, even if the origin and justification of the exemption still remained obscure. It seems to be a case in which all the evidence is on one side, and all the probability on the other. For, besides the improbability of the privilege being granted at any date later than Henry's reign, it is difficult to believe that the *same* abuse crept in, owing to some *different* cause, at *both* Universities: whereas, if William of Wykeham had already secured the privilege for his Foundation, the example set by Oxford might not unnaturally be followed by Cambridge.

B.—THE SENIOR SCHOLAR'S BOOK

This is a MS. book, containing a collection of College customs, some of which survived into the nineteenth century; but the comparative antiquity of the different customs can only be ascertained by internal evidence. In its present form the book seems to be a compilation made in the eighteenth century: but much of it no doubt represents the practices of an earlier period.

There are elaborate directions for a Freshman. It was the duty of the Junior Scholar to meet him on his arrival in Cambridge, to see that he was provided with a cap and gown, and to take him to the Provost with his Eton letter of introduction. The same scholar had to place him in a particular spot in Hall called "Stain Coat Hole," and under the organ loft in Chapel, and to see that he read the "Admission Statutes"; as well as to provide all things necessary for the ceremony of admission, including the presence of a public notary.

While the bell tolled for his admission, the Freshman stood bareheaded under the "Parlour" window or outside the Provost's Lodge, till called in. Then he knelt down, read certain statutes and swore to obey them. Thereupon the Provost admitted him, but did not, as was the custom at the admission of a Fellow, give him the "osculum pacis"; after which the Freshman, rising from his knees, addressed these words to the two Senior Fellows present, "Oro vos (magistros vel doctores A.B.) ut testes sitis hujus meæ admissionis,"; and turning to the notary he added, "et te requiro (C.) ut hanc meam admissionem in protocollum redigas."

The Freshman was next placed in his chamber by the Provost and Vice-Provost; after which he was put under the charge of his Chamber Fellow or Chum. The Chum now shared with the Senior Scholar the further initiation of the Freshman, attending him in and out of his chamber for a week or ten days, "lest he ignorantly alone should commit absurdities." During this period the Freshman "caps the Court and Chapel, goes to Hall and Chapel at the first ringing of the bell; stands bare in the Hall at the upper end of the Scholars' table; reads Greek Testament to one of the Senior Scholars till taken off by the Steward or other Graduate Fellows with these words, 'Parce tyroni'; and writes out the Admission Statutes or Senior Scholar's Book during the week of his Freshman-ship." When the right time comes, he calls on each of the chief College officers with a letter containing the prayer "Oro me hoc tyrocinio liberes"; and then he at once becomes "bibler" and reads lessons in Chapel, but he does not say Grace in Hall for a month after his admission.

Even the older Scholars were obliged to visit the authorities with verses before 8 A.M., if they wished to go out of College, except to St. Mary's or to the Public Schools. Visits were also paid, on stated days, for "Dors," i.e., leave to [lie in bed the next morning, and for "Term out." Under this last head were included not only the absences during vacations, but also periods of holiday at the great Church Festivals; e.g., five days before and five after February 2, and ten days at Whitsuntide.

The distinction between Fellows and Scholars was marked. The latter "stand not to talk with a Fellow in sight of a Senior or M.A. either in the Court, Cow Lane, or nave of the Chapel; nor go into the town in sight of any one of them except he give leave." This last rule sounds like a reminiscence of "Shirking" at Eton.

There were, however, occasions when the Seniors unbent a little. Such were "the four solemn beavers in the year, for the remembrance of which there is a false verse, viz.:

'Andreas, Thomas, Sanctorum, Nativitasque,'

on the eves whereof the Fellows and Scholars meet at six o'clock in the Hall, when each having a 2d. of bread and beer they are to drink charity to each other; on which eves as also on the said feast nights the Scholars keep Canonical hours in Hall and call them Crambo nights, from an old custom of playing then at Crambo."

There was also a Bachelors' Feast in Hall on the first Tripos day; when the Senior of the new Bachelors acted as steward and sat with his hood on; and both he and the next to him had the right of asking two friends to dinner. On this occasion also those Bachelors who were *not* Fellows, even if they were Choristers, dined at the Bachelors' Mess. Yet the ordinary rules were not altogether discarded; for "they withdraw from the hall fire, as indeed all Fellow Commoners, even M.A., while Grace is saying before Meat, and leave the same to the person who comes up as Vice-Provost."

Disputations were held in Chapel every week during term, except at the time of audit. Those for Bachelor and Questionists were on Wednesdays and Saturdays; those for M.A.s on Thursdays; notice of questions to be discussed being in all cases posted on the Hall screens three days before. During Lent there was no M.A. disputation, and only one in each week for B.A.s. Nothing is said as to the disputations of the Scholars.

The book contains many details as to the procedure for taking degrees within the College and in the University. For those who were *not* on the Foundation the number of times on which they must "oppose" and "respond" is specified, as well as the days and hours during which they must sit in the Senate House for examination. It is added that they sit "uppermost of all Questionists, as belonging to King's College; but if any of the Choir sit, whether Choristers or Singing Men, they are to take place of our Pensioners and poor Scholars as being on the Foundation." Yet it appears that the precedence in presentation for degrees, which Kingsmen still enjoy, was then only granted to Fellows. Others members of the College were presented for admission according to the seniority of their Fathers.

C.—PROVOSTS OF KING'S COLLEGE

1441 William Millington.*	1553 Richard Atkinson.
1447 John Chedworth.	1556 Robert Brassie.
1452 Robert Wodelarke.	1558 Philip Baker.*
1479 Walter Field.	1569 Roger Goad.
1499 John Dogget.	1610 Fogg Newton.
1501 John Argentine.	1612 William Smythe.
1507 Richard Hatton.	1615 Samuel Collins.*
1509 Robert Hacomblene.	1644 Benjamin Whichcote.*
1528 Edward Fox.	1660 James Fleetwood.†
1538 George Day.*	1675 Sir Thomas Page.
1548 Sir John Cheke.*	1681 John Coplestone.‡

* These Provosts were ejected, or else resigned to escape ejection.

† Fleetwood vacated the Provostship on becoming Bishop of Worcester.

‡ Coplestone was the last Provost nominated by the Crown.

1689 Charles Roderick.
1712 John Adams.
1719 Andrew Snape.
1743 William George.
1756 John Sumner.

1772 William Cooke.
1797 Humphrey Sumner.
1814 George Thackeray.
1850 Richard Okes.
1889 Augustus Austen Leigh.

VISITORS OF KING'S COLLEGE

William of Alnwick.
1450 Marmaduke Lumley.
1452 John Chedworth.
1472 Thomas Rotherham.
1480 John Russell.
1495 William Smith.
1514 Thomas Wolsey.
1514 William Atwater.
1521 John Longland.
1547 Henry Holbeach.
1552 John Taylor.
1554 John White.
1557 Thomas Watson.
1560 Nicholas Bullingham.
1571 Thomas Cooper.
1584 William Wickham.
1595 William Chaderton.
1608 William Barlow.
1614 Richard Neill.
1617 George Montaigne.

1621 John Williams.
1642 Thomas Winniffe.
1660 Robert Sanderson.
1663 Benjamin Laney.
1667 William Fuller.
1675 Thomas Barlow.
1692 Thomas Tenison.
1695 James Gardiner.
1705 William Wake.
1716 Edmund Gibson.
1723 Richard Reynolds.
1744 John Thomas.
1761 John Green.
1779 Thomas Thurlow.
1787 George Pretyman Tomline.
1820 George Pelham.
1827 John Kaye.
1853 John Jackson.
1869 Christopher Wordsworth.
1885 Edward King.

D.—NOTE TO P. 157

It was not the first time that the appointment of Stephen Upman to the Provostship had been contemplated. Sir Thomas Page died in 1681, at the crisis of the Tory reaction which followed the rejection of the Exclusion Bill; and it seems that Charles II. had then chosen Upman as a representative of the policy at that moment triumphant. But Upman did not possess the necessary Divinity degree; and the following letter, signed by Archbishop Sancroft and Bishop Compton, shows how this difficulty was to be surmounted.

" In pursuance of your Maties Declaration, of the 21st of July Last, concerning Preferrments in the Church and Universitys ; We do humbly Certify our Opinions, that Mr Stephen Upman, Master of Arts and Fellow of Eaton Colledge, is a Person for his Piety, Learning, and Prudence, well deserveing your Matie Letter of Dispensation to your University of Cambridge, to admitt him to the Degree of D{or} in Divinity, in order to qualify him for your Matie Royall Favour in his Election to the Provostship of King's Colledge now voyd by the death of Sr Thomas Page.

W: Cant.
H: London."

Aug. 13th 1681.

Upman however was not appointed Provost. Probably Charles or his advisers came to the conclusion that it was safer to promote a man of less extreme opinions.

INDEX

INDEX

INDEX

U

INDEX

INDEX

Printed by Ballantyne, Hanson & Co.
London & Edinburgh

www.ingramcontent.com/pod-product-compliance
Lightning Source LLC
Chambersburg PA
CBHW021122270326
41929CB00009B/1008